Beyond Small Groups

From Programmatic Meetings

to Flourishing Community

M. Scott Boren

C & M Publishing
Saint Paul, MN

Published by
The Center for Community & Mission
www.mscottboren.org

For more information, please contact:
mscottboren@gmail.com

"I am so happy that my friend Scott Boren has once again written such an important book. He gets it as both a thought leader and practitioner. Small groups are not our goal but a means to much greater purposes: Biblical community and spiritual growth. Small groups simply provide organizational constructs to enable that greater end, and Scott gets that. Read *Beyond Small Groups*, and be freshly and creatively reminded why life really is better connected."
> —Bill Willits, Executive Director of Ministry Environments,
> North Point Ministries, Co-author of *Creating Community*

"As you read this book, you may come under conviction as I did, realizing that some of what we attempt to do in our groups is man-made. Scott explains how we can approach small group ministry in a completely different way to see completely different results. If you are exhausted with trying to find x number of new leaders for new groups to be launched and you desire to see your groups naturally grow and send out new leaders, this book will help you make a radical transition."
> —Randall Neighbour, President, TOUCH Outreach Ministries,
> author of *The Naked Truth About Small Group Ministry*

"You will be stimulated and refreshed as you read this life-changing book. Scott Boren is a student of small groups, having lived, studied, and written about them for decades. This excellent book will help you think beyond small group formulas and techniques to understand the "why" small group ministry. Thanks, Scott, for writing this thought-provoking book!"
> —Joel Comiskey, Ph.D. www.joelcomiskeygroup.com

"Many people are an echo but a few are a voice. Scott Boren is a voice to those of us in the trenches of discipleship and groups. *Beyond Small Groups* will challenge your preconceived ideas about community and spiritual formation. It will cause you to take that critical second-look and uncover hidden realities you didn't notice before. If you are a pastor, groups director, or point-leader, this is a must-read book!"
> —Andrew S. Mason, Founder of SmallGroupChurches.com

"Our hearts sing when we experience the "one anothers" of New Testament community because our God is loving and relational—and we are made in his image. *Beyond Small Groups* is an excellent resource for pastors and ministry leaders who want to see healthy and life-giving expressions of the church. Scott writes with a rich theological foundation and the wisdom of many years of practical coaching and leadership development. I heartily recommend Scott's book to you and hope it will stir your desire to see the church alive and flourishing in your context."
> —Jamey Miller, Lead Pastor of Antioch Fort Worth

Acknowledgments

This book stands on the shoulders of pioneering innovators like Ralph W. Neighbour Jr., Carl George, and Lyman Coleman. The paths ventured here would not be possible without conversations with Bill Beckham, Jim Egli, Joel Comiskey, and innumerable pastors and leaders who carry a great passion for groups. In addition, these words have been shaped by missional church thinking of Alan Roxburgh, Craig Van Gelder, and David Fitch.

I want to thank Randall Neighbour for over ten years of collaboration and for the permission to adapt and update pieces developed while working for the ministry he leads. I am also grateful for the opportunity to work with Andrew Mason and for the contributions of his excellent thinking in this book.

I owe this book to my unbelievably beautiful wife, Shawna. As I reflect on the unexpected adventure that we have traveled to this point, I am beyond thankful that we have been and are now walking it together. I'm grateful that love is not based on what is deserved because there is no way that I deserve you.

Table of Contents

Prologue 9

    1 A Letter to Pastors and Leaders 13

Part 1: Perspective 33

    2 What Do We Want from Our Groups? 35

    3 What Do We Get? 47

    4 Why Do We Get What We Get? 57

    5 How Do We Get What We Desire? 67

    6 How Do We Help People See Groups Differently? 83

Part 2: Presence 97

    7 Why Do We Need New Church Structures? 99

    8 Why Do We Need Christ's Presence? 111

    9 Where is Christ's Presence? 125

Part 3: Practices 141

    10 What Do Flourishing Groups Practice? 143

    11 What Do Flourishing Leaders Practice? 157

    12 What Do Flourishing Coaches Practice? 161

    13 What Do Flourishing Pastors Practice? 169

Part 4: Pilgrimage 179

    14 What Does the Pilgrimage Look Like? 181

    15 What Is the First Step? 191

    16 Who Guides the Pilgrimage? 201

    17 How Do You Prepare the Church for Groups? 213

    18 How Do You Get People Connected? 223

    19 How Will You Initiate Organic Missional Experiments? 239

    20 How Will You Form People for Flourishing Community? 259

    21 How Will You Support Groups So They Flourish? Part 1 269

    22 How Will You Support Groups So They Flourish? Part 2 285

    23 How Will Groups Impact the World? 295

Conclusion 309

Appendix 315

Notes 331

Prologue

Asking great group questions is more important than developing accurate answers to less than stellar questions, ... even if the right questions are more difficult to answer.

The right questions require a shift in imagination. This book aims at shaping your imagination about groups while providing practical guidance for what that imagination means.

Each of us already has an imagination about groups; however, most often we fail to name it, and therefore we fail to see its inherent strengths and weaknesses. This is what leads us to ask the wrong questions. For instance, some ask questions about how to close the back door of the church, while others are looking for how to get back to an ideal of what the church was like in the New Testament. Some have a group imagination that is primarily built around the need for Bible study or a video discussion guide. Others are asking about how groups can be a means for evangelistic growth. The particular imaginative questions you have will determine the practical steps that you take.

The concern I have is that—for the most part—we have adopted imaginations that are shaped by subordinate purposes, as opposed to that which is ultimate. It's not that closing the back door, studying the Bible, or evangelistic growth are inherently wrong in and of themselves. It's that we make them the priority and therefore turn the subordinate into the ultimate goal. This is illustrated by my first book on small group strategy which I wrote in the early 2000s, entitled *Making Cell Groups Work*. It sold well, received quite a lot of praise, and was well received. However, my imaginative questions were shaped by the need to help churches make groups succeed. In doing so, I turned an important subordinate goal into an ultimate end. When we fail to ask ultimate questions, then we will develop answers that are only partially accurate. However, being partially accurate means that they are partially wrong, and therefore the answers are ultimately misguided.

This book offers an imagination alongside a set of practical guidelines that are based on the ultimate goal of participating in the life and love of God. This is the ultimate end or goal and must shape all that we do, even the work of developing groups. Therefore, this ultimate end must shape our imagination so that the way we lead corresponds with the ultimate goal of knowing and participating in God's love.

This book was originally published under the title *Group in Your Church in the Way of Jesus* in 2017, which was a beta test of material that I use to coach pastors and consult with churches. The feedback I received led to three primary changes. First, the book required a new title, one that speaks more directly to the primary point. Second, I needed to articulate an imagination of what it means to go beyond small groups structures into flourishing life. This imagination is based on Ezekiel's vision of the valley of dry bones. Flourishing groups are developed as the Spirit of God moves through and connects the bones, forms the body, and empowers with God's breath. The bones represent the structures we develop, the body corresponds with way people are discipled to fill those groups, and the breath is about the Spirit's work to enliven our structures and discipleship.

Finally, the feedback revealed the need for additional practical handles so that pastors and leaders could more easily see what it means to move beyond small groups. Therefore this version expands the practical guidance, specifically the kind that aligns with the breath of God.

Options for Reading this Book

I encourage you to start by reading the letter found in chapter one. It is written to pastors and leaders when we embark upon a coaching or consulting relationship. After that, there are a few options:

- *Reading Option #1:* Like most books, you can read through the chapters in chronological order as there is a logical progression to them.
- *Reading Option #2:* Chapters 6, 7, 10, and 14 provide a big picture summary of the book's argument. Read these chapters to attain an introduction to the major themes.
- *Reading Option #3:* Read Part 4 first as it provides practical guidance for leading a church through the steps from your current state of group life (whether no groups, a few groups, or floundering groups) to the experience of flourishing community.
- *Reading Option #4:* Review the topics in the Table of Contents and identity chapters that address questions you have about groups. For instance, if you have questions about the role of group coaches, then chapter 12 is a good place to start. Or if you want to know how to develop groups that get Sunday attenders connected, look at chapter 18. For those interested in starting missional community experiments chapter 19 will prove interesting.
- *Reading Option #5:* If you have interests in thinking theologically about groups and church structures, start reading Part 2 and then move into other chapters.

I wrote this book so you that you can flip to the parts that address your questions and felt needs in order to help you work out the implications of a specific chapter. The goal is to merge theory, theology, and practice so that the ideas move beyond concepts in a book and actually have an impact upon your ministry.

If you are interested in coaching or consulting to help you work out these ideas for your specific church and context, visit: www.mscottboren.org.

1

A Letter to Pastors and Leaders

Dear Pastors and Leaders of First Church,

At the beginning of this season of coaching, I want to provide a framework for our conversations, a big picture for what we will be discussing about moving "beyond small groups." Basically, this means that we need to shift from the subordinate goal of focusing on small group structures that get people connected in meetings to focusing on how we participate in the ultimate end of God-inspired, flourishing communities. Let me explain a bit about my journey of seeing the importance of moving beyond.

After I graduated from Texas A & M University, I went to seminary for one semester. I tried to fit in with the training to become a pastor of a programmatic church, however, it was not working very well for me. Even though I was taking classes from some of the best teachers—including a church leadership class with the great Calvin Miller, who had pastored for thirty years—I could not bring myself to conform to the status quo. While studying for final exams, a friend from college told me about a job opening at TOUCH Outreach Ministries, led by Ralph W. Neighbour Jr. This ministry had been the primary pioneer for small-group life in the North American context for about a decade. Neighbour had recently written a book entitled *Where Do We Go From Here* which was selling over 1000 copies per month. This was unusual because it was 468 pages long, written for pastors, and it slammed—with harsh and condemning words—what he called the "programmed-based-design" church. It was not your typical best seller, yet it tapped into a deep hunger for re-structuring the church with small groups as the base.

I was intrigued because I had studied Neighbour's writings during my senior year at Texas A & M. I had even written a sixty-page paper on groups for an assignment that only required twenty. My curiosity extended beyond logical necessities of typical expectations. I applied for the job and was hired to be the business administrator for the ministry. What a joke! While my degree qualified me for such a position, administration is not one of my strengths. (A few years after I had moved on to another role, the competent administrator who followed me found a completed bank deposit slip for $957 which I had failed to take to the bank.) Interacting with pastors, leading training events, and writing materials shaped my interests.

That all started in 1993. Since then, I have studied churches that have experimented with many different ways to organize groups. They go by a variety of names: cell groups, small groups, house groups, organic groups, G-12 groups, short-term groups, campaign groups, semester groups, sermon-study groups, missional small groups, missional communities, growth groups, and even Bible studies. There are some great strategies and supporting resources for them at our disposal. However, finding the "right" strategy and doing it the "right" way will not automatically result in flourishing groups.

Failing? Floundering? Fine?

In 1999, I served as the Director of Research and Development for TOUCH Outreach Ministries. For our meetings, Dr. Jim Egli, the Director of Training, and I would talk while walking through a park near our offices. One day, we discussed why our training and resources were proving quite fruitful in the churches with which we were working in Brazil, South Africa, Russia, Singapore, and many other countries around the world. In these contexts, groups were flourishing with both growth and dynamic, organic experiences of community life, but in North America the results were far from stellar. We were missing something crucial.

That conversation with Jim Egli sent me searching. While churches have sought to develop groups that flourish most often the outcomes are groups that fail, groups that flounder, or groups that are just fine.

First, we have seen far too many churches *failing* with their groups. They go to conferences, purchase the materials, and make groups a priority. They commit to being a church *of* small groups instead of a church *with* small groups. Some even take it a step further and set up groups to be the core base of their life so that they become organic missional communities. However, as many pastors have confessed, they just have not figured out how groups work. Or worse, churches have split or pastors have had to leave because the group vision fell apart. As a result, churches revert back to old ways.

For many others, their groups are *floundering*. The groups have struggled in a clumsy way, riding random ups and downs, never with enough success to celebrate or enough decline to make radical changes. Instead, there is often a perpetual chase after the next programmatic fix. A new book or a new conference offers a formulaic strategy that promises to lead the church into small group bliss. Leaders adopt the new strategy for a season, resulting in an initial upturn in group life, but after six to twelve months, things level out again.

Another set of churches have settled for groups that are *fine*. The groups are part of the life of the church, as no one questions their value, however, there is nothing about them that is distinctively Christian. They are just weekly Bible studies or a nice fellowship groups of people who like one another. The groups work; they might even be growing in number. Yet no one would say that they are actually experiencing the flourishing life of God in their midst. The groups are a part of a program—many times a well organized one—but fine groups are not good enough.

Flourishing Community

In our coaching conversations, we will focus on what it means for groups to flourish in your church and what to do when you find that you are failing, floundering, or in the state of being just fine. A vision found in the book of Ezekiel helps to explain what I mean by flourishing. It reads:

The hand of the Lord was on me, and he brought me out by the Spirit of the Lord and set me in the middle of a valley; it was full of bones. He led me back and forth among them, and I saw a great many bones on the floor of the valley, bones that were very dry. He asked me, "Son of man, can these bones live?"

I said, "Sovereign Lord, you alone know."

Then he said to me, "Prophesy to these bones and say to them, 'Dry bones, hear the word of the Lord! This is what the Sovereign Lord says to these bones: I will make breath enter you, and you will come to life. I will attach tendons to you and make flesh come upon you and cover you with skin; I will put breath in you, and you will come to life. Then you will know that I am the Lord.'"

So I prophesied as I was commanded. And as I was prophesying, there was a noise, a rattling sound, and the bones came together, bone to bone. I looked, and tendons and flesh appeared on them and skin covered them, but there was no breath in them.

Then he said to me, "Prophesy to the breath; prophesy, son of man, and say to it, 'This is what the Sovereign Lord says: Come, breath, from the four winds and breathe into these slain, that they may live.'" So I prophesied as he commanded me, and breath entered them; they came to life and stood up on their feet—a vast army.

Then he said to me: "Son of man, these bones are the people of Israel. They say, 'Our bones are dried up and our hope is gone; we are cut off.' Therefore prophesy and say to them: 'This is what the Sovereign Lord says: My people, I am going to open your graves and bring you up from them; I will bring you back to the land of Israel. Then you, my people, will know that I am the Lord, when I open your graves and bring you up from them. I will put my Spirit in you and you will live, and I will settle you in your own land. Then you will know that I the Lord have spoken, and I have done it, declares the Lord'" (Ezekiel 37:1-14).

Flourishing groups depend on the work that occurs on three levels: the bones, the body, and the breath. (Note: I am using "body" instead of "flesh" due to the various ways the word "flesh" is used in the Scriptures.) In other words, we need to develop structures, be discipled in a way of body life together that corresponds with the group structure, and receive the empowering life of the Spirit. Let's consider each.

Bones

When Ezekiel saw the valley of dry bones, he described his experience by saying, "He (the Spirit) led me back and forth among them, and I saw a great many bones on the floor of the valley, bones that were very dry." Today, many churches have a lot in common with the dry, disconnected bones that Ezekiel saw. People walk through the doors of their preferred religious building on Sunday morning. They sit for an hour, put a little money in the offering, and then return to their "real" lives. Even those who volunteer at the church find themselves only connected to activities and programs. The church ends up being a meeting place for bones that are, for all practical purposes, disconnected and therefore dead.

Over the last thirty years, we have had many "bone prophets" who have spoken to the bones like Ezekiel did when he said, "And as I was prophesying, there was a noise, a rattling sound, and the bones came together, bone to bone." The coming together of the bones is what happens when we adopt a grouping strategy to serve as a base for the way we do church. We have needed these prophets to challenge the status quo of church structures that operate as if the bones do not need to come together.

These group prophets have echoed the words of Moses' father-in-law, Jethro, when he observed Moses' patterns of leadership after the Exodus from Egypt:

The next day Moses took his seat to serve as judge for the people, and they stood around him from morning till evening. When his father-in-law saw all that Moses was doing for the people, he said, "What is this you are doing for the people? Why do you alone sit as judge, while all these people stand around you from morning till evening?"

Moses answered him, "Because the people come to me to seek God's will. Whenever they have a dispute, it is brought to me, and I decide between the parties and inform them of God's decrees and instructions."

Moses' father-in-law replied, "What you are doing is not good. You and these people who come to you will only wear yourselves out. The work is too heavy for you; you cannot handle it alone. Listen now to me and I will give you some advice, and may God be with you. You must be the people's representative before God and bring their disputes to him. Teach them his decrees and instructions, and show them the way they are to live and how they are to behave. But select capable men from all the people—men who fear God, trustworthy men who hate dishonest gain—and appoint them as officials over thousands, hundreds, fifties and tens. Have them serve as judges for the people at all times, but have them bring every difficult case to you; the simple cases they can decide themselves. That will make your load lighter, because they will share it with you. If you do this and God so commands, you will be able to stand the strain, and all these people will go home satisfied."

Moses listened to his father-in-law and did everything he said. He chose capable men from all Israel and made them leaders of the people, officials over thousands, hundreds, fifties and tens. They served as judges for the people at all times. The difficult cases they brought to Moses, but the simple ones they decided themselves (Exodus 18:13-26).

Many of these bone prophets have offered church models for others to mimic. The first of these models arose in the 1960s in Seoul, South Korea, a church that developed thousands of groups in a Buddhist culture. Countless pastors traveled to see how the church operated and returned to implement their structures. One of the early significant models in North America was led by Dale Galloway in Portland, Oregon, who explained his strategy in the 1986 book *20/20 Vision: How To Create a Successful Church with Lay Pastors and Cell Groups*. Another early model arose organically in rural Pennsylvania and resulted in a network of churches around the world. Larry Kreider documents this story and their model in the book *House to House*.

Then in 1989 and 1990 two books about small group models were released that changed the conversation. First came *Prepare Your Church for the Future* by Carl George and then *Where Do We Go From Here* by Ralph Neighbour. The roots of every group model now promoted extend back to these two titles. There truly is nothing new under the sun, contrary to what small-group experts might say about how novel their insights are.

Since that time, books on models (the bones) have dominated the conversation. A few of the most prominent are *Becoming a Church of Small Groups* by Bill Donahue, *Small Groups with Purpose* by Steve Gladden, *Sticky Church* by Larry Osborne, *Activate* by Nelson Searcy and *Creating Community* by Andy Stanley and Bill Willits. Then there are strategies that aim to foster organic, movement growth of networks of groups, often called missional communities. Resources on this topic include *The Forgotten Ways* by Alan Hirsch, *The Church as Movement* by J.R. Woodward and Dan White Jr., *Organic Church* by Neil Cole, and many more. My article, co-authored with Jim Egli, provides a quick introduction to the various ways that the bones have been ordered. You can find it in the Appendix of my book *Beyond Small Groups*.

Most of what has been written and taught in conferences on groups pertains to the assembling of the bones. This is important, and we will talk at great length about the best bone strategy for your church and context. However, in most cases, the way that the bone prophets talk about groups—whether it is a programmatic strategy or something more organic in nature—places the focus on lining up the bones in the right order, as if this alone will result in flourishing community. Of course, these bone prophets know that much more is required, but if you simply survey their writings and what they talk about at seminars, we can quickly see the body and breath get little attention in comparison to the bones.

Body

Then Ezekiel said, "I looked, and tendons and flesh appeared on them and skin covered them ..." The bones are connected by tendons and flesh, what I am calling "body" in this book. At the risk of stretching the image, the structures that we develop in the church operate in the same way. The best structures, the most awe-inspiring strategies, only work when they are connected by a living body. Your specific grouping strategy will flourish because of the people who fill them. Don't ever forget this: small groups are about people, not about making your strategy "work."

With this in mind, let's think about how the body works in various ministries of the church. In some cases, the connective tissue of the body depends only upon the work being done with excellence. We make a list of tasks, recruit and train people for those tasks, and then get to work. The people are connected to the tasks. It is different with groups because they don't flourish because the tasks are done well. They flourish because people actually connect with other people.

This requires people to be formed, that is discipled, to live in a way that fits the goals of those groups. Think of it in terms of playing a sport. If twenty-two basketball players are chosen to play on a football team, they would probably do relatively well because they are good athletes. However, since they have been formed (discipled) through the training required to play basketball, they could never keep up with twenty-two players who have been formed to play football.

Understanding the way that the body connects the bones is not merely about recruiting and training leaders or about getting people connected in groups. Those are issues related to the ordering of bones. "Body disciplers"—these include people like Dallas Willard, Richard Foster, Henri Nouwen, and Eugene Peterson—have taught us that the formation of our lives is about being shaped to embody the kind of life that aligns with flourishing groups. In other words, putting the body around the bones is about being discipled to be the kind of people who can live out God's kind of flourishing community in the structures we develop.

This is especially crucial for our conversations for two reasons. First, those who have been committed to the church have been trained according to the inherited patterns of church life. For instance, many have been discipled in the Sunday school pattern of church life, where people gather in groups on Sunday morning to listen to a teacher expound on a Bible passage for an hour, with little personal interaction and no expectation of shared life outside of the Sunday school hour. Over the last thirty years, numerous churches have shifted from Sunday school to small groups, but all they got was Sunday school in homes. The people in the groups had not been discipled or formed to manifest the patterns of life that fit groups. Another example is found in churches that are highly dependent upon centralized, ordained leadership. While there might be an official commitment to the theology of priesthood of all believers, their discipleship has shaped them to depend upon clergy who carry out religious tasks. Therefore, any meeting that was not led by such a special person is second rate.

A second reason why discipling the body is important relates to today's seven-day-a-week, non-stop world that undermines our ability to do groups well. This is illustrated by two movies starring Tom Hanks. The first is *Forrest Gump* where in one scene Forrest's platoon comes under attack in the Vietnam War and is told by Lieutenant Dan to run. Being that Forrest was very fast, he outran his platoon and ended up alone. Specifically, he could not find his best friend, Bubba. Forrest does a one-eighty and heads back to look for Bubba. As he does, he finds four other wounded soldiers, including Lieutenant Dan, and carries them out one-by-one. He then heads back into the hot zone while Lieutenant Dan commands him to stay. Forrest yells, "I've gotta find Bubba!" Most of us in the Western world do not have time to have Forrest Gumps in our lives who will run into the crossfire of spiritual warfare, risking their own lives.

Instead, our lives resemble the second Tom Hanks movie, *Cast Away.* In an opening scene, Hanks' character, a FedEx executive named

Chuck Noland, is training Russian employees on the value of time. He is controlled by the need to squeeze as much as possible into every minute. Then he finds himself marooned on an island after his plane crashed. This experience of island isolation is actually a metaphorical representation of the life he led before the plane crash. In Western cultures, people do not merely need to join a small group, they need to be discipled in basic relationship skills to be the body of Christ because we have become addicted to the FedEx way of life that Chuck Noland represents. Work, electronic devices, and constant stimulation have trained us to be disconnected from each other.

We can actually see this body formation in the ministry of Jesus. Many body disciplers have taught about the fact that Jesus' ministry focused on a small group of disciples. It was not merely about the willingness of these twelve men to be a part of his group or their desire to follow him. Jesus focused on the twelve so that they might be discipled or formed in God's kingdom ways. Any first century Jewish person would have been formed by the common expectations of the coming messianic kingdom. According to N. T. Wright, those expectations were three-fold. First, God's king would restore Jerusalem to its glory as the Israelites returned from exile. Second, he would drive out the Romans so that Israel might be a great nation again. And third, the presence of God would be restored to the temple. These expectations formed their imagination and therefore their ways of worship, which did not align with the kind of kingdom that Jesus established. The disciples had to be re-discipled, re-formed, to fit Jesus' kind of kingdom. Thus it took three and a half years, and the twelve disciples still did not rightly perceive the nature of the kingdom.

When we are talking about putting the body on the bones (small group structures), we are talking about how our lives are re-formed in order to live in community, to serve as relational leaders, to practice the one anothers, and to manifest the self-sacrificial love of the cross as groups.

The work of body disciplers that is directly connected to the development of groups is exemplified by the book *Connecting Church* by Randy Frazee. Also my work in *The Relational Way* focuses on this aspect of

Ezekiel's vision. The subtitle for that book illustrates this point: "From Small Group Structures to Holistic Life Connections." This is also represented by writings on group leadership that focus on habits that effective leaders develop in order to foster flourishing community. For instance, one might consider titles like *8 Habits of Highly Effective Small Group Leaders* by Dave Early and *Groups that Thrive: 8 Surprising Discoveries about Life-Giving Small Groups* by Joel Comiskey and Jim Egli.

But there is more, a more that serves as the core of what takes us beyond small groups.

Breath

After the bones came together, Ezekiel observed, "There is no breath in them." Ezekiel saw the reality that good is not good enough. While the bones and body were better than a valley of disparate dry bones, the body was still not living. God told Ezekiel to prophesy to the breath. Ezekiel reported, "So I prophesied as he commanded me, and breath entered them; they came to life and stood up on their feet—a vast army." The biblical image of the breath of God is one used to speak of the Holy Spirit. God's Spirit enters into the church just as God breathed into Adam in order to animate and enliven the form of his bones and body.

To speak of breath is to speak of life, energy, vigor, power, and verve. It is the action of God himself moving in God's body. This action, this life, generates desire within those who are aligning the body with the bones. There must be an energizing life that generates the desire within the participants to fully engage so that they might be the kind of people that God has called them to be. This is the fulfillment of the promise recorded in Jeremiah:

"This is the covenant I will make with the people of Israel
    after that time," declares the Lord.
"I will put my law in their minds
    and write it on their hearts.
I will be their God,
    and they will be my people" (Jeremiah 31:33).

The Spirit sparks desire through our imaginations, not by fixing the bones and the body, which could be done out of a legalistic mindset. We need more than the rules that speak to developing structures or guidelines regarding what it means to be "discipled" to do the right things. No group system flourishes out of duty to small group instructions or even obligations to a list of community disciplines. They flourish because the Spirit has ignited the imagination of people so that God's love is written on their hearts and minds.

Groups flourish because God's law of love is poured into God's people, thereby empowering them to live in the love that God is. If we don't grow in love, it really does not matter how great your bones and body are.

Why We Need the Breath

If you break a bone, you get it reset so it will heal. If your flesh is cut, you get stitches. However, if you cannot breathe, you have about three minutes. This is how much breath means to our bodies, and the same is true of Christ's body today.

While groups had been a part of my journey growing up in the church, I realized their power when I attended college. I was a leader in a large student ministry at Texas A & M University. On a weekly basis, hundreds of students led by other students met in groups—on the campus, in apartments, and at our ministry building. Groups served as the foundation of what we did. As I look back on that experience, we did not have to twist people's arms to show up to their groups. People wanted to come! The groups were just fun. Now of course, part of the reason for this was the fact that we were in college. It was a fun period, but it wasn't like we entertained people in typical college-appropriate ways. In fact, on the surface, one might say that we were rather dull. We talked about God a lot. We prayed more as a group than in any church I've ever been a part of. We had extended worship services. We were immersed in the Scriptures. And we saw lots of people's lives changed as we sacrificed for one another.

We did not do groups because they were the "right" thing to do. There was no guilt or a sense of obligation to get in a group. Nor did we do groups because they were good for us. There was just a simple desire to be a part because of the love that people experienced in the midst.

The "bone prophets" have spoken to the need for groups and the various structures and strategies that can bring the bones together. With such arguments I hardly agree. And the "body disciplers" have provided concrete ways to realign our lives with new ways that God is structuring the church. We need such discipleship.

However, the bones and the body only speak to what is right and good for us. They do not speak to the deep desires that arise within us. Many times pastors tell me that the people in their churches are too busy to be a part of a weekly small group. When I first started hearing this, my response was "Does this mean that since they are too busy for weekly groups then they are too busy for weekly worship, and therefore we should only hold Sunday services twice per month?" This response revealed that I was working from a "bone" imagination, as I was trying to force the "right" way of doing church.

After a few years, I started responding differently, something that might sound like this: "What if we started discipling people to live in contrasting ways instead of 'baptizing' the busy American culture. What if we were shaped to live well, to live in community as God created us to live?" This response is based in the "body" imagination, as I saw the need for Western Christians to understand how the church had been co-opted by Western culture.

The "breath" imagination takes us further as it addresses our God-shaped desire to live in love. We can follow the right rules and embrace good life patterns, but if our desires, passions, and wants are not part of the equation then the energy for God's kind of community will wain. Think of it this way: if the single mom with three kids who has to work two jobs to make ends meet does not "want" to be a part of a group because she does not find in them a sense of joy, fulfillment, and even fun, then it does not matter how much you teach on the biblical basis for community or the fact that group life will be good for her.

The same extends to our work as group leaders, coaches, and pastors. If pastors and volunteer leaders do not experience a sense of love, joy, and peace (along with the other fruit of the Spirit) in group life, if there is no innate energy that stirs up desire to love others in community and on mission, then there will be no passion for God or for groups. I'll take ten people who gather because they live in love for God and others over 10,000 who do groups out of a sense of duty.

Now when I hear excuses about people being too busy for groups, I wonder, "What is happening in groups that is not compelling, attractive, and evocative?" God's breath is utterly beautiful, completely attractive, and perfectly alluring because "God is love." When the "breath enters," we come to "life and stand up on our feet—a vast army" just as Ezekiel saw. This is what makes groups flourish and stirs up desire for groups.

Four Facets of the Breath

The understanding of God's breath of love is not merely about good feelings for God and other people. To understand the breath of God, we need to examine the way that the breath enters in and through a church. This will shape our coaching interactions.

After the conversation I had with Jim Egli about groups in North American churches, I began my research by identifying thirty-five North American churches with whom we had worked and listened to their stories to ascertain the differences between churches that failed, floundered, or got stuck in being fine against those that flourished. I compared the journeys of these churches to understand patterns and studied how they organized the structures (bones) and the various ways that they discipled their people in those groups (body). This opened up an imagination to see how the breath (living in love) enlivens groups.

In order to understand what I was observing in these churches about the breath, I looked outside the bounds of typical ways of talking about the Spirit to understand better the ways that the Spirit moves. Specifically I explored four things.

First, I sought to understand the principles of organizational and cultural change and how effective leaders develop a process for leading people into groups. Through interaction with change leadership experts like John Kotter, Ronald Heifetz, and Robert Quinn, I discovered how the development of groups is about leading people to live differently in order to embody a new way of being the church. This revealed how hidden systems of church life either create space for God's love or block it. The way that pastors lead, in other words, can promote a culture of love and when this is done, there is room for the Spirit to generate the kind of life that naturally results in flourishing. On the other hand, when pastors lead through force, subtle manipulation, a cult of personality, or aggrandizing sales pitches, they are actually cultivating a culture that blocks God's breath of love.

Secondly, I took a deeper drive into what it means for the Spirit to move through the church as a missionary congregation. When a missionary moves to a country like Indonesia, she assumes that she doesn't don't know how they think and live within their culture. Out of love, she would pay attention to the people in the local context. With regard to groups in Western settings, we need a similar mentality. We need to love as Spirit-discerning missionaries in our own culture. Thus I explored sociological themes that explain the way we live in Western contexts and how that influences the way we do church and the way we develop groups. For instance, the sociologist Kenneth Gergen uses the image of a "saturated self" to describe modern identity. We are over-saturated, over-informed, over-committed, and over-stimulated. When we add groups on top of this way of life, what do we really get? Part of the answer is summarized by the words "failing," "floundering," and "fine" because we only have time for a religious program called a small group meeting. There is no time nor space for love, and therefore no time for flourishing.

A third thing I explored was the importance of spiritual formation and how this shapes the way we live in community. Being that we have been discipled to do church in a certain way, and we have been formed by a broader culture which is over-saturated, over-informed, over-committed, and over-stimulated, we need to think of the development of groups in terms of how the Spirit forms us. To move beyond failing, floundering and fine groups, we must embrace the way that the Spirit forms people to live according to God's breath.

Finally, I dove into how the triune God is the embodiment of community and what it means for the people of God to participate in the mysterious community of the Father, Son, and Spirit that has always been and will always be. The kind of community that God has for us is that which can only come as a gift by the Spirit. I asked what it means for the Spirit to draw groups and a group system into participation in God's life, God's community, and God's mission in the world, based on the assumption that the Spirit is alive and active.

These four topics give shape to four facets of God's breath, even though they are not directly related to how we typically speak about the work of the Holy Spirit. Each of these identify hidden elements that are crucial to visible results. Bones and body are tangible and visible. The breath is unseen and below the surface. For instance, leading change in a church is more about addressing the hidden factors of culture and interpersonal relationships than it is about following a change formula. Or consider the hidden impact of an over-saturated life upon group involvement and how the Spirit is at work to change our everyday experiences, not just what we do or don't do when we meet formally as a church. Spiritual formation is not about going through a fixed set of classes or curriculum; it is about listening deeply to the Spirit's work in people, in groups, and in our common lives. If we take God's triune life seriously, then God's way of working in the world is a hidden mystery that is more relational (and messy) than productive (and strategic).

Groups flourish not because we invest endless energy in external bones and body factors like curriculum, videos, training sessions, strategic planning, etc. Those things are important, of course; however, if that is what makes groups flourish, churches would not be struggling with groups as they do. Groups flourish because the hidden life of God's breath shapes how we engage one another in life together. If you don't get anything else from this book, let this point sink it: *the hidden produces the visible flourishing.*

The hidden breath can be illustrated by the analogy of a sailing vessel. First, the various grouping strategies that a church adopts or develops operate as a part of the hull and rigging of a sail boat— corresponding with the bones from Ezekiel's vision. The crew that is equipped to sail the ship is required to make the boat work—the body. However, for that boat to sail well, there are many other aspects that are much less obvious and much harder to define. Some are related to how the boat works beneath the surface (unseen organizational systems of the church). Some are related to the way the crew is empowered to fulfill the vision of the ship (the Spirit's formation of God's people) and how the captain leads that team (change leadership). Some are related to the waters in which the boat is sailing (missionary understanding of culture and church). Then there is the movement of the Spirit (the winds of the triune God) that fills the sails and cause the ship to move forward.

These hidden aspects of sailing (the breath of God) are woven into those that are more obvious (the bones and the body) because the tangible and concrete—the structures and discipleship processes—depend upon God's unseen movement.

Perspective—Presence—Practices

Investing most of our energy in external factors while ignoring the hidden life is akin to identifying the fruit of the Spirit (Galatians 5:22-23), developing lists of ways to be loving, joyous, peaceful, etc., and then putting great effort into the external actions that look loving, joyous, and peaceful. The fruit is a natural product of the hidden life of the Spirit. Likewise, flourishing groups are not the product of our efforts to prop up our external efforts to make groups work. They are a result of the hidden work of the Spirit that gives life to the external.

This hidden breath works with the development of the bones and the body, which is ignited by a three-part conversation between the Perspective we have about groups, the Presence of God who is with us, and the Practices that the Spirit uses to shape us to participate in God's life.

We need a Perspective that helps us embrace the memory that the God of love is at work in the world and that God's mission is first of all God's mission, not ours. This deepens our imagination regarding the way that the Spirit writes God's ways on our hearts. (See Part 1 of *Beyond Small Groups*.)

The reality of God's Presence with us empowers us to be with God and with one another in love. In contrast to functionalist relationships where we do groups for God and for others so that we can accomplish a set of purposes or attain some kind of goal, we need to develop the capacity of simply being with God and with others. (This is covered in Part 2 of *Beyond Small Groups.*)

The third thing that we need is a set of Spirit-shaped Practices that equip the church to be a people of God's breath. These practices guide those who have the responsibility of developing groups—senior pastors, group point leaders, staff pastors, volunteer visionaries, and group coaches—so that they can learn what it means to lead their churches into the way of Jesus. (I introduce this in Part 3 of *Beyond Small Groups.*)

Perspective, Presence, and Practices work together in a circular trialogue making space for the Spirit to shape us for participation in God's love and work in the world. We might illustrate this way.

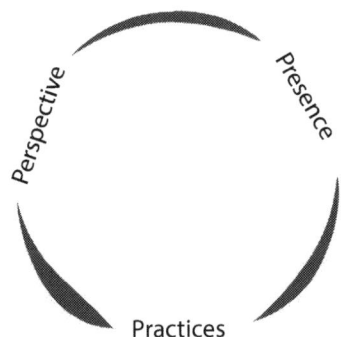

While recognizing the value of the bone prophets and the body disciplers, Perspective, Presence, and Practices opens paths for the Spirit to move the church on a serendipitous journey. This introduces the idea of the Pilgrimage that provides a practical process for leading your church beyond small groups.

The Pilgrimage

When we embrace the three-part movement of Perspective, Presence, and Practices, the Spirit opens space for us to move forward on a creative journey or what I am calling a Pilgrimage. Far too often groups flounder because pastors and leaders operate from a decision-based perspective. The goal, it is assumed, is to get from here to there so that we might arrive at a destination called "an effective grouping system," and to do so quickly. If church leaders decide to make groups a priority and if pastors and volunteer leaders work hard enough at implementing their chosen strategy, the bones, body, and breath will fall into place.

Instead a Pilgrimage perspective provides a framework for pastors and leaders to see that the bones, body, and breath are developed through the ups and downs of the journey itself. They converge and develop as the people of God learn together what it means to be God's people in groups within their local contexts, by the power of the Spirit. The goal is to enter into the beautiful ways of God where the Spirit leads the church into a customized, contextualized, and organic way of living in love with God and with others. It's a fluid, organic, and unpredictable way of embracing the way of God.

In our conversations, we will walk through eight priorities that facilitate this Pilgrimage, each of which seeks to answer a specific question about the journey. (These questions are explored in Part 4 of *Beyond Small Groups*.) They are:

Question: What Is the First Step?
Priority: Work from Reality

Question: Who Guides the Pilgrimage?
Priority: Lead as a Team of Dialogical Learners

Question: How Do You Prepare the Church for Groups?
Priority: Think Systems

Question: How Do You Get People Connected?
Priority: Provide Subversive Connecting Experiences

Question: How Will You Initiate Organic Missional Experiments?
Priority: Foster Missional Community Experiments

Question: How Will You Form People for Flourishing Community?
Priority: Develop a Spiritual Formation Environment

Question: How Will You Support Groups So They Flourish?
Priority: Establish Hidden Support Systems

Question: How Will Groups Impact the World?
Priority: Invest in the Hidden, Indirect Work of the Spirit

As we work through these eight priorities, we will interact with various resources that apply to the bones and body. These will serve as the tools of a *Beyond Small Groups* toolbox from which we will pick and choose as we seek the filling of the breath.

May the Spirit guide our conversations and open our eyes to see what the Father-Son-Spirit is doing in our midst. I look forward to the journey.

Scott

Part 1

Perspective

2
What Do We Desire from Groups?

What do you want from your groups? Do you want to become a church of small groups? Or a church with 80% of your people in groups? Or an "organic" church? Or a "sticky" church that closes the back door? Or a church with exponential group growth? Or a pure cell church? Or a church of missional communities?

These are some of the goals that have been promoted, serving as rally cries to motivate churches around the vision for small groups. These are the things that we want, but are they what we really desire?

We have far too often settled for rally cries that spark energy in the short term, but they end up being cheap batteries that fail to spark our deep passions over the long haul. What we say we want is often misguided when we fail to let the desires that are part of the created order shape our dreams for groups. If the wants take center stage, our desires get covered over.

We Want Groups

Churches do life as an organization of sub-groups. In many cases they are formal: leadership teams, worship teams, Sunday school classes, home small groups, youth groups, etc. It's only natural that churches would get stuff done in groups as they are part of the warp and woof of how good living works. All organizations operate as a system of groups. Businesses, governments, teams, classrooms, volunteer foundations, and, yes, churches work as a network of smaller groups.

We often miss the reality of how groups pervade our lives because they are always present, whether they are healthy and life-giving or not. We are born into a small group called a family. We go to school in groups called classes. We play in groups called teams. We organize our work in groups. Our friendships naturally cluster in groups. We even eat in groups, something that is easily illustrated—for good or bad—by our high school lunch breaks.

Small groups are everywhere. And they are in your church whether or not you actually have a specific grouping strategy. Whether you are a church of a century and a half or a year and a half; whether you are a church of 2500 or 25, you have groups.

This is just the way relationships naturally work because we cannot connect with everyone at the same level. We even see this in the life of Jesus. He did not relate to the entire world 2000 years ago, as he came to the people of Israel. Within Israel, he related to people at different levels. He surrounded himself with three intimate confidants and nine other close friends. Jesus then related to a large group of up to 70 people who followed him in his ministry (See Luke 10). Then there were others who were connected to him, symbolized by those in the Upper Room after his ascension. Beyond this, he related to the crowds of people who did not know him personally (e.g., the crowds who heard the Sermon on the Mount or the 5000 who were miraculously fed). Those around Jesus formed a web of connections, and thereby the smaller groups closest to him knew him in a way that those who were further away did not.

We want a strategy to make groups work. In most cases, this means that we want a formula that we can replicate, a mechanistic program that we can implement. While working for one of the first organizations that promoted small group strategies in the North American setting in the 1990s, we developed more resources, conferences, and tools than anyone. We studied small group churches that were flourishing in places like South Korea, Singapore, East Africa, and Columbia. We analyzed their systems and programs. We adapted them for the North American context, and many churches adopted those systems and programs. They got what they wanted, but they did not get what they desired. Actually, our desires played a very small part of that conversation.

What We Need

Even though groups are foundational to the way we do life in the North American context, and even though we have developed some great resources over the last three decades, the systems and programs that look like those we observe in churches in South Korea and other countries fall short of the life they experience there. We say we want small group strategies, but the strategies fail us because we don't see what is going on beneath the surface, and therefore we fail to see what we really need.

We live in an era of chronic isolation and disconnection. It does not take much effort to get a basic understanding of how sociologists describe Western life to see what is going on. Over the last few decades, cultural observers have used images like the lonely crowd, bowling alone, the saturated self, a society of strangers, intimate strangers, the myth of individualism, and many others to describe common life. There has never been an era in the history of mankind when humanity has practiced a way of life that is characterized by such pervasive isolation.[1]

While we are "hardwired for relationships," and we intuitively know it, our way of life fosters a set of practices that train us to live as if we don't need each other. In describing this way of life, the authors of the classic book *Habits of the Heart* write about the mythology of individualism using the characters of cowboys and private detectives as individualistic heroes to illustrate their point:

Both the cowboy and the hard-boiled detective tell us something important about American individualism. The cowboy, like the detective, can be valuable to society only because he is a completely autonomous individual who stands outside it. To serve society, one must be able to stand alone, not needing others, not depending on their judgment, and not submitting to their wishes.[2]

This mythology shapes us. Our logical conclusions about the need for belonging and connections don't necessarily form the way we practice life on a daily basis. The environment in which we live forms us without our even knowing it. For instance, we tend to operate as if we are able to construct ourselves from nothing so that we can do what we want to do and be whomever we think we should be. We change jobs. We relocate. We create identities online. We switch marriage partners. We try to form and reform ourselves as if we were a blob of Play-doh. If we were to look in the mirror and ask, "Who are you?", the honest response would be, "Who do you want me to be today?"

In the midst of this reality, we need to go beyond what we want and listen to our desires. Then we can align our wants with these God-created desires.

What We Desire

When we take an honest look at how we do life and then compare that to the biblical call to be the church, it does not take long to see the disparity. We could look at many different scriptures to illustrate this point, but this one highlights the point as concretely as any:

> Therefore if you have any encouragement from being united with Christ, if any comfort from his love, if any common sharing in the Spirit, if any tenderness and compassion, then make my joy complete by being like-minded, having the same love, being one in spirit and of one mind. Do nothing out of selfish ambition or vain conceit. Rather, in humility value others above yourselves, not looking to your own interests but each of you to the interests of the others (Phil 2:1-4).

In verse three, the word that is translated "others" is the Greek word *allelon*, which literally means "one another." This is one of the 59 "one another" verses in the New Testament. (See list on the next page). The church is called to be a people who live in community with each other and manifest God's love to each other in these ways. This stands in sharp contrast to the patterns of life that describe our culture.

We are created for the one anothers, so much so that we have built within us a deep hunger for them. When you are hungry, what do you want? The answer is obvious: you want food. If you were to say that you want _____ (insert the name of your favorite restaurant), no one would think that you want the actual restaurant. You want the food that is served by that restaurant. The restaurant is simply the form used to provide that food.

When we say that we want groups to flourish in your church, what is it that we really want? We don't actually want the form called "small groups" or "missional communities." We want belonging, community, life together, connection, prayer, sharing, sacrifice, the presence of God together, mutuality, discipleship, leadership development, spiritual gifts, mission. In other words, we long to love and be loved. What we want could be summed up with this Venn diagram.

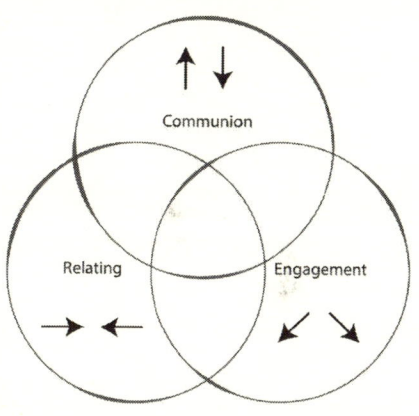

Communion with God, relating well to one another, and engaging our world with the Gospel sums up our longings for group life. Or it could be described this way: Loving God together, loving one another, and being a witness to God's love in the world. One of my mentors put it this way, "If you love God, love each other, love those who don't know Jesus and train others to do the same, your group will flourish."

Some kind of basic explanation like this for what we want to see in groups can be found in almost every book on small groups and missional communities from the last half century. For instance Bill Donahue writes of four basic components that he hopes to see in groups:[3]

Love. "Love is expressed in a variety of ways in group life. First,

One Anothers

Accept one another: Accept one another, then, just as Christ accepted you, in order to bring praise to God. (Rom. 15:7)

Admonish one another: Let the word of Christ dwell in you richly as you teach and admonish one another with all wisdom, and as you sing psalms, hymns and spiritual songs with gratitude in your hearts to God. (Col. 3:16)

Bear one another's burdens: Carry each other's burdens, and in this way you will fulfill the law of Christ. (Gal. 6:2)

Bear with one another: Be completely humble and gentle; be patient, bearing with one another in love. (Eph. 4:2)

Build up one another: Let us therefore make every effort to do what leads to peace and to mutual edification (original=build up one another). (Rom. 14:19)

Care for one another: . . . so that there should be no division in the body, but that its parts should have equal concern for each other. (1 Cor. 12:25)

Comfort one another: Therefore encourage each other (original=comfort one another) with these words. (1 Thess. 4:18)

Confess faults to one another: Therefore confess your sins to each other and pray for each other so that you may be healed. The prayer of a righteous man is powerful and effective. (James 5:16)

Be Devoted to one another: Be devoted to one another in brotherly love. (Rom. 12:10a)

Encourage one another: Therefore encourage one another and build each other up, just as in fact you are doing. (1 Thess. 5:11)

Fellowship with one another: But if we walk in the light, as He is in the light, we have fellowship with one another. (1 Jn. 1:7)

Forgive one another: Be kind and compassionate to one another, forgiving each other, just as in Christ God forgave you. (Eph. 4:32)

Greet one another: Greet one another with a holy kiss. (Rom. 16:16)

Be Honest with one another: Do not lie to each other, since you have taken off your old self with its practices . . . (Col. 3:9)

Honor one another: Honor one another above yourselves. (Rom. 12:10b)

Be Hospitable to one another: Offer hospitality to one another without grumbling. (1 Pet. 4:9)

Be Kind to one another: Be kind and compassionate to one another, forgiving each other, just as in Christ God forgave you. (Eph. 4:32)

Love one another: Let no debt remain outstanding, except the continuing debt to love one another . . . (Rom. 13:8)

Members one of another: So in Christ we who are many form one body, and each member belongs to all the others. (Rom. 12:5)

Pray for one another: Therefore confess your sins to each other and pray for each other so that you may be healed. The prayer of a righteous man is powerful and effective. (James 5:16)

Be of the same mind with one another: May the God who gives endurance and encouragement give you a spirit of unity among yourselves (original=same mind among each other) as you follow Christ Jesus . . . (Rom. 15:5)

Serve one another: You, my brothers, were called to be free. But do not use your freedom to indulge the sinful nature; rather, serve one another in love. (Gal. 5:13)

Spur one another on: And let us consider how we may spur one another on toward love and good deeds. (Heb. 10:24)

Submit to one another: Submit to one another out of reverence for Christ. (Eph. 5:21) we express love to God through prayer and worship and by giving him praise. We express love to one another as we serve one another and care for one another in our group."

Learn. "Learning about Christ and about his will for our lives is a key component of group life. All groups learn—they learn the Scriptures, they learn about one another, and they learn about themselves."

Serve. "Service and good works are part of any vibrant, healthy small group. Your group must decide how you will express Christian love to your community or to others in the body."

Reach. "Groups must make decisions that ensure the group's purpose and vision are carried out. That means reaching others for Christ."

Steve Gladden writes in his book *Leading Small Groups with Purpose* that his dream for what he wants to see in small groups is based on the experience of the early church recording in Acts 2. There he finds the five purposes of the group: Fellowship, Discipleship, Ministry, Evangelism, and Worship.[4]

Joel Comiskey has performed, by far, the most research on the worldwide growth of the cell church and has written over twenty-five books on the topic. While the cell church has not taken off in North America like it has on other continents, the hopes and dreams of what leaders want to see happening in the cell groups looks much the same as those stated by Donahue and Gladden. Comiskey writes,

> Cells are groups of three to fifteen people who meet weekly outside the church building for the purpose of evangelism, community, and spiritual growth with the goal of making disciples who make disciples, which results in the multiplication of the cell.[5]

Similar things are stated about what leaders want to see from the groups that are commonly called missional communities. Mike Breen promotes the Up-In-Out dimension of group life. Reggie McNeal summarizes it this way:

> The up-dimension includes worship and efforts toward helping members maintain a dynamic and growing relationship with God,

including a personal relationship with Jesus as Savior. Typical in-dimension emphases of community life are the nurture and care of each other, praying for one another, encouraging one another, and attending to the physical, social, economic, and spiritual needs of other members. Out-dimension expressions of service and witness vary from group to group, depending on the particular mission of the community. Some communities target the homeless and others minister in night clubs, some in gated communities, and others convene Alpha groups in their living rooms and office conference centers.[6]

Almost all the resources on small groups and missional communities share the common emphases on loving God, loving of one another, and sharing the gospel in the world; however the desires for Communion, Relating, and Engagement that I'm promoting here are subtly different.

What We Desire: Communion with God

Right before Jesus went to trial and then to the cross he prayed:

I'm praying not only for them
But also for those who will believe in me
Because of them and their witness about me.
The goal is for all of them to become one heart and mind—
Just as you, Father, are in me and I in you,
So they might be one heart and mind with us.
Then the world might believe that you, in fact, sent me.
The same glory you gave me, I gave them,
So they'll be as unified and together as we are—
I in them and you in me.
Then they'll be mature in this oneness,
And give the godless world evidence
That you've sent me and loved them
In the same way you've loved me. (John 17:20-23)

The longing of our hearts is for communion with the Father. There is a deep-seated desire in our being that can only be met when we are living in unity with God. This goes far beyond praying the sinner's prayer so that we can go to heaven when we die. This is about the experience of union with God that is a kind of dance with God in the here and now.

This kind of communion cannot be captured by our efforts in prayer and worship, while they are essential. This is about learning to live in personal interaction with the Father through the Son by the Spirit. And this kind of union moves us toward oneness with others. We cannot be connected to one another without communion with God. Dietrich Bonhoeffer put it this way:

> Christian community is not an ideal we have to realize, but rather a reality created by God in Christ in which we participate. The more clearly we learn to recognize that the ground and strength and promise of all our community is in Jesus Christ alone, the more calmly we will learn to think about our community and pray and hope for it.[7]

We only connect to one another as Christ, by the Spirit, stands between us. If we lack this communion with Christ by the Spirit, then connecting to each other will only be something we manufacture via our efforts.

What We Desire: Relating with Each Other

Jesus prayed that we might be one with others in the same way that Jesus and the Father are one. Our communion with God unites us in love to one another. This manifests creatively like a great painting. I'm a fan of the Impressionists. Prints of Monet, Renoir, and others bring life to a room. However, when I first saw an original in person, I entered into an experience that no print can reproduce. Prints, being flat cannot replicate the brush strokes or the depth of the paint on the canvas. The light bounces off the paint in such a way that the images come to life. The characters sitting around the tables looked as if they were inviting me to join them. I stood mesmerized because I didn't just view it. It pulled me into it. In a similar way, the experience we long for in our groups is like being pulled into a work of art. We are not mere observers, but we are participants in a unique masterpiece where no two are the same. Connection is not a cheap print replicated from a past experience or a formulaic concoction promoted by another church across the country. Connection cannot be copied, replicated, or mimicked. Every connection experience is unique, a one of kind expression of God's love.

This is far more than the development of a small group program or of some kind of organic missional community experience. It actually is not something that we produce at all because we cannot make it happen. It's something that we enter, that we participate in as we love the other in the presence of Christ. We love each other through Christ who stands between us by the Spirit, in the same way we are loved by Christ.

This is mystery. This is the reason why I use the awkward word "Relating." It does not role off the tongue naturally like "Communion" or "Engagement." That is purposeful because every time I teach or write about it, it creates a pause, reminding us that while we know what it means to relate, in all honesty, we only enter into it when we come to realize that we actually don't have the ability to relate. It is a mystery that occurs when the space that stands between us is filled with Christ and then the Spirit connects us to one another. We don't control it because it is a gift that lies beyond our grasp.

What We Desire: Engagement with Context

According to the prayer of Jesus in John 17, the way that the world will come to believe that Jesus is the manifestation of God is through our connection with one another as we commune with God. Our love for each other demonstrates to the world that we belong to Jesus, that we are his disciples (John 13:35).

Jesus prayed that we might live in unity, in oneness with one another as we are one with the Father, which results in being "witnesses" of Jesus. This is not about developing an evangelism program so that we can get converts to join our groups. This is about living in such a way that our lives bear witness to Christ, so that we put on display the beauty and love of Christ in the midst of the world. This witness occurs as the church engages the world in conversation, as it lives in self-sacrificial love with those who do not know that love.

What We Really Desire: Beyond

The prayer of Jesus in John 17 is a prayer that the people of God would go beyond merely attending meetings or talking through Bible study questions. As Jesus lived in communion with the Father by the Spirit, so the church. As Jesus lived in relationship with others by the Spirit that unites, so the church. As Jesus lived in engagement with the world as a witness to God's life, so the church.

A group leader who had tons of experience leading Bible studies went through training to guide her group into this new experience of beyond. In the meeting, she asked questions, modeled transparency by sharing about her own life, and made sure there was plenty of time for prayer. She connected with people outside the meeting and tried to create a safe place for people to be real. She called her pastor after a three months of leading in this way and told him that she was tired of taking the risk of leading this way. She planned to return to the old Bible-study pattern if something did not change in the next meeting. That night, a member of the group shared how he was HIV positive, which he had contracted while participating in a lifestyle that he was ashamed of. Up to that point, no one in the church knew about this. The group surrounded him, laid hands on him, and prayed. Two ladies who were friends of a group member were visiting the meeting that night for the first time. One stood up and blurted out, "This is crazy" and left. The other opened up about how she had been abused as a child. As they listened, she began her journey of walking with Jesus.

This is a taste of what lies beyond.

3

What Do We Get?

We want our groups to move beyond programmatic meetings. We want Communion with God, Relating well with each other, and Engagement with our context.

However, let's ask this crucial question: Is that what we get? It's easy to confess that this is the aim of our groups, but it's much harder to be honest about what we actually experience. Too often we end up with wishful thinking.

Since I was eight, I've been a Texas Rangers baseball fan. In 1972, the Washington Senators franchise moved from Washington D.C. to the Dallas area and changed their name. Up until the mid-1990s, the Rangers waffled between futility and mediocrity from year to year. Nonetheless, you could not shake my commitment. I would do chores on our farm in North Texas while carrying around a little blue transistor radio, hanging on the narration of every pitch.

Before a season in the early 1980s, I listened to my favorite player, Buddy Bell, tell a reporter how they had a real shot at winning the World Series. Since I knew everything possible about the players and coaches, my logic told me that they were fated for another year of futility. Nonetheless, my heart leapt with hope. Within a few weeks after opening day, it proved to be false hope; it was another year of baseball mediocrity.

When I read books that are published on various forms of group life in the church, I sometimes hear Buddy Bell's words of unfounded hope ringing in my ears. While on the surface, we cast the vision for Communion, Relating, and Engagement—or whatever language one might use—I look at the evidence regarding small group implementation in North America over the last fifty years, and the results have not lived up to the promises. In fact, it seems like we are more interested in hopes and dreams than we are in dealing with reality.

In his classic on the vision for community, Dietrich Bonhoeffer challenges this mindset with these words:

> Those who love their dream of Christian community more than the Christian community itself become destroyers of that Christian community even though their personal intentions may be ever so honest, earnest, and sacrificial. ... Those who dream of this idealized community demand that it be fulfilled by God, by others, and by themselves. They enter the community of Christians with their demands, set up their own law, and judge one another and even God accordingly.[1]

I remember the first time I bought into such dreams. It was 1992, and I was reading about how churches around the world were expanding small groups so fast that they were spreading like an ant hill that had been recently stomped. As a young pastor-to-be, I interviewed a church consultant who helped churches develop organic, multiplying groups. He told me how within ten years his church would be so large it would have to gather annually in the local professional football stadium, which held about 60,000 people. It never happened.

The next year I attended a groups seminar in the Midwest. The pastor had signs posted around the building with the vision for 2000 groups by the year 2000. He told us during his talk that a vision can only be a vision if it seems unrealistic. I guess it was just too unrealistic, because it never happened.

Some promote hope by saying that their methods will get 100% of your people in groups. Others claim that if you follow their instructions you will get 125% of your people in groups, that is more people will come to your groups than attend on Sunday. Others say that the hope is not found in a small group of 10-15 but in a mid-sized group of 20-35. Still others argue that the goal is to create movement growth.

Then reality sets in. A small group pastor from the east coast confessed, "After about three years into small groups, I became angry with the small group experts. I did not want to read anything they said. They painted a picture of small group grandeur. They promised that the new structure would make everything great." This pastor was not speaking from failure. Actually she was sharing from a place of success and strength after they had started over 100 groups and over 80% of the church was in groups. Even more, this church was seeing conversion growth and leadership development through their group system, so much so that it was held up as a model for others to follow. However, these results did not match the deep longing within her. She did not like what she had actually gotten.

Group Stories

It is a great thing that groups have become so widely accepted that books, conferences, and web resources are so prevalent that it's hard to know where to start. Their seems to be an endless supply of group recipes developed by renowned small group chefs within model churches or from experts on the secrets workings of the first century church. However, as the old saying goes, "The proof is in the pudding," not in the recipes. It really does not matter what the recipe looks like on paper or from the perspective of pastors who organize those groups from church offices. It's a great thing that we have so many grouping recipe options at our disposal, because it gets pastors moving in that direction. However, normal people in your church will not give their lives for a small group recipe. Just as no one goes to a bookstore and purchases a book of recipes for the recipes themselves, the same is true of groups. The point of the recipe is to experience of the food that results from the recipes.

The point of small group strategies is to produce a kind of flourishing life that draws people into God's beauty.

The problem is that we cannot understand the groups that a church has developed in terms of a recipe. When this occurs, we can only understand the bones. Instead, we must understand groups in terms of a story, which emphasizes the body and breath. Who we are formed to be as the body and the power of God's breath results in a compelling and attractive the story.

The story of your groups is what makes groups group. If the story is storied well, then the groups will group well. If it is storied poorly, then ... well you get the picture. A group is an experience, a living parable, that tells a story.

Think about it this way: while we, as pastors and leaders, ask all kinds of strategy questions, these are not the questions that the group leaders nor the group members are asking—single moms with three kids, overworked accountants who are afraid their job is on the line, teachers who work with kids who are being neglected, (insert a description of one or two people in your church). The life that they live together in the groups is what makes the groups work. If the groups are not working at that level—at the level of the story that they experience—then it matters very little how we tweak the actual strategy.

Small groups depend upon relationships. The specific strategy cannot produce loving relationships. The strategy can create environments that promote the development of these loving relationships, but only relationships beget relationships. It's organic and fluid. It cannot be forced, contrived, or controlled.

Of course, the strategies that we implement can either promote or hinder the stories. But the strategies don't *make* the stories, as if we are in control of group story production. Rather, the strategies that we adopt are more like those of a corn farmer, who works with the natural ways of God's creation, as much as possible, to facilitate an environment where corn can flourish. He does not make corn; he simply makes space for corn to produce corn.

In the same way, we are in the business of creating space for Communion, Relating, and Engagement to flourish. We work with the way that God wired us, created in his image, where what comes most naturally to our souls can actually occur. When we create systems that promote this, we offer opportunities for the stories of God to be lived.

Now let's consider four common stories that pervade the life of almost any grouping strategy or model (as listed in the Appendix).

Four Common Group Stories

The way these stories are told in specific situations in local churches are always unique; however, these four stories provide us with a way to understand the kind of life we actually live in our groups.

The first story is called *Personal Improvement*. This is the group experience where individuals participate because it is personally beneficial. A group might say that it wants to live out Communion, Relating, and Engagement, but the reality is that the people are involved because they are drawn to a topic or to a group of people like themselves. Participation is high until it becomes inconvenient. Little to nothing in group members' personal lives is required to change to participate because each "me" lies at the center of the vision for the group. The key distinctive characteristic of this story is that people attend as long as it benefits them. Instead of Jesus at the center, each individual is at the center of the group and will participate at the level he or she deems beneficial to their well being. Communion, Relating, and Engagement might be the official confession, but it's not the way the story really works.

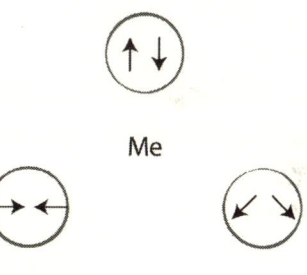

Lifestyle Adjustment identifies the second story. Group members view involvement in this kind of group as not only beneficial, but also it is crucial to their well-being. Therefore they are willing to adjust their schedules to prioritize attendance at a weekly or biweekly meeting. Usually this manifests in what is commonly called a "Bible study." We study what we should be, but it does not go much further than that. People tend to make longer-term commitments to attend such groups because they're good for one's spiritual journey. But the group usually vacillates between good and mediocre. It's not great enough to brag about, but

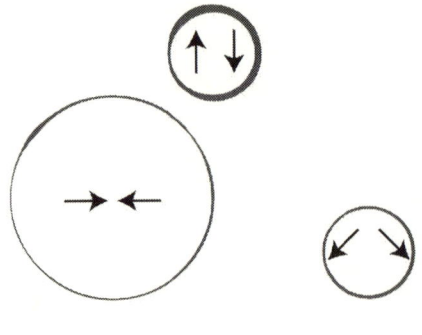

neither is it bad enough to stop attending. It's a good-meeting group that tends to focus on one aspect of group life, Communion, Relating, or Engagement. The above illustration shows how the Relating component is the emphasis.

In this case, the meeting becomes a place for focusing on Bible study and fellowship. Other groups might focus more on prayer or even outreach projects. And if the leader leads well enough, people will continue to make schedule adjustments to prioritize the meeting.

The third story is called *Relational Re-vision*. In this narrative, groups have a sense of urgency to operate according to a distinct set of practices that will form them into a community that stands out in our world. They recognize that Communion, Relating, and Engagement do not come naturally in an individualistic, fast-paced culture that dominates modern life, and they know that they have to make space in their lives for the Spirit to form them into a community that tells the story of the way of Jesus. This calls for commitment to Spirit-shaped practices that will train the group to live in distinctive ways that stand in contrast to the common patterns of the broader culture. In this way, they will discover unique ways to live out the dream of Communion, Relating, and Engagement. We could illustrate it this way.

Jesus

The point of this illustration is to demonstrate how the Spirit (depicted by the arrows pointing to Jesus) moves through us to form us into a community in the way of Jesus. We don't do this simply because we commit to it. It is a work of the Spirit that calls and empowers us into a different way of being a group.

Missional Re-creation describes the final story. As a group begins to practice these distinctive patterns of Communion, Relating, and Engagement, they become integrated around the presence and leading of Jesus by the Spirit. As this occurs, the group will follow the Spirit into creative patterns and structures as members engage the community. They will engage the neighborhood, determine needs, meet those needs and, as a result, develop creative ways to live out the way of Jesus. Through the dialogue with those in the local context, the actual forms and patterns of life will be shaped by the context. A few from one group might meet with a group of shift workers at a bar they frequent after getting off work early in the morning. Others will adopt a home for mentally-challenged individuals. And still others will come around a family that lives in a mindset of poverty and walk with them into a new way of being. The specific form is not the point. The key distinctive is that the group has learned how to live out of an integrated wholeness of the way of Jesus—Communion, Relating, and Engagement—and the presence of Jesus manifests in creative life by the Spirit.

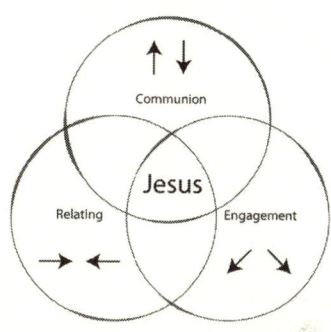

Comparing the Four Stories

Churches that promote the *Personal Improvement* story emphasize groups that fit into the normal patterns of life within the broader culture. For most in the Western world, this involves fitting groups into our over-saturated, over-informed, over-committed, and over-stimulated lives. For busy people, they create once-a-month groups. For people who fear commitment, short-term groups are the answer. For independent types, they are invited to start any kind of group they want. The focus lies on developing groups that fit the natural wants of individuals.

Lifestyle Adjustment groups focus on moving people into a meeting structure or closing the back door. It is an enfolding system. The strategy aims to gather Sunday attenders and keep them connected. Usually this story is heavily dependent upon a recruitment strategy so that there are enough groups for people to join.

While the church might publicly cast vision and set up support systems for living out *Relational Re-vision* or *Missional Re-creation*, most churches in the North American context do not go beyond the story of *Lifestyle Adjustment*. A good small group meeting is all that we get. We want and hope for more, but an honest look at what goes on in groups reveals that we fall short.

The stories of *Relational Re-vision* and *Missional Re-creation* make the meaning of "beyond small groups" concrete. Those living out these "beyond" stories recognize what we desire for our groups (outlined in chapter 2) will not come simply because we say we hope for it and attend a weekly meeting. They also recognize that the broader culture is a lived story that shapes how they do life at work and at home, and for the most part this cultural story is contrary to the way of Jesus.

The Story	Personal Improvement	Lifestyle Adjustment	Relational Re-vision	Missional Re-creation
Experience	Better Self	Better Friends	Formation	Organic Mission
Cost	Minimal	Attendance	Accountability	Sacrifice
Goal	Connections	Assimilation	Conversation	Engagement
Discipleship	Events	Curriculum	Practices	Experiments
Kind of Group	Short Term	Weekly Meetings	Discovering	Creative

This table names the differences between the stories. When we live out the stories of *Personal Improvement* and *Lifestyle Adjustment,* small groups are simply a programmatic meeting added on top of our regular life. The experience of the group is to attain a better self and better friends. These are good, but not good enough. God is calling us to be formed by the Spirit for the sake of participating in God's mission in the world. In the first two stories, the cost is minimal and is focused on meeting attendance. God is calling groups to go beyond that to accountability and sacrifice. In the first two stories, the goal is making connections and assimilating people for the sake of closing the back door of the church. God is calling groups beyond that into creative conversations around God's presence and engagement with others in our contexts.

Discipleship in the first two stories depends upon events and curriculum, whereas God offers more to groups when they embrace practices and creative, organic experiments.

In the first two stories, groups are short-term meetings that are programmatically designed to serve as a spiritual "good and service" provided by the church to those who want it. If the group is made up of the right people, the leader does a good job leading the study, and the people in the groups are friendly, then participation will be high. God is drawing groups beyond this into the discovery of God's gifting, power, and creativity in order to foster groups that change the world.

In summary, we long for the alignment of the bones and body with the breath of God that results in groups that live in a kind of love that contrasts with the patterns of the world. This is our deep hope, but instead we get programmatic meetings characterized by patterns that look a lot like the world. The group meeting is merely added on top of normal life. Why is this the case? This sets the stage for the next chapter.

4

Why Do We Get What We Get?

I had packed up everything I owned in my aging Honda Accord, left the familiarity of Texas, and trekked across the Western states. I drove up Interstate 5 and crossed the border and began my final leg into Vancouver, Canada. I was about to begin my degree in New Testament studies working under the direction of Gordon Fee, the author of the some of the best New Testament commentaries from the last fifty years.

My questions were two-fold. First, I wanted to understand the New Testament church so that I could confirm what I had already been teaching: that they met in small groups in homes. Finding answers to this question was quite easy because the common historical conclusions of New Testament scholars confirms my assumptions. The early church was a movement of small groups that primarily met in homes. Although some argue that they met in mid-size groups of twenty to forty in homes of the more wealthy Christians—and I'm sure this occurred in some locations—archaeological and historical research has demonstrated that most homes could only handle ten to fifteen people.

My second question was much more complex and has taken me

years to answer. I wanted to know why the early church got what it got. In other words, why did the early church experience the vision of Communion, Relating, and Engagement as they did? Why did they live as a parable of *Relational Re-vision* and *Missional Re-creation*? Answering this question helps us to understand the story that the early church told so that we can better understand the story that we tell today through our groups. Then we can better see why we get what we get in our groups.

The Story of the Early Church

In Luke's chronicle of the early church, we are told that early Christian movement was referred to as "the way" (Acts 19:9, 22:4, 24:14). When we look at how the church operated in the first century, this way was clearly lived out from house to house. It is also clear that they experienced some kind of organic, viral growth where incredible numbers of people believed in Christ and new churches were multiplied. This occurred with very little institutional or administrative oversight. Some have used these historical observations and concluded that since the modern church is organized so differently from the early church that these structural differences serve as barriers to the organic, viral expansion of the church. Therefore the way to get what the church in the New Testament got is to remove these institutional barriers.

However, if we look beneath surface of the historical facts about how the early church operated, some other factors about the way must be considered. Let's look at three. First, the early church was a movement with no social standing. In fact, it was considered a cult that undermined the mores of the majority culture. As an upstart, fledgling group proclaiming that a poor Jewish man, who was conceived out of wedlock, died on the cross, and then rose from the dead, where else would they have met but in homes? There is a reason that Paul claimed that the gospel was "foolish" after all (1 Cor 1:23). To meet in homes or other ad hoc places was the only option the early church had.

A second thing that stands out when one looks inside the world of the New Testament church relates to the role of the home in that culture. In the first century world of Jesus, Paul, and the other apostles, the home was a public place that was integrated into daily life. A carpenter did not go to a factory to do his work. His work would be connected to his house or to the house of another carpenter. Education, play, social interaction, eating—all of this would have been part of home life. To meet in the home of a church member during that time would have reflected daily life patterns. It would have been quite natural for early churches to meet in homes because of the role the home played in general society.

Thirdly, while we understand that churches in the New Testament met in homes, we don't have much evidence that reveals how they met. Actually those who want to get specific about what happened in these groups are speaking from silence. For instance, many argue that there were only small group house churches and that there was no preaching or teaching in larger gatherings. How can we actually know this? Jesus taught in larger groups, as did Paul which is illustrated by the story of him teaching all night in Ephesus (Acts 20:7). But there is a lot that we just don't know. It seems that church experts tend to project their preferred model of church life back upon the early church and thereby fill in the blanks.

While the New Testament, first century history, and archeology reveal that early Christians met in small groups in homes, to understand what went on in church life, we can only imagine how life centered around the home might have shaped the way that churches would have operated. This does not provide us with a model to follow, as if meeting in homes today will take us into small group panacea. Instead it helps us read the story of the early church and see how they lived out *Relational Re-vision* and *Missional Re-creation*.

Understanding Their Story

If we read between the lines, we can peek into some aspects of the life of the early church. While we don't have access to anything like a bulletin or a Bible study guide, we can see patterns. To see them, we have to try to let go of our modern expectations about how a church is supposed to operate. When we do this, we can see some of the ways that they practiced Communion, Relating, and Engagement, and thereby told the stories of *Relational Re-vision* and *Missional Re-creation*.

First, they ate together. The early church was not centered around a Bible study. In fact they did not actually have physical Bibles, and the New Testament was not written yet. A meal was crucial to their life together. People connect, talk, and share life over meals. Before, during, and after this meal, stories would have been shared, including stories about Jesus. And I might add that the Lord's Supper or Communion meal was a part of this. So the presence of Christ was woven into the common meal.

Second, they experienced what sociologists refer to as repetition of contact. This is a way of talking about how social capital is built through multiple, but short, interactions with one another. In the world of the first century, repeated social interaction with those who live nearby would have been the norm, both inside and outside the church. People would have worked in the fields together, interacted over their trades, and shared common life with each other. Dropping in and out of each others' lives would have been an accepted pattern. Therefore, when the Bible talks about the "one anothers" these would have been put into practice in many different ad hoc ways on a daily basis. It was not limited to some kind of organized form of house church life that the apostles programmed for church members. Consider the fact that a town like Ephesus was only about four miles long and less than two miles wide, with a population of about 300,000 people. Houses were built next to one another on narrow streets. Being a part of the home life of one's neighbors would have been part and parcel of daily life. "Dropping in" on one another would have been the norm.

Third, the church experience was public. Today we think in terms of insider church experiences and outsider ministry. Things like prayer, worship, Bible study, communion, etc. we do with one another as insider activities. Outsiders cannot see what we are doing. Then we have outsider activities like evangelism, outreach to the poor, and social justice projects—these are the things that usually take on the label of being "missional." To understand church life in the first century, we have to let go of this insider/outsider mindset. For instance, as they met in homes with windows that had no glass panes and were built adjacent to other homes on a street only six feet wide, a house church meeting would have been on public display. So imagine a church of twelve people worshiping in the home of a tanner. If they were praying for someone who was sick, neighbors could hear their prayers. If they were worshiping in song, people in the streets would be able to understand what they were singing. Think of the Apostle Paul preaching all night in Ephesus and the man falling from the second floor window (Acts 20:7). After Paul prayed for him and he came back to life, many people would have observed it. It was a public spectacle in a physically small city (by today's standards). The rumors would have spread quickly. The entire life of the churches was on display as a witness. Everything that the church did—both insider stuff and outsider stuff—was missional because it all demonstrated the love of God to the world. Evangelism was not just something the church went out to do. It was something that was happening all the time.

The fourth thing that the early church got was failure. The first century church was far from some kind of perfect model for us to follow. Just read 1 Corinthians. Paul was writing to real people with real problems. Groups are messy. There is no ideal way to do church that is going to eliminate this reality. And we need to quit talking about church as if we will suddenly find the New Testament secret to group life panacea. The more I look into the life of the early church, the more I see how much churches today have in common with them.

The fifth thing that I've observed that the early church got was wiki-like creativity. Typically, group organizations are conceived as being either high control or low control. In a high control group system, the oversight of the groups tends to be centralized and vertical. There is usually one type of group that is driven by the leadership of the church. In a low control system, the structure is flat and in some cases there is very little to no direct oversight. The metaphor of a free-market has been used to promote the idea that groups will organize around the ideas that individuals most value. A wiki-like structure is different from both of these options. Wiki is Hawaiian for fast and mobile. It was an idea developed to promote an open-source contribution of information to a website. Wikipedia is the most popular example. While to the casual observer it might look like a low control system, it actually has systems in place where information is confirmed and checked both by other people and by those who oversee the changes in content. The development of the early church was quite similar. It grew very fast, as the growth was not centrally controlled, but neither was it out of control.

Understanding Our Story Today

By looking back at the church in the New Testament, we can see various ways that the church lived out the way of Jesus in their real lives. Now let's consider how we group in our real lives today. After all, groups are about real life. They are about how we follow God when we wake up and head off to work; about how we relate to our friends, our neighbors, and our family; about the stuff that we call secular, not just the stuff that we do on Sunday when we go to worship or when we walk into a small group meeting. If we want Communion, Relating, and Engagement, then we must understand how we do life, not merely techniques to make Communion, Relating, and Engagement work in group meetings.

The common patterns of life in the modern world are vastly different from that encountered by Paul, John, and Peter as they were leading house churches. To illustrate this, consider the board game Clue. Each room represents a different part of life: work, family, work friends, kids, extended family, hobbies, etc. Each room operates according to a different set of rules. When in the room called "work" you interact with a specific set of people who do not enter into any of the other rooms with you. In addition, you have to follow a specific set of practices that are distinct from the practices in the other rooms. In some extreme cases, each room requires a person to put on a different mask to be effective.

The size of each room will vary depending upon their priority to your life. And this might change depending upon your life stage. For instance, if you have young kids,

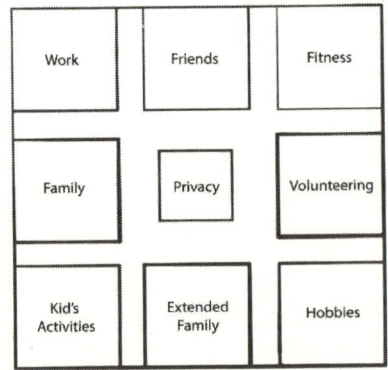

then the kid room will be large. If your job demands that you work 75 hours per week, that room might take up half of the board.

Where are God and the church on this board? To answer this question, try to think like a person who has not been a part of a church for at least ten years. They start coming to your church because they realize that they need God and to be a part of the church. Because the rooms of their life are established, church is like a sun room, added onto the outside of the house. It's an addition to the board.

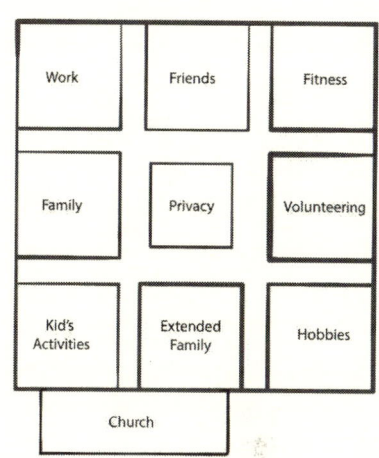

While we preach that God is the Lord of all our lives, the way we typically do our day-in/day-out living reveals how things really work. This is not an evaluation of Christian morality and whether or not Christians practice a distinctive moral standard from the broader culture. This is a way to illustrate how we practice common life in a world shaped by a secular mindset. Church is an add-on, a separate room that operates according to its own rules, one that often is viewed as having little impact on the way we operate in the other rooms. In fact, some pastors have gone as far as to admit that what they do on Sunday is meant to help people live a better life out there, in the "real world."

Now consider where small group involvement falls on this board. I would argue that we treat it as an addition to the addition. In many cases, it's like a closet added to the sun room of church.

For serious Christians, the way to follow Jesus gets interpreted as making the church room larger. Just like a workaholic might make the room called "work" larger than the rest, we often operate as if the goal of the church is to help people make the room "church" larger and larger. And the way that many do small group ministry follows this pattern. Those who are most committed to effective groups make the group closet larger.

As long as people view life in this fashion, all we can hope to expect from any group methodology are the stories of *Personal Improvement* or *Lifestyle Adjustment.* Groups are merely something we add to the rest of life.

Now this does not mean that the church should become the central room of the game board. The issue is not that simplistic. We cannot ask people to quit their jobs and move into a commune. The goal of using this game board metaphor is to demonstrate how normal life is lived and how groups are treated as an additive. In this way, we can begin to understand why we get what we get from our groups.

Take, for instance, the role of the home in this game board. The modern home is a private place that is meant to be a solace from the other rooms of life. As stated earlier, this was not the case in the culture of the first century. The home was the place that integrated all of the activities of life. In fact, this is still the case in many parts of the world. It is naive to think that if we simply start doing groups in our homes that we will suddenly change how we are following Jesus. Meeting in homes is a good step, but it won't change the stories that we live.

Leading people beyond small groups is about trusting that the Spirit is at work in our midst and that it's not a quick fix. This is why we need to embrace the reality of all four stories. They help us see where people really are, while at the same time recognizing the fact that God does not want to leave us there.

Understanding God's Story

God is at work, even in a world where it seems like *Personal Improvement* and *Lifestyle Adjustment* are the only realistic options. This is founded on the fact that God is a God of overflowing love, who is on mission in the world to draw up all of creation into his endless love. Therefore, it is not helpful to conclude that the first two stories are irrelevant, worthless, or even carnal. There is a role for these two stories in most church situations in the West because the God of mission meets us where we are, not just where we think God wants us to be. We live these stories because we are formed by habits. And changing these habits won't come about by pulling ourselves up by our boot straps and committing to live out *Relational Re-vision* and *Missional Re-creation*. They change because God descends into our situation and, by the Spirit, trains us up in a new way.

At the same time, we cannot be satisfied with the first two stories, as if getting people into groups—even 100% of your people into groups—is a worthy goal. There must be more.

All four stories are part of the way of Jesus because the Spirit of God is drawing us from where we are further along the way. We don't get to take the next step on the way from where we wish we were. Jesus works with us where we are. This means that the Spirit is leading and working to move us beyond the life of adding the "Christian thing" on top of our already overly-packed life that is dictated by all kinds of things going on in each room.

We don't move into the third and fourth stories only because we have good intentions to do so or because we develop a clear vision for them. Nor do we move into them because we want to be missional, because we change the name of our groups to missional communities, or because we have a vision clarity about the people we are going to reach. Groups rise and fall through our life together, the lived experience, not because we mandate something called community or announce that we want to be missional.

All four of these stories can be happening at the same time in your church. This is the problem with prescribing an ideal small group model. It forces people into a structure that does not honor their stories. Small groups don't work because we pen people, like cattle, in the right kind of form that is supposedly tested and proven to unlock the magic of Communion, Relating, and Engagement. Groups work because we have generated a space where people can live out the story they are living in now and then move with God on a journey into the next story.

We cannot force, cajole, promote, or preach people into the way of Jesus. The stories of community are not told from the center of the organization or the top of the pyramid. The stories of God are generated from the fringes of the people of God. They are told by people through "aha" moments where they see something new and unexpected about how God is at work through the power of loving others at cost to themselves. We don't make this stuff happen. We simply offer them environments where they might see it for themselves.

5

How Do We Get What We Desire?

I'm a fan of adventure stories, my favorites being those of J. R. R. Tolkien, *The Hobbit* and *The Lord of the Rings*. In the opening chapter of *The Hobbit*, we are introduced to the primary character, Bilbo Baggins, a self-proclaimed risk-avoider who does not go on adventures. In fact, he prides himself on staying to himself, not bothering other hobbits, and living in mediocrity. The story opens:

This hobbit was a very well to do hobbit, and his name was Baggins. The Bagginses had lived in the neighborhood of The Hill for time out of mind, and people considered them very respectable, not only because most of them were rich but also because they never had any adventures or did anything unexpected; you could tell what a Baggins would say on any question without the bother of asking him. This is a story of how a Baggins had an adventure, and found himself doing and saying things altogether unexpected. He may have lost the neighbors' respect, but he gained—well, you will see whether he gained anything in the end.[1]

If *The Hobbit* had chronicled Bilbo sitting at home pondering his safe life, it would have been 250 pages of boredom. Instead, it is a tale about Bilbo's reluctant adventure with a small group of companions to take back stolen treasures from a fire-breathing dragon. Adventures are adventures, after all, because they are full of ups and downs, struggles and victories, missteps and overcoming failures. This adventure takes them through a wooded forest where they are bound by large spiders, captured by three huge trolls, imprisoned for trespassing, and almost drowned as they floated down a raging river. And all of this occurred before they even get anywhere close to the dragon!

Adventures like *The Hobbit* teach us about life, leadership, and the church. For me, and many like me, we begin leading with assumptions that resemble the life of Bilbo at the beginning of the book, one that is defined by predictable outcomes, minimal risk, and getting results without having to give up the safe life. Or if we are moving into something different, we want a strategic plan that will make the path clear. In other words, we want promises of a successful destination before we take any steps. If that cannot be done, then we keep what we already have. But life and following God do not work that way.

If you want your church to foster groups that tap into our desires, to move from the groups that tell the stories of *Personal Improvement* and *Lifestyle Adjustment* and into the stories of *Relational Re-vision* and *Missional Re-creation*, then think about the way forward as an adventure. The Spirit of God is found in the unpredictable winds and waves, where we meet God, live in God's love, and share that love with others.

Embracing the Adventure

Adventure stories are adventurous because they are unpredictable. Aristotle has taught us that a great story introduces events that occur "unexpectedly and at the same time in consequence of one another." In other words, as the reader turns the pages, they cannot forecast what is coming, but upon reading what does occur, they make sense retrospectively.

Or to put it another way, such narratives do not work according to mechanistic predictability. They are driven by the characters as they encounter the presence of others and the circumstances along the way. We know that there will be a resolution to the story, however, we don't know how that will occur.

We can also see this as we read the Bible. Taken as a whole, the Scriptures are a grand narrative that moves like an adventure story, with the cross as the climax. Leading up to the cross are a series of conflicts. The cross and the resurrection serve as the culminating zenith to which all of the previous conflicts point. That which follows the cross and resurrection are demonstrations of how the climax of this grand story plays out. The climax of the cross rolls forward. This is called the resolution of the story, and it's the place where the church finds itself in the present.

Like acts in a Shakespearean play, when we read the Bible as a whole, we could imagine it as divided up into five acts. N. T. Wright breaks it up this way:[2]

- Creation
- Fall
- Israel
- Jesus
- Church

This climax of the cross and the resurrection defines the life of Jesus and the life of the church. We are trying to understand the implications of the scandalous foolishness of the cross and how we can live faithfully into this story. If we understand the cross rightly, we will see that there could never be a more unpredictable event in the history of the world. For the God of creation to take on human flesh, to come as a servant of servants, and then to die on a cross was and is absolutely inconceivable. No one in any culture in history imagines any deity in such a way. We only need to read the Gospels and see how none of those around Jesus had such an expectation. The fact that Jesus actually died, allowing himself to be viewed as a disgraceful criminal, the worst of the worst of society, is shocking.

Yet this is the defining act in the grand story. And here we see the defining movement of God. It's absolutely unpredictable. However, as we see in the writings of the New Testament, in retrospect, it makes sense.

The church today is part of this grand story. The defining moment of the unpredictable scandalous foolishness of the cross rolls forward toward God's final resolution as the person of Christ revealed on the cross must define the story of the church. This is what it means for Jesus to be the head of the church (Col 1:17).

However, when it comes to groups, this often is not the case. While the cross reveals how God comes and reveals himself in the unpredictable, adventurous way of the self-sacrificial love, that the way of Jesus is a way that is personal, there is a tendency in the church to develop groups in a way that mechanizes and de-personalizes groups. We make them about mechanics and techniques.

For instance, when churches develop groups based on a model developed by another church, they are aiming to replicate the techniques and mechanics of leadership training, curriculum, and organizational procedures that have proven effective.

Or consider when churches set up an ideal vision returning back to a pure New Testament model that supposedly will provide exponential movement growth. The ideal structures become rules or techniques that we try to replicate to make groups work.

Either way, we de-personalize groups and therefore undermine the very thing that makes groups work in the first place, the personal. We remove personal presence and the encounter with one another and with God which are the very parts that make any story worth being a story.

Groups are about knowing and loving God while we know and love others, not about techniques and strategies.

However, we continue to look for the next technique to make groups work. The supposed goal is to set up an abstract mechanism that will produce results independent of the specific people that are part of the groups. If the people within the structures do the structures in the right way, then you can expect the results you want. Those who are leading within the vision need not have the character of Christ or be empowered by the Spirit. In fact, some even promote their vision or way of doing groups by saying that this fact is one of the best attributes of their system. The magic is found in the structure itself. All one needs to do is to push play on their DVD. Or if you organize groups geographically, then you will foster simplicity. Or if you remove the barriers to growth, groups will grow all by themselves. Or meeting from house to house and as a whole church will return us back to the way of the early church (Acts 20:20).

The Story of the God is Personal

If we are going to get what we desire from groups, then we must embrace the way that God is revealed in God's story. Jesus did not provide us with a mechanistic formula for how to organize the church. He did not leave us a leadership model to reproduce. And he did not prescribe a way of life that will make the church work. Instead he gave us the cross and the resurrection. In our understanding of this climax of the story, we see that the cross is a manifestation of the relationship between the Son and the Father by the power of the Spirit. And then upon Christ's ascension, the Father sends the Spirit to remind us of all things that the Son has taught us. In other words, the Spirit comes to reveal to us the life of Christ so that we can participate in the life of Christ.

God is calling us into the waters of the personal presence of the Spirit so that we might hoist our sails and respond to the movements of God. Thus we are called not to an ultimate destination of something that we might label as "an effective grouping system." Instead we are called to the ultimate destination of knowing Christ and him crucified. Anything that stands in the way of this, according to the words of Paul, is "manure" by comparison, even if it produces an incredible group system (Phil 3:7-11).

As we know Christ by the waters of the Spirit, concrete structures, procedures, structures, and curriculum will be adopted (that is we might very well replicate something developed by another church) or developed (we might birth something new), but these things are not the center. They are peripheral to our knowledge of Christ.

The adventure story of your church that emerges as you sail the waters will be shaped by our being with Jesus and how the presence of Christ by the Spirit forms us as a community, as individuals, and as leaders. We cannot get around this fact. Because Christ's presence defines the way that God works in the world, we must embrace the fact that God's church and the effectiveness of the church depends upon the character of people who live in love by the Spirit, not the system that we develop. Knowing who Christ is matters. Because of that, who we are matters.

Navigating Your Adventure

Stories, whether on the macro level of the Bible, the micro level of specific books of the Bible, or the specific situation of your church, operate as a series of challenges and responses to those challenges. While the climax of the cross defines and brings ultimate resolution to the grand story, the story is not finally resolved. We are living in-between, in that part of the story where the ultimate victory has already been won, but that final victory has yet to manifest.

Your adventure story will be told as you enter the waters of life and learn the art of sailing. When a captain determines that he needs to change course in order to arrive at a new set of coordinates, he uses a nautical chart that shows water depths, surface obstacles, common water lanes, and navigational aids. The captain charts a course that is unique to his position, his destination, and the particular capabilities of his vessel. On water there are an infinite number of courses to take and each is unique to each trip, not just to each ship. In other words, no two trips will be the same, even if they begin at the same starting point and aim at the same destination. Weather, water currents, prevailing winds, and other factors will constantly impact the course a ship steers. As the voyage progresses, the crew will regularly re-evaluate the course and make adjustments as necessary to ensure that they arrive at the proper destination.

If we are sailing a ship of the church into groups, then thinking in terms of maps, blueprints, and predetermined destinations, will prove useless. We need to develop navigation skills that fit the situation. In addition, when sailing—as opposed to a ship that is powered by propellers—the captain and crew have to learn the skills of tacking, that is moving forward without going in a straight line. The way forward in the development of groups is not one of clear, predetermined paths, but one of leading people forward when it might look like you are going in the wrong direction.

Understanding the Challenges

One of the key navigation skills that you will need relates to how you understand and interpret the challenge of getting something beyond the normal stories that most live in their groups. If you don't understand the challenge rightly, you will try to address that challenge in the wrong way.

The following table delineates three types of challenges or problems that we face as leaders. Let's look at each in turn.[3]

Challenge	Problem	Solution	Source
Technical	Clearly Understood	Known	Leader
Discovery	Clearly Understood	Discoverable	Leader & Followers
Adaptive	Unknown	Unknown	Followers

Technical Challenges

Techniques are actions leaders take in order to address technical challenges. These are problems that we face where the nature of the problem is clearly understood and we know how to address the challenge. Most often techniques are developmental in nature. Churches experience developmental change when they seek to improve what they are already doing. Pastors read a book on preaching. Sunday school teachers attend a workshop. Children's workers travel to a conference. Prayer coordinators visit a church to learn about a new prayer ministry. We want to take the situation from one level to the next as illustrated by the graph on the next page.

The key to understanding the nature of techniques is the fact that they depend upon experts. The pastor or some kind of specialized trainer is the one who has the answer for the right way to solve the problem.

When we treat grouping as a technique, we think that we know

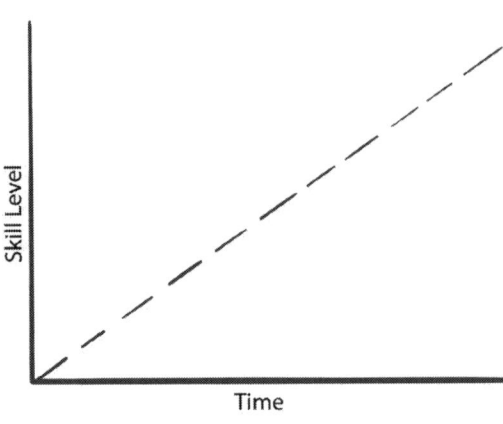

the nature of the problem. We need to "close the back door" or we need to get people connected and discipled. A small group strategy promises to do this if we just follow the "a + b + c = intended outcome" methodology. There is some truth to this, as there are some important techniques to learn. But as you develop skills, you discover that some, if not most, of the challenges we face in developing groups are not technical in nature.

Discovery Challenges

A more complex challenge is that which requires discovery. Instead of simply implementing a predetermined formula, discovery requires us to learn something new. The problem remains clear, and we know that we do not currently have the resources within us to address it, but we know that someone does.

Discovery of a new way invites us into a time of transition from one state of being to the next. The goal of the transition is clear and the steps to get there are laid out. We just need to shift from one way of operating to another.

In the church, transitional changes transpire when leaders discover that current methods do not work and that new methods are required. Examples might include the adoption of a new worship style, hiring a new staff member, adding a second worship service, replacing the Sunday evening service with a training center, or building a larger worship center. Transitional

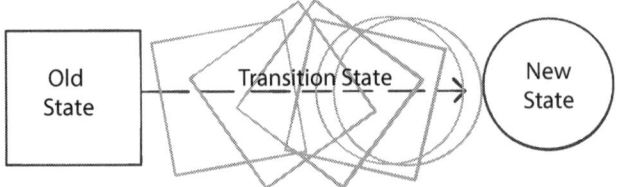

changes have set beginning and completion dates. They can be managed with the use of budgets and time lines.

When we treat groups as a discovery challenge, we know the nature of the problem—we need to learn to develop a group system—but we don't know how to do it. But someone does. There is an expert out there somewhere who can come and tell us how to design the "right" group system. They can provide us with the strategies, the manuals, and the structures that will take us from our current state and into flourishing groups.

In reality, a discovery challenge is just a slightly different form of a technical one. The difference is that we are not trying to improve the situation. We are trying to move from one situation to another. If your goal is to develop groups that experience the stories of *Personal Improvement* and *Lifestyle Adjustment*, then you will primarily be facing technical and discovery challenges. There are plenty of great strategies readily available to you that will take you that far.

However, if you want to see your groups live out the stories of *Relational Re-vision* and *Missional Re-creation*, then you are facing something much bigger. When we face these challenges, we look for answers from authorities, hoping someone "in charge" will provide a strategy to solve the problem we face. Pastors feel the pressure to act, to make something different happen and thereby overcome the problem. But groups that move into *Relational Re-vision* and *Missional Re-creation* are based on the reality that groups are about people not about strategies, curriculum, and structures. People come with unpredictable challenges and the manual got lost somewhere along the way.

When we look for answers from an authority, more barriers inevitably arise, creating a perpetual loop of frustration. Ronald Heifetz, an expert in adaptive leadership, writes, "In response to our frustration, we are likely to perpetuate the vicious cycle by looking even more earnestly to authority, but this time we look for someone new offering more certainty and better promises."[4] We must imagine beyond our traditional ways of thinking about group implementation and understand the adaptive nature of developing groups.

Adaptive Challenges

Adaptive challenges are different because they call for transformation of the character of those involved, thereby requiring us to change our way of being, not just our doing. "Transformation is the radical shift from one state of being to another, so significant that it requires a shift in culture, behavior, and mindset to implement successfully and sustain over time. In other words, transformation demands a shift in human awareness that completely alters the way the organization and its people see the world, [their ministry, the church and themselves.]"[5]

Church transformation is necessary because of the definition of the challenge. First, the challenge is such that a predetermined formula cannot address it. There is no set path that can be copied, no plan that can be reproduced. Secondly, the problem or challenge is not fully understood. With technical challenges, the problem is clear and there is a solution available. When facing an adaptive challenge, the challenge itself is an enigma. In order to define the problem, new learning is required.

A third attribute of adaptive challenges is that the solution is not found through the work of an expert—as in a church consultant who has a church formula—or a positional authority—a pastor or key leader who has traditionally been the source of solutions. Instead the work is done by the stakeholders, the common people of the church.

This means that the path is not predetermined, nor is the end result known from the onset. Change leadership expert, Robert Quinn, writes about this:

> Since they [leaders] are taking the organization where no one has been before, no one can know how to get there. No one has the necessary expertise. Furthermore, without the normal assumptions of equilibrium and expertise, the traditional principles of good management no longer work. Since there is no safe path, no way to be in control, they are forced to move forward one blind step at a time. ... They then experience exponential learning about self, others, and the organization.[6]

Quinn's observations points to leadership that is not based on experts, but on leaders who have the ability to create generative environments where people discover together the way forward. Instead of a leader controlling the way forward, the people create it together. The role of the expert is not that of providing a solution but of offering people a way to learn together.

Adaptive leadership gives us the space to treat the people we lead in our groups as people. They are more than leaders, or potential leaders. They are far more than disciples who can contribute to the life and success of the local church. They are complex, unpredictable creations of God who long to love and be loved. And the way that this occurs is always new, because the challenges that arise with people are always new.

Adaptive challenges require more than a change in the way we do church. They require us to change. They call us to become different, and as this occurs, we are able to write a different kind of story. The way the story usually progresses looks like this:

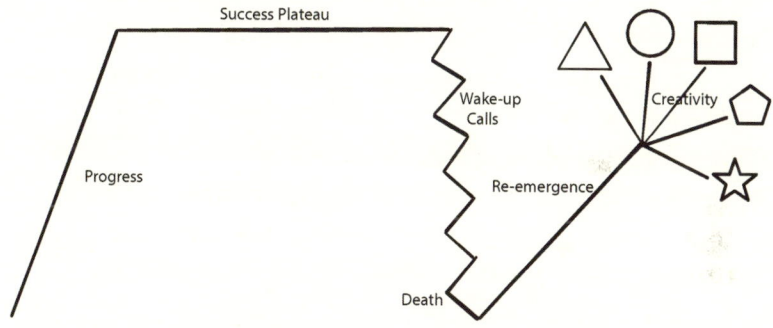

At first, the progress might begin in a predictable fashion, but the wake-up calls and the transformation through death are always unpredictable and unexpected. Most of the time we tend to search for technical formulas for adaptive challenges because we want to continue to tell the stories of success and growth that we told in the past or that other model churches seem to be experiencing in the present. As Heifetz and Linsky claim, "[T]he single most common source of leadership failure we've been able to identify—in politics, community life, business, and the nonprofit sector—is that people, especially those in positions of authority, treat adaptive challenges like technical problems."[6]

Failure is a cruel, but necessary teacher, which is part of the story and often it is the only way that we can learn to write a new narrative and thereby address the adaptive challenges. However, through this, we become different. We become the kind of people who live in a way that aligns us with the hopes and dreams that we have for our groups.

Technical and Adaptive

Most grouping strategies offer technical solutions, offering ready-made programs and fixed strategies. These technical approaches tend to lower the small group bar to make connecting in *Personal Improvement* or *Lifestyle Adjustment* groups as easy as possible for people. Technical/programmatic groups are like motor boats where we set a clear course and take control of the outcomes. Connecting small groups focus on how to develop systems that have the aim of closing the back door, making the church "sticky," or getting more than 30% of your church in small groups.

On the other hand, many recognize the adaptive challenge of living in community and on mission in our culture today. They tend the raise the grouping bar and call people into a distinct way of living that either fits *Relational Re-vision* or *Missional Re-creation*. The adaptive nature of such groups operate more like small sail boats who are tacking back and forth to navigate the winds of the Spirit and the currents of time. Missional communities, on the other hand, are designed to equip and release people to live out the gospel in their neighborhoods and grow through organic relationships. (An older label for this kind of group is "cell group.") Those who advocate for missional community focus on things like creating a way of life that is in contrast to the dominant culture, embracing a set of spiritual practices, developing a discipleship culture, experimenting with ways of engaging the neighborhood, and thinking outside the box with regard to how the church can be the church. Some take this so far as to abandon traditional forms of church life.

In most cases, churches tend to think in either/or terms, and therefore they choose between a group strategy that promotes Connection Community or one that aims a Missional Community. We opt for a grouping program that offers a technique or we view the entire process as being so radically different that all of it is an adaptive challenge. Those who want quick results for the established church are drawn to the technical options, while the more prophetic types lean toward those that are adaptive in nature.

It is my contention that most churches actually need to think in terms of both/and, both Connecting Community that is technical in nature and Missional Community that tends to be adaptive. As will become clear in later chapters from both theological and practical perspectives, churches need both because Missional Community is something that arises out of experiments performed by those who possess a sense of urgency to think outside of the box. In most cases, only five to ten percent of the church will have this sense of urgency. Connecting Community then becomes a preparation ground for the majority of the church so that they can move into Missional Community when they are ready for it.

For instance, if you are leading a church in the West, no matter the tradition, the people who comprise the church have been shaped according to a set of cultural expectations about what the church should or should not provide for them as spiritual consumers. This is not a critique of their perception of the church. It's just reality. People attend if they find the church experience beneficial—even if they only attend to appease a sense of guilt. If they don't find it so, they attend elsewhere or quit going altogether. Many connecting small group programs have been developed to meet these needs and to keep people from church jumping in a consumeristic world.

Of course, no pastor or leader is satisfied with this. We know that there is more for our groups than simply closing the back door or getting 80% of the church in groups. We want life together in community and on mission that goes beyond a programmatic group experience. In response to the desire for more, it is commonplace for churches to develop a vision for communities that are missional, that do life together in the neighborhood, that minister together in the midst of daily life. As many have said, such a pattern of group life is different from the more programmatic approaches to groups because the focus lies on equipping people to do this community on the margins. Such groups share community and the gospel with those who may or may not be interested in attending a traditional church service.

However, if you throw people shaped by consumeristic expectations regarding groups into something called missional community, you will get consumeristic experiments that are called missional. The wiser approach would be to develop underground missional experiments with those who are ready for such while providing connecting small group experiences for the majority of the people. Then as the missional experiments develop and grow into something concrete and observably effective, those within the connecting small groups will shift into missional community life.

Therefore, the imagination about grouping and the process for either starting a group system or taking your groups beyond calls for both Connecting Community (what has been labeled "small groups") and Missional Community (what many call "missional communities"). The names used are irrelevant, as will become clear in the chapters that follow. The point is that both work in tandem to guide into something that is beyond.

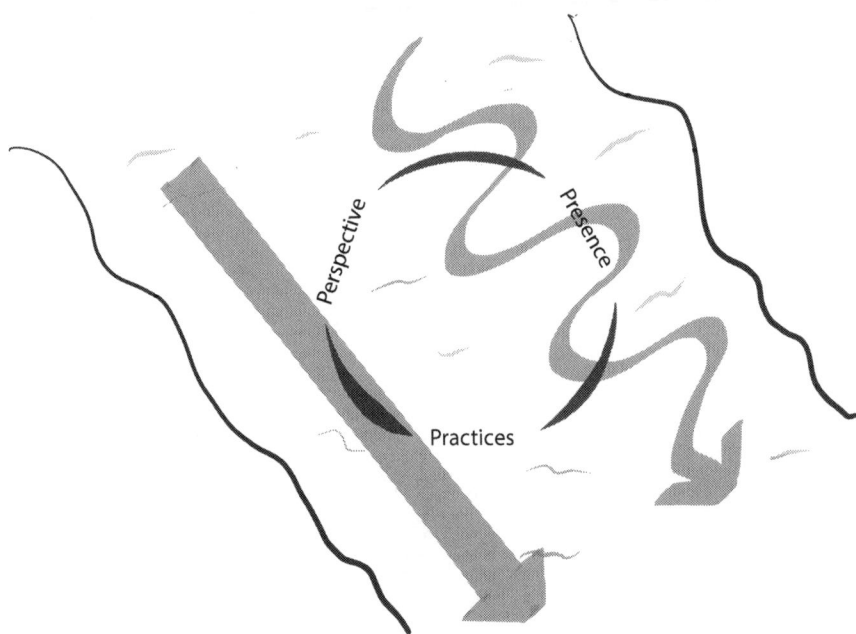

Therefore the technical and the adaptive work in tandem, Connecting Community alongside Missional Community. At the risk of stretching the analogy to the point of being silly, motor boats that progress in a straight line work alongside sailboats that tack with the winds of the Spirit to move the church into the river.

As we move forward, we need techniques, discovery, and adaptation. We must learn the skill of interpreting challenges so that we can address them properly. This is why we need both Connecting Community in tandem with Missional Community, which will be fully explained in Part 4.

6

How Do We Help People See Groups Differently?

In our over-saturated, over-informed, over-committed, and over-stimulated world, life patterns that actually make groups flourish do not fit. While people have built within them the God-given desire to live in love with God and one another, most don't have the time and emotional space in their lives to participate in what they desire, to live according to the way that God created humans.

Therefore, leading people into group life is not merely about developing and managing a small group strategy. It's not about getting people to attend group meetings or about getting a certain percentage of Sunday attenders into groups. It is about making a way for people to embrace change. It is about guiding people to see a different way of doing life, to imagine and participate in a way of living in love that challenges the status quo. We must shift our perspective about groups from an add-on meeting that we might or might not attend to participating in what God is doing as we walk with others.

Making this change requires helping people "get it." Of course, some will while others will continue doing what they have been doing. Jesus said, "Whoever has ears to hear, let them hear" (Mark 4:9).

He also told the disciples, "Blessed are the eyes that see what you see" (Luke 10:23). "Getting it" is about someone having an "aha" moment when they hear or see the reality of God and God's action in a different way. It occurs when a leader meets with you and explains how they are called to listen to people instead of talking all the time during the meeting. You think to yourself, "I know that I've said this at least twenty times in different training sessions; why did it take so long for them to 'get it'?" Or a group member who works eighty hours a week confesses that he is a workaholic and that God has called him to sacrifice income for the sake of investing in relationships. You wonder, "Has he been listening to any of the sermons over the last ten years?"

Leading people into groups is not about multiplying groups, getting the back door closed, raising up leaders, or even discipling group members. Those are derivatives of creating an environment so that people can have these "aha" moments where they see and hear what God is up to in the world.

Different Ways Individuals See Groups

Change involves a shift in perspective. A person can have all kinds of logical arguments about the truth of small groups and still miss the point. While information is important, it is never enough. Commitment won't get you there either. People can be trained and even mentored in obedience, but if they only obey because they are supposed to, they are small group legalists who have not had their desires transformed.

"Getting it" involves a shift in vision, an ability to see to such a degree that people's desires and passions change. This is where the four stories of group life (introduced in chapter 3) are crucial. There are basically four perspectives that people "get"—that is ways of imagining, perceiving, or viewing—groups. These are lived experiences that shape the kinds of changes they imagine about participating in groups. The following goes deeper into these four stories so that we can better understand how people "get groups."

The Story Personal Improvement
This is the small group experience where individuals participate be-

cause it is personally beneficial. The people involved are either drawn to a topic or to a group of people like themselves, and participation is high until it becomes inconvenient. Little in their personal lives is required to change to participate in this kind of group. In some cases, quite the opposite is true: They expect their personal lives to be enriched from the "goods and services" provided by the small group experience. They only see the group as something that adds value to their life, and therefore the only change required is to add meeting attendance to their schedules. In *Missional Small Groups*, I illustrated how these stories might play out as a testimony. I've included them here as well to illustrate my explanations. Here's the first for *Personal Improvement*:

> We get together because life is tough in this world, and we need a few friends. It is not always convenient for us to meet every week, but we do meet when we can. Usually we meet in short six- or seven week periods, or we meet a couple times a month. We get together, talk a bit about God or study the Bible and share what is going on at work and in our family. I am not sure that we are close, but it is good to have a place where we can share a little about what is going on in our lives. Being in my small group has improved my life.[1]

Those who tell this story "get it" as far as they see the need for more than attending church on Sunday mornings, and they will continue to "get it" as long as the group does not require too much effort. However, living in this story alone usually ends up in disappointment unless people are led to see that groups can be more.

The Story of Lifestyle Adjustment

This story is a logical extension of the first, as group life is viewed as beneficial, and therefore the group members are willing to adjust their life schedules to prioritize the attendance of a weekly or biweekly meeting. Usually, this involves a longer-term commitment to group membership, along with the development of friendships over time. This story usually plays out in such a way that small group members attend meetings until they hit a time of conflict or struggle in the relationships within the group. While they adjust their lifestyle to prioritize a regularly scheduled small group meeting, they typically do not adjust their lives to make room to work through relational issues unearthed within a group. As a result, they either stop attending, attend meetings but in a way that is disengaged, or look for another group comprised of people with more compatible views and personalities. Here's how this story might be experienced:

> This group has become a priority to us. We have adjusted our schedules to meet together at least every other week, but usually we meet weekly. In our meetings, we either study the sermon preached by our pastor or use a Bible study guide that we all find personally beneficial. We truly enjoy each other's presence, and we put a high priority on the group and the members in the group. We even do something social once each month. We rise to the occasion when someone has a need, and there is a sense that we are friends.[2]

This story is the most common way of perceiving how groups work. The point here is not about the fact that most stop at this story. In our over-saturated, over-informed, over-committed, and over-stimulated world, being a part of such a group requires a shift, a change in our way of life. For some the change might be minimal, while for others it is monumental. At the same time, the hope is that we can provide a way for people to see something more.

The Story of Relational Re-vision

While the shift from the first story to the second often looks like a continuous progression, the move to this third is discontinuous. Living this story requires intentional practice. Because the habits of the average person in North America are so contrary to a life of mutual love and self-sacrifice, nothing radical or Kingdom-like will be experienced if a group does not choose to practice a distinctively Christian way of life. The *Relational Re-vision* story is only told as a group develops a new set of rhythms, like a person might do when first learning to play the guitar. Hours of intentional practice are required. Here is where a group discovers distinctively Christian practices such as:

- Worship
- Encountering the presence of God together
- Communion
- Hospitality
- Mutual generosity
- Making time for each other
- Entering the neighborhood

While working with a traditional Lutheran church who had tried a myriad of small group strategies over the years, I introduced the four stories of group life. They were well versed in the first two, but when I introduced this one, the "lights" went on. There was a collective "aha" throughout the room. They told me, "That's why groups never took off for us. We just did meetings, and that was not enough." A person might relate their *Relational Re-vision* story in this way:

Our group has a weekly meeting, but I am not sure that you would call it a meeting in the formal sense of the word. When we get to-gether, it is the culmination of the rest of the week when we have been in one another's lives. It is a time of sharing what God has been doing, praying for each other, and talking about how God is using us in our everyday lives. Yes, we do have a weekly lesson, but the leader usually only asks one or two questions from it. The most important part of our group, however, is not the meeting; it is how we are connected the other six days of the week. I have never been part of a group in which people are so willing to sacrifice time and energy for one another. And this connectedness actually spills out into our neighborhood. It seems like we are always interacting with, praying for, and serving people who live near us. And in some ways, they are just as much a part of our group as those of us who call ourselves Christians. I am not sure how I was able to do life before having this group. This might sound a bit utopian, but it is far from it. Sometimes it is hard. Recently, we have had to wrestle with some relational conflict and hurt feelings. In the past I would have run away from such encounters, but not this time. It was not easy, but we pressed through. We are still learning what it means to be God's family.[3]

The spiritual practices done as a group (which are introduced in chapter 10) create an environment for the Spirit to open people's eyes to see what God is up to in the world. The point is not to disperse more information. Nor is it a call to more commitment. The point is to make space for the Spirit to spark people's imagination so that they might be stirred from within to shift and participate in a different story.

The Story of Missional Re-creation

As groups begin to live out the story of *Relational Re-vision*, they practice rhythms of community and mission with God that result in unexpected, creative patterns of group life. The gifts of the Spirit arise and empower the group to love each other and their neighbors in ways that break the mold of what a group should look like. Members engage the neighborhood and determine needs, meet those needs, and as a result, that experience will change how they exist as a group. Some will develop into house churches of fifty. Others meet in groups of five at a coffee shop. Others will adopt a home for mentally-challenged individuals. And still others will gather around a family that lives in a mindset of poverty and walk with them into a new way of thinking and living. The key is not the form that the group takes but the ability of the group to see what God is up to and join in on that. Here is how it might be described:

We have developed a way of connecting with each other and God that has resulted in some rather unpredictable developments. Two couples and a single person in our group live within walking distance of each other. As a group, we decided to adopt their neighborhood. We started with a block party. At first it was hard because no one knew us, but after that first party, we created a small presence in the community. Then one person started a summer children's Bible study. As she got to know the neighbors and their needs, we began to pray. Now we have come around a single mom who has three kids, and we include her as much as we can in the life of the group. She has yet to fully understand who Jesus is, but we feel led to embrace her and the kids and see what God does in her life.[4]

This story manifests as group members see what God is doing and the group responds. Such an experience is about learning to move with God, as the Father, Son, and Spirit dance in order to redeem all things, and the ways that we join in surprise us.

Different Ways Churches See Groups

The four stories are not only about how individuals and groups see groups. They also give us perspective on how groups are viewed by the church as a whole. As I shared in the letter in chapter one, I worked with Ralph Neighbour and his team for ten years as a writer, researcher, and consultant. Ralph was the person who introduced the American church to the concept of the cell church model, providing practical instructions on how to set up a church structure similar to those found in churches like Yoido Full Gospel Church in South Korea, Elim Church in El Salvador (over 200,000 members) Dion's Robert's church in the Ivory Coast (over 200,000 members) and others. This strategy is characterized by groups of people who live out the bones, body, and breath of God's beyond story.

Our process, resources, and conferences revolved around the promotion of a model. However, as with any one specific model, we actually experienced manifestations of the four stories where churches lived out the model differently. The following offers examples of four different churches who all adopted the same model but told four different stories.

Church Improvement Story

Second Church was a successful church located in a mid-size city in the south. Its senior pastor was one of the best and brightest leaders in the region. Traditionally, this church had grown through Sunday School, which required building more and more physical space for classrooms. After the last addition, they filled up all of their new Sunday school classrooms the first week. What were they to do? This church came to us to find a new way to connect people so that they did not have to build more buildings. From us they found a way to improve their already good church experience.

Second Church learned how to prioritize group life, set up the structures, and do the training. They were able to get 80% of their 2000 people into groups. They were so effective initially that the senior pastor even became one of our conference leaders. People loved small groups, and it was exciting right up to the day they hit a brick wall. It did not provide the improvement they desired. So Second Church went looking for new strategies. They created all kinds of groups that people would join because they were based on interest or self-improvement. Cooking groups, biking groups, and quilting groups popped up over-night. Anything that would get people connected by tapping into what people already wanted is what Second Church created. This church focused so much on getting people into groups that they failed to assess what was actually going on in the groups. As a result, they just devel-oped a new structure that told the same story as the old one.

Church Adjustment Story

The leadership of a church of 150 attended a group conference at a model church. They were sold on the idea as a way to grow their church and impact the people in their very large city. They attended our training, bought our resources, and even invited Ralph Neighbour to personally train their leaders. Groups were established because the pastor asked the people to make group life a priority, and they obeyed.

The church prioritized the groups by modifying the weekly sched-ule of church life. They closed the mid-week service so groups could meet during the week and changed the Sunday night service to a week-ly training time for group leaders. They adjusted everything about the church calendar and asked people to adjust their lives according-ly. Small groups became the primary tool for growing the church and helping people connect. They followed the practical steps we taught in our seminars, and they followed our recommendations to a tee.

However, the resulting story was rather uneventful. The groups weren't bad, but they weren't anything to write about either. The groups did not merit being elevated to such a central role in the church strategy, even though they followed all of the rules. As a result, the leaders went searching for other strategies, started tweaking how the groups were organized, reworked how they wrote the weekly curriculum, and de-emphasized the role of the groups in the life of the church. However, adapting the small group rules did not change the story. The groups were stuck in a never-ending reality of average.

Church Re-vision Story

The Hills Church in Northern California was a small traditional church that had recently took on a new name. The pastor came to us recognizing that they had no potential to grow, little money to maintain what they had, and no passion to engage the people in the culture. The leadership learned the same principles, language, and structures as the previous two churches, but this church understood the need to revise its culture and church rhythms to fit the new structure. They began by asking hard questions about their expectations of people and how they participated in the life of the church. They realized how they could use their weekly Sunday services as a launching point for something new, and then they transformed what was a very good Sunday evening service into an equipping time so that people would understand what it meant for them to participate in group life.

Next, they helped people process the expectations of being committed to participate in the life of the church community. They did far more than get people into groups. They established what they called The Community Practice, which included practical ways that they were going to live in community, including statements such as:

• We will center our time together around the presence of Jesus.
• We will work through conflict even when we want to run away.
• We will make room in our lives for each other so that we spend time together outside the meeting.

- We will speak honestly to one another.
- We will open our lives and not keep secrets from one another.

This church was less worried about assimilating a high percentage of their people into groups and more concerned about establishing a way of life together that is distinctively Christian. They realized that this might seem radical and the groups would not grow as quickly. From this experience has come a group of people who understand what it means to live in such a way that they actually love one another in distinctively "Jesus" ways.

Church Re-creation Story

In a church in a Southwestern state, the college minister developed his department of the church around our teachings. He took his time and did not expect to restructure the entire church around this strategy. Instead, he invested in leaders, challenged them to count the cost of discipleship, established accountability structures within groups, and developed a leadership training process. They were doing much more than developing groups. They were inviting people to enter a journey of learning what it means to be on mission.

Eventually, this college ministry grew and was birthed out to plant a new church. They did not set out to start a new church. They simply worked with the people they had and developed a way of life and then discerned God's leading in the midst. Today, they have a school of discipleship where they challenge young people to take a year off work or school and go through intensive training that exposes them to churches in foreign countries. In addition, they have a network of churches that have been planted around the world that have been shaped by this re-creation of the bones, body, and breath. The "normal" in their groups is to live out this story of *Missional Re-creation* in ways that are distinct in their culture.

Seeing Beyond Small Groups

When Moses led the Israelites out of Egypt, the call was to return to the Promised Land, a journey which would have normally taken three or four weeks. However, by following the cloud by day and the pillar of fire by night, God led the people on an indirect path, one that took them through the wilderness for forty years. On this journey, they had to learn to trust God for what he was doing so that they might see and know God's ways. They may have gotten out of Egypt, but the ways of Egypt remained in them. The way that they perceived who God is and how God works was filtered through their experience of Egyptian slavery. The wilderness experience served as a time of preparation to get the slavery out of them so that they could rightly see what God was up to.

The journey toward flourishing groups is much the same. It begins with a confession that we are not satisfied with *Personal Improvement* and *Lifestyle Adjustment*. While these stories are better than the modern slavery of the over-saturated, over-informed, over-committed, and over-stimulated individualism, they are not expressions of the small group Promised Land. They are wilderness stories that prepare us to cross the Jordan River and to enter the stories of *Relational Re-vision* and *Missional Re-creation*.

The call is to help people see the movement from one story to the next by drawing in individualists—those looking to get their consumer-driven spiritual needs met through a church program—and helping them attain a different perspective that moves them from the wilderness into the Promised Land of *Relational Re-vision* and *Missional Re-creation*.

Do not assume that people will move through the four stories in the same way. Some will enter this journey through more traditional means, through a weekend worship service, while others might come to Christ in organic relational ways, through the relationships in a group that is living in mission in the community. Because almost every American, whether Christian or non-Christian, comes into a church experience with preconceived notions about what the church is about, no one in the modern West comes to Christ or the church with a blank slate about what it means to be a part of a church. Most have expectations about what God can do for them and what the church should do to improve their lives. Therefore, while the journey through these stories might look very different in a mega-church of 3000, a mid-sized program based church of 300, a traditional family church of seventy, or a house church of thirty, people will need to discover ways that culturally-shaped church expectations need to be reframed.

The key is to communicate the next step for people. If you "raise the bar" too high, then the challenge will create too much stress and people will disengage. Often, the phone calls that I receive from pastors start off like this: "We committed to doing missional community two years ago. We don't want to foster more ingrown church life that does not care about our city. And we did our research. We learned from the best of the best about how to do seven-day-a-week church where people are doing life together in missional community. We attended training seminars, purchased online modules, and we read all we could."

Thus far, this sounds very promising. Over the years, I've found that churches that do the best job of developing groups that live out mission and community do their homework before they get started. However, the tone shifts at this point with something like this: "But ... after we trained our key leaders, determined our mission focus, aligned our programming, and equipped all of our small groups to become missional communities, um ... well ... not much has changed. Our new "missional communities" were too much for people. So they are just doing what they have always done. There are a couple of groups we would describe as missional, but honestly, the members are kinda tired. What do we do next?"

They did not help people see a compelling new story of what their group could be. They cast the vision of a radical program and then asked people to commit. Yet the story remained the same.

On the other hand, many pastors tell me how they want their groups to be more than they are, but their people are content with what they have. The average church person expects pastors to provide great connecting experiences that will keep them happy because they treat the church as a provider of spiritual goods and services. While there is nothing wrong with excellence, we must recognize that perfecting connecting experiences may not actually move people further on the journey because it will make group meetings too easy. Connecting is not a destination but rather an important stage of seeing God's work in the world. However, these pastors tell me that their connecting groups are stuck. People are not being discipled as they hoped, and they are mired in running a program.

In both situations, the goal is the same: lead people through the four stories. The specific ways this is done will vary, but the first step is to understand the need to help people re-imagine groups. Practical steps for doing this will be provided in Part 4. The following questions set the stage for what is to come.

- How will people get started in a group, even if they only want something that resembles the *Personal Improvement* story? Make the path clear and communicate it often. It is especially important that the senior pastor publicly promote this path.
- How will people grow into and beyond the story of *Lifestyle Adjustment*? Since many, if not most groups get stuck here, how will you equip and support the groups that want more?
- How will you empower those who are looking for more than a weekly small group meeting? What kinds of experiments will you offer as examples? How will you support and learn from those experiments? These are questions related to the story of *Relational Re-vision*.
- How will you respond to the work of the Spirit that results in unpredictable expressions that are ministering to people who are not part of the church on Sundays? These are questions that pertain to the story of *Missional Re-creation*.

The Freedom of the Four Stories

Embracing the four stories can make all the difference in how we see God's movement to develop flourishing communities. It frees us from typical approaches that focus on numbers, growth patterns, and percentages of involvement. It places our emphasis on the life that actually produces God's mustard seed growth. I consulted a small church of fifty members in Pennsylvania that embarked upon a small group journey ten years before they contacted me for support. They hired me to assess why they were not growing in the ways that the church consultants had promised. In our first discussions about their history, they shared the titles of books they initially read, which promised spiritual and numeric growth, relational evangelism, and "success" if they launched small groups. A decade later, they remain a congregation of fifty that couldn't figure out what they were doing wrong.

During my initial visit, I found a few things that hindered their growth and suggested some steps to address these issues. However, beyond the numbers, I found that they were doing a lot of things right. There was so much good going on in this small church! Sadly, it was all hidden beneath the discouragement that resulted from the focus on numbers.

Beyond the numbers, we discovered that group members were sharing life together; they were counting the cost of being in relationships that mattered; they were investing in people who did not know Jesus and helping them find the cross and then Lordship; they were involved in their communities, sacrificing their lives with the poor; and they practiced simplicity and mutual sharing. The bones, body, and breath of the church revealed that they were actually living out the story of *Missional Re-creation*.

This church is practicing an alternative way of being the church, a way that stands in stark contrast from our culture and from the "easy believism" found in many churches in their area that are experiencing typical success. What they developed is beautiful, but it does not fit conventional expectations. They are a mustard seed movement of something different, a remnant that is now asking far more powerful questions and is forming a grass roots movement of group life that moves beyond small group structures.

Part 2

Presence

Perspective

PRESENCE

Practices

7

Why Do We Need New Church Structures?

Jesus said, "Neither do people pour new wine into old wineskins. If they do, the skins will burst; the wine will run out and the wineskins will be ruined. No, they pour new wine into new wineskins, and both are preserved" (Matt 9:17).

Through the years, many have called for the church to develop new church wineskins, new forms of life, instead of holding on to the church structures of the past. This is a valid argument. When we hold onto the structures and institutional forms of the past, we can miss the fact that patterns and practices of our old structures blind us to new opportunities. However, there is much more going on in this passage than an invitation to develop new structures. When we reflect on the meaning of the relationship between the wine and the wineskins, we are able to see how the presence of God relates to our development of grouping structures.

It's About the Wine, Not the Wineskin

Jesus' short parable about the wine and the wineskin—one that is partnered with the parable of the patched garment—is told in response to a specific question from John the Baptist's disciples: "How is it that we and the Pharisees fast often, but your disciples do not fast?" (Matt 9:14). If we fail to see whom Jesus was addressing and what specifically he was addressing, it is too easy for us to read our own meaning into Jesus' words. The question raised to Jesus that day was not about religious forms or the structures of Jewish life. There is nothing here about how the Temple is organized or how the synagogues should work. It is a question about how Jesus' disciples practiced their faith. To this Jesus responds: "How can the guests of the bridegroom mourn while he is with them? The time will come when the bridegroom will be taken from them; then they will fast" (vs. 15). This section of Scripture—which is included in a very similar way in all three of the Synoptic Gospels—is really not about religious structures at all. While John's disciples wanted to ask about the way that Jesus' disciples practiced their faith, i.e. how they were being discipled, Jesus turns the conversation to something else entirely.

He answers with a poetic statement about his presence. The presence of the bridegroom—this is an image of the expectant Messiah who would come to save his bride Israel (see Hosea)—calls for a different response. While the Pharisees and John's disciples were looking forward to the Messiah, here, Jesus is saying that the Messiah has already come and therefore everything changes.

In this context, we read about the wine and wineskin. Jesus was saying that the disciples were practicing their faith differently because Jesus was present with them. The presence of God's saving Messiah changed the way that the followers of God were to respond. To put it clearly:

Jesus' Messianic Presence >>>>>>> New Faith Practices

To clarify what Jesus is saying, it's also helpful to see what he is not saying. Jesus did not say that new wineskins result in new wine. Of course, this observation is obvious. Even those of us who have not ever set foot on a vineyard know that wine is a product of grapes and grapes are the fruit of grapevines. Even stating that wine is not the product of a new wineskin is so obvious that it is ridiculous.

However, stating the obvious is necessary to hear Jesus' poetic point. No new form of religious practice will magically produce some kind of new life in God. For instance, getting together in a small group, or in a missional community, or in a triad for discipleship—while necessary just as a new wineskin is necessary—won't produce new wine. They are just wineskins for the wine.

We, in the church, have become experts at wineskin making, and this is especially true when we think about groups. However, no one wants to "drink" our creative wineskins. If we are missing the presence of Christ in our midst, then we could apply the words of the Apostle Paul to ourselves:

> If my group reaches lost people and grows but there is no love, we are only a growing shell of emptiness. If my group raises up new leaders and multiplies but there is no love, we are only multiplying a form of spiritual cancer. If my group gets serious about discipleship and dives deep into the Word but there is no love, we are puffed up hoarders of information. If my group serves and goes forth on mission but there is no love, we are like a chicken with its head cut off. If my group gets lots of people in my church connected but there is no love, we are no better than a peddler of the next product that "everyone must have."

Without the wine of the love of Christ that is empowered by the Spirit, the kind of self-sacrificial love expressed by Jesus on the cross, then any new church structure will fall far short of what we hope and long to see. New church structures are important only when we put them in the proper place.

New Wineskins Arise from New Wine

This does not diminish the importance of new wineskins. To extend the parable, if new wine is put in an old wineskin the wine will leak. This is true because new wine expands and thus causes the wineskin to stretch. If the wineskin has already been stretched, then the additional stretching from the new wine will create holes, thus leaving the new wine on the floor.

Therefore, there is the problem of old wineskins. We have an affinity for the things that we know, and we know how to do church. We like the predictability of the church structures that we have inherited. With all of the talk from the last five decades about how ineffective the institutional church is, about how people in our culture are no longer listening to what the church has to say, and about how the church as we know it has been relegated to a provider of spiritual goods and services, the basic way that we do church remains the same. Even the promises of the "bone prophets" prove empty because, when you enter into what they are doing, the end result is merely a tweaking of what we already know how to do. The old wineskin remains, even though we might market what we are doing as new.

Church innovation for the sake of church innovation might look creative, but there have been many creative ventures that were simply good ideas of man. Of course, God uses these ideas. However, the new wineskins that will arise in your local context, and that are best suited for the people who live in your neighborhoods, will manifest as you and your people live into the wine of God's presence. This will result in fresh expressions of the church, ways of being God's people that arise from within God's people. The practical way that groups might enter into this reality is explored in chapter 19.

The Problem of Old Wine

In the early 1990s I was a part of a new wineskin, an organic/missional experimental church in Houston. We did not call it organic or missional, which are common descriptions of such churches today, but that's what we were. We did not fit the normal patterns of church life as we experimented with innovative ways of forming and living in community.

We saw many people embark upon a new relationship with Jesus, and we had a very strong leadership core. Those who came to Jesus for the first time through the relationships in our church joined our life quite easily. To them the wineskins that shaped our life as a church were all they knew. I remember one person returning from vacation and sharing her shock at how the traditional church she visited operated.

In addition to new Christians, we also had many join us who had been a part of traditional churches. Those from this category, myself included, did not flourish in this new wineskin experience quite as quickly. It was not hard for us to commit to the vision because many of us were fed up with traditional church forms. Some had been hurt by church life, and others were simply burned out from programmatic ministry leadership. Our vision for this new way of being the church was compelling and, for most, easy to commit to. We wanted the presence of Christ forming us by the Spirit, and we committed ourselves to the innovative ways that were being generated. That part was simple.

However, the complexity arose as we realized how we had been shaped and formed by the life of previous churches. We didn't suddenly leave behind these patterns when we moved into this new experimental church. We brought "old wine," if you will, with us. And that included things like expectations, patterns of leadership, and participation habits that were woven into the way that we did church. It proved impossible to leave such things behind simply because we choose to do something else.

The way we were present in our former church life had formed us and because of this formation the old wine we brought with us was poured into a new wineskin. Let me illustrate: Some tried to get the church leadership to perform traditional roles, even though they were told up front that the leadership would not do those things. Others would ask where we did Bible study, and the leaders would lay out all of the places where the Bible is woven into the life of the church, but because we did not have a specific ministry called "Bible study" they could not get it.

The old wine was characterized by a "for" mentality. God was supposed to do something for us. Church leaders were supposed to provide a set of spiritual goods and services for us. And then we were supposed to do something for God and for each other.

However, we were learning to be with God and with each other. This new wine of being with, as Jesus was with his disciples, did not meet our expectations. It was too slow. It was too mundane. It was too rudimentary. Those from an unchurched background found it life-giving and even fun. Those of us from a churched background wanted to see God produce more fruit. "God, use us" we would pray. All the while, Jesus was trying to invite us into his presence and into the presence of one another so that we could be with each other.

The wine of God's presence manifests as he is with us. Doing something for the world and for others comes about as he is with us. Otherwise we turn Jesus into a commodity.

Being with God and others occurs as we learn to hang out, to slow down, and to simply embrace presence. In my book on small group leadership, I offer the practice of "Hang Out" as being central to effective group life. When I train group leaders, I find that people are most resistant to this practice when compared to the others. People offer their resistance for two reasons. Some reject it because they want to make a difference in their community, as they are overwhelmed by the needs for discipleship, and they want to do all they can for the sake of the Gospel. Others see how busy their lives already are, and they just don't have the time to give to what looks like a waste of time.

Being with God and others is not necessarily productive. Yet it is the way that Jesus does something for us and for the world. And it's the way that groups flourish.

Understanding the Old Wine

To see how the old wine hinders us from receiving the new wine of being with God, let's think about this from a different perspective. If someone has been a successful section manager in a department store and then takes a new job managing a small retail store, the old "wine" of the former job doesn't disappear. Some work patterns might transfer well, but many will not. In a large department store, the manager of a specific department has a very limited role that focuses on one section of the store and has the support of various other management divisions that make the whole store work. Whereas in a small boutique, the manager has to take care of almost everything. One cannot simply choose to change and expect to flourish in the new role. And providing some kind of up-front training will only set the right course. The new employee must do the hard work to embrace and be shaped by the patterns of work that fit the vision and strategy of the new employer.

The employee could have been very successful in their former role, but when you put them in a new role (a new structure) they naturally will continue operating according to old patterns because those patterns proved effective in the past. When stress rises, they will even more ardently depend upon those old patterns; the first thing we do is to return to what we already know how to do, even if we logically know that it won't work.

Many Christians today are frustrated with the traditional church experience. They know they want something else. The natural response is to look at a different structure of church life. Who is to blame them when there are so many church structure prophets promising entry into the church promised land with the adoption of their strategy. While these prophets might very well have experienced something akin to ecclesiological bliss, others adopt their methods and find themselves wandering around in the land of banality.

After a couple years, they go looking for another strategy. This never-ending chase has plagued the grouping movement for decades. We maintain the same wine while looking for new wineskins.

Jesus' disciples faced this same challenge while trying to figure out what Jesus was up to. They followed him because he gave them a vision for the kingdom of God. However, they brought with them a definition of what the kingdom of God should look like. For instance, Simon the Zealot—like all Jewish Zealots of the time—would have assumed that the kingdom of God would come when the Israelites rose up and violently drove out the Romans. Matthew the tax collector—whose vocation required him to collaborate and compromise with the Roman authorities—would have had a more realistic vision of trying to work with the power players in the Roman government. As the Gospels clearly illustrate repeatedly, none of the disciples assumed that the cross was going to be part of the vision of the kingdom. They wanted the Messiah to do something for them, and for Israel. Self-sacrificial love manifested by God being with them did not play a part in the common Jewish vision for God's Messiah.

The twelve disciples all brought with them a preconceived under-standing (a wine) that defined what it meant to follow God. Even though Jesus gave them a new structure (the small group of discipleship) for three years, all except John rejected "God with us" when Jesus went to the cross. Afterward, the fishermen in the group of disciples returned to their old life patterns—they went fishing—when they did not know what else to do. The natural tendency within us all is to return to our former comfort zone—old life structures—when God is trying to form new wine within us. New forms of church life are not alive because of the new forms. We only learn a new way of being the church by slow-ing down enough to be with God and with each other. In that way, we discover how God is reshaping us from the inside out.

Old Wine Tastes Better

In Luke's version of the wine/wineskin parable, there is a sentence not found in either Matthew or Mark. It reads:

> "No one pours new wine into old wineskins. Otherwise, the new wine will burst the skins; the wine will run out and the wineskins will be ruined. No, new wine must be poured into new wineskins. And no one after drinking old wine wants new, for they say, 'The old is better'" (Luke 5:37-39).

The final sentence of a parable like this is crucial to understanding it. It's a bit like the punch line of a joke. If you skip it, you miss the meaning. This is especially the case when it is unique as compared to that of the other two Gospels.

On the surface, this sentence could be interpreted to mean that the new wine is less valuable than the old from a kingdom perspective. However, if this is the case, then Jesus is contradicting himself. Since Jesus is the new wine, what does it mean when he claims that people say "the old is better"? Does the old wine taste better than the new wine that Jesus offers?

The answer is, "Yes." If you know much about wine, Jesus' obser-vation isn't actually shocking. Wine that has not been aged is tart and even bitter. It's not something anyone wants to drink, especially when old wine is readily available.

Jesus is simply using a common experience from life to explain what it means to be his disciple. The question to which Jesus is responding is about discipleship. The disciples of John the Baptist were asking why Jesus' disciples did not fast. In other words, why weren't they doing the normal stuff that might open the door for the Messiah to do something for the world? (Note: this is not about following rules. This is about trying to figure out the right way to be Israelites in order to clear a path for God's Messianic deliverance.) As we observed above, Jesus' response was to say that the bridegroom had come.

However, there is a catch. The wine of Jesus being with them, that is the way of life that he offers, does not fit common expectations, and therefore, it will taste like bitter wine to most. Being with Jesus—following a Messiah on a journey to the cross—will not be something people are lining up to do. The old ways where people have a hope that God will simply do something for them will always be more attractive, at least on the surface. Once they taste what it means to be with Jesus, many will return to what they already know.

Before we condemn "those faithless ones," it's important to recognize that this is a normal part of life. The old adage "You can't teach an old dog new tricks" is appropriate. The old wine represents those patterns of life with which we become accustomed. We don't think about them. They are just habits that make the life as we know it the kind of life that we like. This is one reason why we experience culture shock when we move to another country. Nothing "feels" right and therefore we "feel" lost. It's only natural that we are drawn back to what we find comfortable.

When Jesus offers the new wine of his presence, most of the time it will not "feel" right. It will cause a kind of culture shock within our souls. When Jesus showed up 2000 years ago, he was always stirring the pot. His wine was tart and bitter. While his presence was, and still is comforting, it is rarely comfortable. When God gets up close and personal, we begin to see the world in a different light. Then, and only then, do we need new wineskins.

The emphasis here is not on the new, the next, or the novel. The emphasis lies on the fact that the disciples were with Jesus. This is the only reason that there is new wine and therefore a need for a new wineskin. Jesus was not a future expectation for them. He was a present reality in their midst.

Neither is God now a future expectation because we are in Christ, the Spirit lives in us, and we are with God. God literally surrounds us. To be a disciple of Jesus is to be with him. This, if we are honest, causes angst. The presence of God is not something that we can control. It's like wine that is organically produced from grapes. While we can mechanistically control the production of wineskins, we cannot manufacture the wine of God's life with us. It is merely a gift that we receive.

However, rarely do we think that being with God is enough. We expect results. We expect to do the stuff that Jesus did. We want to make a kingdom difference in the world. Sometimes it feels like the old wine can get more done than the new. The list of things that need to change in the world are endless. We need new wine and new wineskins all over the place. Some of these places might include:

- Personal issues
- Relationship patterns
- Work Struggles
- Political concerns
- Violence and war
- Racism
- Famine
- Then there are church structures that so many want to change.

The common path to making a difference in these arenas is to attack them head-on, to make a plan, and develop a strategy and structure that will change things. In no way am I saying that such efforts are unnecessary, but we find ourselves in a never-ending loop of trying to fix one thing after another. We end up doing what we think God wants us to do, but we are doing it without him. God is up there telling us what to do, and it's up to us to pull it off down here. And while we do a lot of good things this way, this is not the way of Jesus.

The wine of God in Christ did not come to force change upon the world. God entered into our life from the inside, at the lowest levels of society and he changed it from the bottom up.

However, the change Jesus brought is veiled. It's only seen by those who view that the world is different because God is with us. They realize that God did not come to fix the world, or at least he does not fix things like we try to fix things. The first goal of God with us is to be with us, not to change the world. Changes in the world—new wineskins— are derivative. The world is simply different because God is with us and being with us is the point of it all. This changes the world, but in a way that we don't expect. It's slow. It does not feel productive. It's hard to measure.

Thus it tastes like tart, bitter wine. We get impatient with the way the new wine works. How does church leadership put on their annual report the ways that they were with God? How do we talk about leadership by saying that Sabbath rest is crucial to leading God's people? How does a pastor convey to his church that spending extended time with God is more important than being available to answer the phone 24/7? What happens when people call the church office to learn that the pastor is spending time in the neighborhood, getting to know people on their turf?

We are tempted to return to the old wine. We get busy, caught up in the rat race of trying to make a difference, of trying to change things for the better. God's goal is not to fix everything externally while we remain alienated from being with God. He comes to be with us, and as we are with him, then, usually in small ways, new wineskins develop that fit the patterns of being with God.

Receiving the New Wine

The Father sent the Son to offer the world God's new wine. Then the Father sent the Spirit to "teach us all things and remind us of everything Jesus has said to us" (John 14:6). The way that Jesus was with the people of Israel when he walked the earth is the way that God is with us now. It's a way to the cross. We only receive this new wine of Jesus with us now by the Spirit as we walk with the Spirit to the cross (Luke 9:23). This is why learning to live and lead out of the presence of God with us is so crucial.

8

Why Do We Need Christ's Presence?

It was the Compline Service, the high-church service of a self-confessed high church of high churches. I had been hired to coach the small group pastor in the development of a group system, and my first task was to enter into their world. While I had attended liturgical churches in the past, this experience was new to me, and it opened my eyes to something I did not expect to see.

At one point in the service the priest brought out the thurible which carries the incense. As he swung it toward the congregation, he said, "Receive the Holy Spirit." Three times he did this, right, middle, and left. When he spoke these words in my direction as I sat on the left, a warm blanket of peace came over me. While in college, I had spoken disparagingly of churches with such "smells and bells," but this experience of God's presence was as significant for me as a challenging sermon at a Baptist church or when I had been prayed for at the end of a charismatic service.

Following this, the priest prepared the bread and wine, and we walked to the altar to receive them. As I did, I became aware of God being with me in a deep way, as if fresh water was being poured inside my soul. It was free. I was living into the life that was given to me by Jesus, the true source of life. It was gift.

It literally felt like I had been invited to sit at a table in the presence of the Father, Son, and the Spirit. I belonged there, not because I had done anything to make it happen or to earn it. It's just where I belonged.

I was participating in the free gift of being with God.

Of course, such an experience is not unique to the high-church tradition. I've had other such encounters from a variety of traditions. However, that night the gift of God's presence became an all-consuming reality. That Compline Service was not dependent upon that which men or women can produce. It was dependent upon an uncontrollable, relational, free encounter with God.

Such a free encounter with God's presence is foundational to faithful churches throughout history. It's just that other church traditions have been formed to encounter God in other mysterious ways. For some, the presence of God primarily comes through the preached word. Others facilitate the mystery of God's presence through worship. And still others tend to emphasize an encounter through altar ministry at the end of a service.

This encounter during the Compline Service caused me to ask a question regarding groups: What does the presence of God we are experiencing here have to do with the work of developing and overseeing groups?

It is quite common to view communion, sermons, and calls to repentance as a work that we cannot produce, actions that require the presence of God to show up. However, when it comes to developing groups, that work gets thrown back upon us to make happen. We imagine that there are some

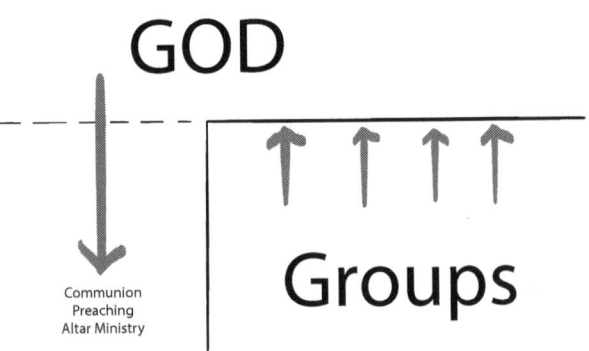

things that depend upon God's presence in the church while there are other things that we have to get done.

God is above and there are certain sacred places where God is at work. God comes down to meet us in those sacred places. However, when it comes to getting groups going in our church, that really is up to us and our organizational skills. If we do the right things in the right way, then our group experiences will rise up to a higher plane of spiritual experience. They won't live up to our sacred experiences of the Eucharist, a sermon, or an altar call—depending upon your tradition— but they will be better than simply a good Bible study.

That day, I asked, "What if the way we lead people into groups— if in fact we want to group them in the way of Jesus—depends just as much upon God's presence as a communion experience does?" Or to put it in concrete terms: What if the job a pastor does on Monday morning while overseeing groups depends upon God's presence just as much as what he or she does while leading the church in communion on Sunday?

The Presence of God Matters

One of the names given to Jesus is "Immanuel," which means "God with us." The story of God was and is shaped by the personal presence of the divine. God did not speak to the world from a distance. He pulled up a seat right beside us and started a conversation. This is the way that God relates to the world.

In the New Testament, a word often used to describe the encounter of the presence of God is the Greek word *koinonia*. A bit difficult to translate, it means something like "participate with," "commune with," "share in," or "take part in." Those who belong to God take part in, join in, or stand in communion with the divine life. Peter called the people of God those who are "participants (*koinonia*) in the divine nature" (2 Peter 1:4). Paul concluded his second letter to the Corinthian church by writing, "May the grace of the Lord Jesus Christ, and the love of God, and the fellowship (*koinonia*) of the Holy Spirit be with you all."

The gift of the presence of God is not merely a heavy power over us. It is a presence of communicative dialogue, of being with each other in love. God is including us in the love that he eternally is as Father, Son, and Spirit. We are invited to join in on this love through *koinonia*.

To be a participant or sharer in the divine nature is to be one who has been included in the divine presence. Imagine it as if you are a child that has been adopted by a wealthy family. You are a full participant in the life of the family. You have the right to be present in every room of the home and with every person in the family. You can eat at the family table, sit and talk with your new father, and even raid the fridge at midnight. You have a new name, which means you can be present and receive the presence of any other.

During that Compline Service, I met God. I cannot document how I met God in a scientific way, but I knew that I was relating to the Father, Son, and Spirit in a tangible and even experiential way. I was participating in God's life. I was having fellowship of the Holy Spirit.

The presence of God matters. It's what makes the church more than an organization with a good message and some good works. The Bible makes this abundantly clear. Jesus, the ultimate manifestation of God's nature, showed up as the personal presence of God. John summed it up by saying, "The Word became flesh and made his dwelling among us. We have seen his glory, the glory of the one and only Son, who came from the Father, full of grace and truth" (John 1:14). Later we read where Jesus proclaims how he is the manifestation of God's presence:

Jesus answered, "I am the way and the truth and the life. No one comes to the Father except through me. If you really know me, you will know my Father as well. From now on, you do know him and have seen him." Philip said, "Lord, show us the Father and that will be enough for us." Jesus answered: "Don't you know me, Philip, even after I have been among you such a long time? Anyone who has seen me has seen the Father. How can you say, 'Show us the Father'? Don't you believe that I am in the Father, and that the Father is in me? (John 14:6-10).

To show us what it means to live the kind of life God intended for us, he came himself. He did not announce it from a distance. He got up close and personal. The fact that Jesus showed up as God's personal presence demonstrates that this is the way that God works. In the concluding sentence by Jesus at the end of Matthew, we read "And surely I am with you always, to the very end of the age" (Matthew 28:20). Even though Jesus was about to ascend, he said that he would never leave us. In addition, in the only recorded discussion of Jesus about the church, Jesus stated, "Where two or three are gathered together in my name, there I am also" (Matthew 18:20). The presence of God is the driving force of the church.

This claim is simply built upon the narratives and poetry of the Old Testament. From the famous words of Psalm 23, "Even though I walk through the darkest valley, I will fear no evil, for you are with me," to the cloud by day and the fire by night that led the Israelites through the wilderness, to the holy of holies in the tabernacle, the presence of YHWH marked the people of God.

One of the most compelling passages of Scripture regarding the importance of the presence of God is a dialogue between Moses and YHWH in Exodus 33. It reads:

> Moses said to the Lord, "You have been telling me, 'Lead these people,' but you have not let me know whom you will send with me. You have said, 'I know you by name and you have found favor with me.' If you are pleased with me, teach me your ways so I may know you and continue to find favor with you. Remember that this nation is your people." The Lord replied, "My Presence will go with you, and I will give you rest." Then Moses said to him, "If your Presence does not go with us, do not send us up from here. How will anyone know that you are pleased with me and with your people unless you go with us? What else will distinguish me and your people from all the other people on the face of the earth?" (Exodus 33:12-16).

The distinguishing mark of the people of God throughout the biblical narrative is the fact that God is the main character who personally acts. The Bible begins with "In the beginning God ..." The climax of the Bible is all about what God did in Christ through the Incarnation, the cross, and the resurrection. The end of the Bible is all about how God will restore all of creation, the new heaven and the new earth. God. God. God.

God is the lead actor in the story. Now by the Spirit, God is the lead actor of the work you do in the development of groups. The Spirit holds together the story with various actors who never seem to quite get how the story works. The Spirit goes before us and enters into us to draw us up into the life of God, "in Christ," using Paul's language. We might illustrate it this way:[1]

God, the Spirit, comes into our groups—and into the way that we strategize, oversee, and develop groups along with the traditional

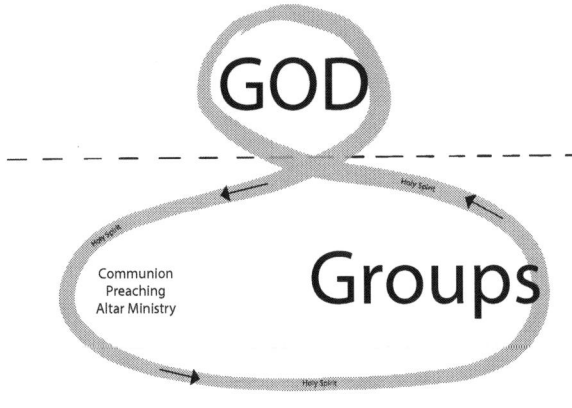

ways that we experience the presence of God in church—and draws us up into the life of God, that is with the Son before the Father. This is God's ultimate aim.

The church is not the protagonist of God's story. The people of God play bit parts in what God is doing. This does not diminish the church's (or any individual's) importance or value to the story. It simply acknowledges the fact that God acts. God initiates. We join in on his action. We do this via *koinonia*.

Disruptive Presence

How then does the presence matter when it comes to developing and overseeing groups? It's easy to say that we believe that God is with us and that the call on our lives is to be with God and with one another. It's another thing to weave this mindset into the way that we operate when we do the work of overseeing groups. In most cases, the way that we lead in the church is shaped by being for. We preach for people. We recruit leaders in order to produce a program that provides a ministry for those who will benefit from it. We do outreach projects for those outside the church. And we develop a group system that offers a spiritual product for small group consumers.

This should not be surprising because our culture—at least for those living in the world shaped by Western consumerism—has trained us to play the roles of either providers or consumers. As soon as someone moves into the role of a leader in the church—whether paid or volunteer—we automatically put on the hat of a provider of spiritual goods. We are doing something for the sake of others. This is like a perpetual loop from which we cannot break. It is ingrained in us. In fact, to challenge the notion that spiritual leaders are not called to do things for others is hard to embrace.

We can only see an alternative if there is something (or in this case someone) who breaks into our perpetual loop and reveals a different way. Otherwise, we are stuck continually trying to lead people with this "for" mentality.

We are only able to discern the presence of God as God with us by the revelation of God. Without this insertion of God—like that experienced by Mary and Joseph in Bethlehem—we will use God with us in order to provide some kind of ministry for others. As a result, any new idea is simply an incremental advance of being for people. Left to ourselves the most we can expect is *Personal Improvement* or *Lifestyle Adjustment*. Our understanding of God, God's ways, and our ability to enter into the way of God are bound by the limits of what we already know how to do. We end up projecting our best intentions upon the way of Jesus. And to challenge our best intentions feels so unnatural. Why wouldn't God want us to do the best we can to do stuff for people?

To illustrate this in a slightly different way, consider how cultures throughout history have projected their best ideas of humanity upon their understanding of deity. We need not go beyond Greek mythology to see how the gods were extensions of their best life experience on earth onto the life that *could not* be experienced. The experience of earth was cast upon the experience of heaven, just in a supposedly perfected way. If a human culture deems power and wealth to be of utmost importance, then their god is a perfection or ultimate expression of that power. If the ultimate human power looks like a violent monarch who gets his way by inflicting fear, then the ultimate power of the universe is simply a perfected version of such a monarch.

On an individual level, we read the Bible and see that God is called "Father." For some this is a good thing because they have or had good, faithful fathers. For many others, however, this is a hopeless expression. The name Father does not stir up positive images. Their experience here on earth has looped them into a perpetually limited understanding of what it means for God to be Father.

Only if God redefines Father according to the way that the Father is Father can we understand who God the Father is. Only if God breaks into our loop from the outside can we see God for who God is. This applies to both those with good earthly fathers and those with horrible father experiences. God's Fatherhood is analogous to faithful father-hood in this life, but it is as different as life on the moon would be from life on earth.

The Church Father Hilary stated, "God cannot be apprehended except through himself." To extend this to the way we lead, we cannot apprehend the way that God would call us to lead except through God himself being with us to show us how to lead. We are not leading in the way of Jesus by compiling our best ideas about leading and then going about the work. We are not left to ourselves to figure out God's mission in the world. Just as Jesus disrupted the loop of the people of Israel in the first century, the way of Jesus depends upon Jesus breaking into our loop to show us the way to be with God and with one another.

Jesus disrupted normal patterns through weakness, becoming the servant of servants, and dying on a cross. God came to be with the world. He did not come to fix the world, even when people asked him to fix it. He did not embrace the mentality of doing something for oth-ers so that they might consume his spiritual services. He instead invited them to be with him and be with others.

This disruption is not something we plan so that we can go from one level of triumph to the next. Often we are most aware of God's interruptive presence when we hit a wall. Our groups are not working like we wish they would. The strategies we have learned through various models just don't pan out. Then we cry out to God and the Spirit leads us into a kind of death.

When we don't like what we are getting from our grouping stories of *Personal Improvement* and *Lifestyle Adjustment*, this creates a series of wake-up calls. This reality generates a sense of urgency within us to seek out God's leading and presence, and thereby the Spirit leads us to the cross. Many times, we are only open to what God wants through failure. There we learn that grouping techniques and strategies might be good things, but they will not get us where we want to go. It's at this point that we realize that we are sitting before the cross, depending upon the Spirit to raise up something that we cannot produce.

Point People to the Cross

The way to embrace the presence of God with us is to foster environments for people to go to the cross. I won't expound on this extensively, as I've written an entire chapter on this in *Leading Small Groups in the Way of Jesus* (see chapter 10). God's presence by the Spirit leads us to the cross, to death. Our job, as leaders, is to trust the work of the Spirit. We don't need to make this happen. We are more like spiritual friends who walk with people as the Spirit is with us. As we walk, we are not to point others to ourselves, but to the cross.

This means that our job is not to recruit more leaders, or train more leaders, or multiply more groups. Those are good things, but they are based in "for" ministry. Our job is to learn the art of being with people on the journey to the cross and help them discover what the Spirit is calling them to be and do. As a result of this "with" ministry, new leaders will arise, new groups will be started, and people will be transformed. If we aim at producing something for God, for the church, or for people, we will miss the mark. But if we work with God and with others, then the disruptive presence of God with us will produce something that we never thought possible.

Presence and Prayer

There is an ancient Latin rule of the church that reads: *lex orandi lex credendi*, which means "the law of praying is the law of believing." To put it into a slightly different vernacular, "the way that we pray is the way that we believe."

In other words, our theology is not merely a confession of agreement with an orthodox list of beliefs. Our beliefs about God are manifested and even cultivated by our communion with God.

So often what we believe is used as a kind of litmus test that we pass in order to get to the place of doing something for God. If we confess the right beliefs about God, then we are qualified to work for him. As a result, it seems that our beliefs have little to do with what we do in the church outside of that which we preach or teach.

While worshiping at the Compline Service, I realized that we pray that God will help us to believe while in church on Sundays, because we know that we depend upon God to do what only he can do in the transformation of lives. However, do we pray in the same way on Monday morning when we are thinking about how we lead the church?

We might say it this way: The way we pray is the way we lead. In the same way that we cannot separate our prayer from our beliefs, we cannot separate our prayer from our leadership.

The way that we pray as we lead the church reveals what we believe about how God leads the church. Recently, I surveyed about twenty-five books from the last two decades that are commonly considered to be some of the best on the topic of church leadership. It is remarkable how little ink was used to talk about the relationship between prayer and leadership. Endless pages spent on the crisis that we face in the church. Strategies upon strategies outline five ways to make your church outreach oriented, eight steps to church transformation, six patterns for the church of the future, etc.

Prayer is in most cases virtually absent. Where it is present, it is tucked away and presented as if this is something that we already know how to do. Or the focus lies on praying that God will help us live up to our full potential as leaders.

As a result, church leadership gets thrown back upon us. It is something that we must accomplish for the sake of God's work. Those of us who are not "great" leaders—which is most of us—read the books by those who are—which is very few—and we try to figure out how to become like them. (Maybe I'm the only one who has done this, and if so, then ignore this.)

I'm no longer interested in trying to lead like those who get the most done for God. I don't want to implement a list of leadership habits or laws. I'm not sure that God is that interested in my ability to be a great leader.

Too often we pray by offering words up to God as a transaction. God did his part on the cross and in the resurrection. Now we pray that God will help us do our part so that we can do something for the world just as God did something for us. We are saved by grace, by the miracle of the work that only God can do. Church leadership is about our efforts, our strategies, and our skills. Prayer is something that we do so that we might be as good a leader as possible. Consider Jesus instructions regarding prayer as abiding:

"I am the vine. You are the branches. Anyone who abides in me and I in him this one bears much fruit for without me you are not able to do anything." (John 15:5, my translation)

The image of the vine and the branches is one of connection and flow of life. The branch only has life as it is connected to the vine. It is a biological metaphor of relationship, of communication. We only have life as we remain, live, abide, exist in Jesus. Only as we live into the truth of God with us are we able to do "anything." Of course this is hyperbole, as is common in the writings of John. However, the point is that we cannot do anything that carries forth the life of the vine without being in direct communication with that vine. The fruit of the kingdom cannot be fruit that we are able to conjure up. God's fruit only comes out of God's life. Jesus continues by saying, "If you remain in me and my words remain in you, ask whatever you wish, and it will be done for you" (John 15:7).

If read through a for view of God's presence, leaders pray in order to get the fruit that is promised. Since God is a missional God who wants to change the world, he wants to produce that fruit. Therefore we pray that this will occur. If we need leaders, then we pray that God will develop them. If we need life in the community, then we pray that God will send us forth. If we need to close the back door, we pray accordingly. If we pray the right way, then we will get the right fruit.

Abiding in Christ then is something that we do for God and for other people so that God will do something for us and for others. This mindset shapes how we posture ourselves toward God. It's like a contract where two parties map out what each will do for the other, and they sign the contract in order to protect the self. While each will do something for the other, the contract is done for the sake of the self. Prayer is done within a posture of self-protection. God is up there, while I am down here. I do my thing because I'm commanded to and then God will do his thing.

Ultimately, this presence of "for" requires the leader to pray for God to make the leader into a hero. Being that God was present as a hero doing what no one could do, God seemingly wants his leaders to be equally heroic, doing what normal Christians cannot do. They take a leap of faith, adopt a zealous lifestyle, and lead as a renegade. The myth of the religious hero calls pastors and leaders to be for others in ways that the others cannot. The hero is present as the center of the story, one who stands out above others and is self-sufficient, courageous, disciplined, quick-witted, battle-ready and excellent in all he does. He stands against the status quo and leaps into the fray of God's mission. His actions and choices turn out "right." He wins. He succeeds. He is for.

Abiding prayer is with prayer, as opposed to praying as a consumer of spiritual goods where the leader seeks God to do something for him/her, the world, or the church. God is not the grand benefactor in the sky doling out spiritual goods for leaders to purchase if only God is appeased or asked in the right way. God calls us into a love relationship with him, and love by definition is about communication. It is about sharing of life with the other. It is about being with the other. Ethicist and pastor, Samuel Wells, writes, "God's fundamental purpose is to be with us—not primarily to rescue us, or even to empower us, but simply to be with us, to share our existence, … Being with us is the nature of God—the grain of the universe."[2] God works for us but the for is a subset of being with.

Abiding is about being with God. It's about recognizing the fact that the Other is with us in the here and now. Prayer as communion with God is about having open communication with the God who is here, not there. God is not up there and out there somewhere we cannot reach. God is near, *Immanuel*.

When reading John 15 about the vine and the branches through the presence of with, it becomes obvious that the point is not about what cannot be done. The point is not about what we can get from God. The point is not about doing the work of God. It's not even about God making a difference through us. The point is about the branches "remaining" in the vine. The point is about being with God. It's about abiding in the reality of indicative, the reality of what is, which is not something that any human agent can increase. The branch is part of the vine by definition. It cannot live without its connection to the vine as its very life is directly related to its union with the vine.

Leaders abide in order to be with God and this open communication penetrates all other aspects of leadership, which has as much to do with Monday morning when we arrive at the church office as it does with our ministry on Sunday morning.

9

Where Is Christ's Presence?

Matthew 18:18-20 records Jesus saying, "I tell you the truth, whatever you bind on earth will be bound in heaven, and whatever you loose on earth will be loosed in heaven. Again, I tell you that if two of you on earth agree about anything you ask for, it will be done for you by my Father in heaven. For where two or three come together in my name, there am I with them." Jesus promised his presence to those who gather in his name, which means that people gather with a focus on Jesus and a commitment to seek what he has done and is doing. Another way to say this would be gathering "under his rule." To seek the rule and leading of Jesus requires his presence, and therefore he promises that he will so lead when two or three gather in this way.

When we read this passage from the perspective of the goal of making groups successful or making the church work—for example, the goal of getting 80% in groups or multiplying a certain number of groups each year—then we might interpret this passage as being about the presence of Christ in our midst during group meetings and our Sunday worship gatherings. Of course, this passage applies to these settings. As mentioned in the previous chapter, the presence of God is crucial to our corporate gatherings and to our group meetings.

However, in the broader context of this passage, Jesus' promise of presence applies to aspects of our life that we commonly label as secular. In the teaching, Jesus was addressing activities and relationships that we typically imagine occurring outside of the domain of church life. To get inside the way that Jesus is present with his people, we must begin to develop an imagination about how Jesus is present in the midst of our everyday secular lives. The presence of God pervades common patterns, everyday habits and our taken-for-granted relationships, whether we see it or not.

Jesus in Secular Places

Previous to the promise of Jesus' presence where two or three are gathered, we read:

> If your brother or sister sins, go and point out the fault, just between the two of you. If they listen to you, you have won them over. But if they will not listen, take one or two others along, so that 'every matter may be established by the testimony of two or three witnesses.' If he refuses to listen to them, tell it to the church; and if they refuse to listen even to the church, treat them as you would a pagan or a tax collector (Matt. 18:15-17).

Then we are told that Jesus would be present when doing this, as two or three are gathered. From these instructions, we can derive a formal process of church discipline, which is appropriate. However, within the imagination of informal community life in early churches, these instructions are less about formal policies regarding how to handle those who are living in sin and more about the ordinary ways that Christ followers relate to one another in love. Today, when our churches are focused on gathering disparate individualists into formal meetings, we often wait until a problem is so bad that we are forced to confront another in a formal "churchly" way. As a result, we must depend upon formal confrontation policies in order to deal with sin. However, this instruction from Jesus and the promise of his presence is not as "churchly" as we might assume. For instance, to "go and point out the fault" does not usually occur in official church buildings or during official church meetings. Jesus' words speak to the practice of healthy communication in the midst of the messiness of daily life.

I draw this conclusion because the larger context of the entire chapter addresses topics that we don't usually place within the domain of church. Matthew 18 is comprised of five topics grouped together in the form of a discourse. All of these topics deal with how people relate to one another in the midst of secular life. These topics include:

• Relating to children
• Not doing anything to cause others to sin
• Going after those who go astray
• Confronting someone in sin
• Forgiving others

In the middle of these practical instructions, Jesus tells them, "whatever you bind on earth will be bound in heaven, and whatever you loose on earth will be loosed in heaven. Again I tell you that if two of you on earth agree about anything you ask for, it will be done for you by my Father in heaven. For where two or three come together in my name, there am I with them." The presence of Christ is the key to connecting the will of heaven to the stuff of daily life. His presence gives his followers the authority to bind and loose according to the will of heaven. These five topics illustrate five ways that disciples are to live with one another according to that will. But without the presence, we lack the ability to walk in these five ways. Without the presence, we focus on "how" questions: How do we treat the children? How do we live in holiness? How do we reach the lost? How do we confront? How do we forgive? And we develop all kinds of solutions and techniques to fix the problems we face. With Christ as a part of the conversation, we can engage the adaptive challenges we face in our relationships (see chapter 5) and follow Jesus into innovative options in the midst of that which we deem as secular.

Presence and Place

Because Jesus descended to unveil the nature of God as "with us," Jesus demonstrated that God's way is to enter into our ordinary places and to show us what God is truly like. This revelation occurs in the physicality of places we embody. God is alive in the material world, in the earthy reality of day-to-day living that we define as secular. God is near—right here, right now—with me in this coffee shop while I'm writing today. He is with you as you read these words. If you are about to make a phone call, cook a meal, or clean a toilet, God is with you. God is present at our work, when we are watching our kids play soccer, and as we interact with neighbors.

However, in most cases, we don't think in terms of God being with us in the here and now in this place at this point in time. Instead, we tend to think of our relationship to God in terms of space. God is out there somewhere or up there in the great beyond. With this imagination, we tend to conclude that we must have a special spiritual experience to ascend to God's level in order to be with him. As a result, church becomes a special event, at a special place, at a special time, led by special people. If we get all of the specials right, then we might rise to God's presence. This point was illustrated in a slightly different way in the previous chapter.

This kind of space imagination also gets applied to the way we relate to others. For instance, when it comes to the command to love others, we might think of if in terms like this: "I will love the entire world just like God does. I will even love my enemies and pray for those who want to do me harm, as Jesus commanded. And I will minister to anyone who crosses my path who needs the love of Jesus." But what does it actually mean to love the entire world? How might we love our enemies when the only enemies that we can imagine are those we view on CNN? With such a space imagination, love has no specificity. It's just an inner feeling one has toward any and all, and if I feel prompted to love someone who crosses my path, then I'm committed to do so.

This notion is exacerbated by three things that are unique to life in modern society. The first is the way we are shaped by patterns of cities and suburbs. People drive ninety minutes per day to and from work. They spend another forty-five minutes in the car carting around kids. They go to a mall and purchase things from people they don't know and will never see again. They buy food from stores owned by corporations from other states. They worship on Sunday at a church that is thirty minutes away, and members of small groups all live twenty minutes apart. Life is just a combination of various spaces because the place in which we live is so complex and so large that we cannot process all the various parts. Therefore living into the physicality of our world and meeting God there is lost.

The second is the crazy experience of social media. We have friends, followers, and chats with an endless list of people. We don't need to know them, touch them, or talk to them. To "belong" we only need to like their posts or send an encouraging emoji, and somehow we are connecting.

The third issue is the fact that in most cases, we do not know those who live near us. Our neighborhoods are not places of neighborliness. They are simply where we lay our heads after a long day at work. The sense of living in the neighborhood has disappeared, something that is quite unique to modern society when compared to any other time in history. As a result, the physical place we call home has very little meaning or value.

My point here is not to deconstruct these common experiences of life. The point is to challenge the notion of relating with a spacial view of others so that we might hear again the call back to being with God and others in the places where we live.

The Places of Jesus

Jesus did not relate to the Father with a spacial imagination, as if he was talking on a phone with the distant first person of the Trinity who could be anywhere, but where exactly, no one knows. He related to the Father who was present in the place where he stood by the power of the Spirit. God the Father was with him in his local place of first century Israel. In addition, Jesus did not reveal God by ministering to and connecting with any and everyone. He came at a specific time in history to a specific location in the world and to specific people in that location.

His ministry was shaped by place, and those who were with him in those places. We can understand how he came by looking at four different places where people experienced his presence, and this can help us re-imagine how Jesus is present with us in our ordinary, secular lives.

These four places are not identified as towns or buildings. They are, instead, places of relating to different groups of people in different ways.

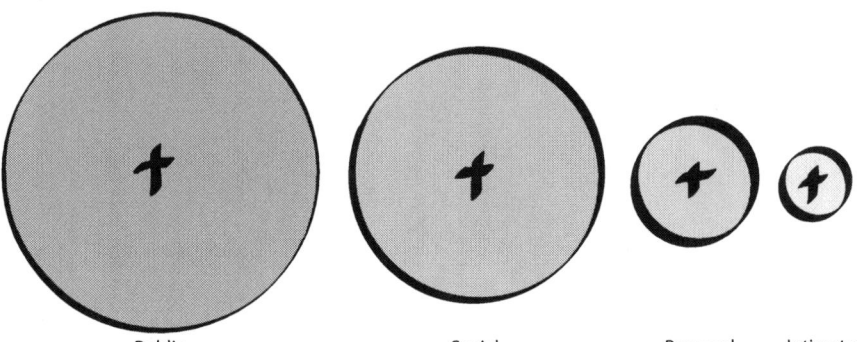

Public   Social   Personal   Intimate

The first place was public in nature as it included crowds that followed him at a distance: the thousands of people he fed miraculously, those he healed, and those who heard his sermons and parables. His critics and enemies were here also. Those who threatened Jesus were not enemies who lived thousands of miles away in another country or critics who wrote disparaging remarks on Facebook. They were in the same villages and towns, sharing the same place with Jesus.

On another level, the social, Jesus related to the committed. Included in this circle were the thirty to 120 men and women who were attached to his ministry. Some of them supported him financially. Some he touched and transformed radically, like Mary Magdalene. Luke tells us that he sent out seventy-two in pairs to carry the news that "the kingdom of God is near." He assembled this smaller group of people to teach them the meaning of the kingdom. These people heard his parables and were repeatedly exposed to his preaching.

As a subset of the seventy-two, there were the twelve whom he mentored. These men received his most concentrated relational efforts. He ate with them consistently, stayed at their houses, and told them the secrets of the kingdom as he explained the parables. The twelve were loved by Jesus on a personal level. He expressed this love by correcting them, challenging them, and even getting angry with them. They saw a Jesus that others could not see.

The smallest grouping included Peter, James, and John. These three men were connected to Jesus on an intimate level. They saw things and heard things that the other nine did not. They were also the only ones who were privileged to see Jesus in the glory of the transfiguration. When Jesus was agonizing about his upcoming Passion, he invited his intimate circle to be with him in his struggle.

God revealed himself in these four places in the local life context of towns and villages in first century Israel. God came in the flesh to be with humanity in the way that humanity was created to relate. Jesus was present in these four domains because we were designed to relate with others in these four ways. The next section expounds on this.

How We Relate

The anthropologist, Edward Hall, was a pioneer in the science of proxemics, which is the study of territory between people as it applies to how people connect. Hall found that there are four distances that determine how a person relates to others: intimate, personal, social, and public. Of course, no one analyzes their friends according to these categories. Hall writes in his book, *The Hidden Dimension*, "We sense other people as close or distant, but we cannot always put our finger on what it is that enables us to characterize them as such. So many different things are happening at once it is difficult to sort out the sources of information on which we base our reactions."[1] In a world where we struggle with being with others, a basic understanding of the physical distances that are natural in our relationships can help us see where Jesus was present in the first century and how he remains present by the Spirit today. God meets us in the normal ways of creation, in the normal patterns of life as we relate to one another. Jesus came and connected with people in these four places, and this continues to be the normal way that Jesus is present in our midst today.

The Public Place

People connect on the public level when they identify with a broad movement. For instance, an individual might publicly belong to a national association to which he pays annual dues but does not attend any official meetings. He is a member in good standing and supports the goals of that association, but he has not invested time and energy into the accomplishment of its goals. We participate in this public place in various aspects of life, including workplace affiliations, club memberships, social media interaction, and many others. The kind of connections here are a mile wide and an inch thick.

If the church were to ignore public belonging, people would lose a sense of being a part of God's salvation of all things. New Testament historian Wayne Meeks writes of the first churches, "One peculiar thing about early Christianity was the way in which the intimate, close-knit life of the local group was seen to be simultaneously part of a much larger, indeed ultimately worldwide, movement or entity."[2] We are part of a global work of God.

Of course, many Christians limit their experience of God's presence to the public place. They identify with the movement of the church through periodic attendance and by the giving of some offerings, but they are little more than casual attendees. Some criticize traditional forms of large group worship because of this, even concluding that there is no need for it because the house church experience should be enough. Others have argued that the purpose of the large group worship is to get people funneled into groups. I think both miss the point because we fail to see that the goal of all four places is to provide venues of presence. Each is just a different kind of presence.

We gather to worship to enter into God's presence. We hear the Word read and preached to receive God's presence in our midst. We receive communion to receive God's presence. This is what churches all over the world, in every tradition and generation, have done. We tap into God's movement to redeem all things by his presence as we do this.

The Social Place

Connecting on this level occurs with 30-120 people. The social place occurs in the local environments where we engage two sets of people. The first are neighbors, those who live in proximity to us. "A neighbor is someone you know well enough to ask for (or provide) small favors."[3] The second includes those in our networks who do not live nearby, i.e. family members, co-workers, and friends.

In modern life, one way we connect to neighbors and those in our networks is through "third place" experiences. The first place is the home and the second is the work or school environment. Third places are environments for social connecting where people choose to gather without external expectations. These include coffee shops, cafes, bars, restaurants, community centers, senior centers, stores, malls, markets, hair salons, barber shops, recreation centers, pools, movie theaters, libraries, and parks.

As cited above, common life that is shaped by cities, social media interaction, and neighborhood isolation has influenced our experiences in social places. Connecting in the social places in our neighborhoods is the most natural, however, our spacial ways of living collapses it. We need to learn again how to relate socially in our neighborhoods and in our networks because the Spirit of God is at work there.

The church can provide third place experiences for social connections. Small groups most naturally begin as this kind of place for people. In addition, connecting socially can also occur at the level of the mid-sized group, 30-120 people that facilitates small talk. Churches have experience doing this within its buildings, but this can also be something that churches help facilitate in the neighborhood.

The Personal Place

The personal place is where people share private thoughts, personal dreams, and feelings to a smaller group of ten or twelve. Here people experience a degree of transparency, but not naked transparency. Small groups are the most logical place for people to move into personal connections with others. However, the reality is that most small group members will only connect socially, especially during the early stages of group formation. Group members will gather looking to make friends, and they are checking out each other to see if it's safe enough to enter the personal domain.

As people are given the freedom to connect socially with others in a small group, some—if not many—will enter into the personal place and become family with each another. For a group to move from the social to the personal, the group members must move through the common stages of group development. At first, it will need to form as a group. It will go through a process where the group members get to know one another. During this forming stage, people assume that they like each other because they have not spent enough time together to reveal any faults.

Then comes the storming stage, or as M. Scott Peck calls it, chaos. After a group has been together for six to eight weeks, the group members will start rubbing each other the wrong way. Jim will tell an offensive joke or Tom will show up late every week. Cathy will whine and complain repeatedly about the same issue while Tammie is just "too happy" all the time. Group members have a choice. They can ignore what they feel and stuff their reactions. This is the only option for many Christians in small groups, and as a result, they ignore the issue at hand and the group cannot enter into the personal space. Or they can be offended and hold a grudge against the offender. This only heightens the chaos, and many times it leads to gossip and slander.

If group members choose to work through the chaos of conflict, it will enter into the norming stage, which is a period of community. This is the time a group becomes family for one another. Members become comfortable and lower their defensive postures. They share more openly and reveal their needs. Transparency that is found in community feels good, but it does not come naturally. (I explore the nature of group conflict with an entire chapter on the subject in *Leading Small Groups in the Way of Jesus*.)

The development of this community in the personal place is not primarily something that occurs within a formal group meeting, although a formal meeting is important. Most often, it is discovered through ad hoc interaction, conversations over meals, shared outings, and other things that friends do with each other.

The Intimate Place

This realm of life is usually only shared with two or three other people. Here the walls come down and we become "known" at a much deeper level than what occurs at the personal level. "In intimate belonging, we share 'naked' experience, feelings, and thoughts."[4]

Will Miller uses the metaphor of refrigerator rights to help us imagine the intimate place. He writes, "How many people in your life right now have refrigerator rights in your home? How many of the people you encounter every day see you unshaven or without makeup? How many people hear you express yourself in that blunt, unguarded way you do with your family? How many can you talk to at a genuine, deep, intimate level? And how many people grant you refrigerator rights? How many people confide in you—tell you about the things that really matter to them?"[5]

Refrigerator rights or naked intimacy is that which occurs in the most ordinary places of life, those that often look the least like church. In fact, it requires such a high level of trust that most small groups don't attain it. I would argue that it's not the goal of a small group in the first place. While such sharing at this level is often encouraged in small group literature, it is not always appropriate. For instance, if a man reveals his struggle with lust in the presence of women, it can cause a great deal of discomfort. It will often create greater distance and mistrust in the group. In this situation, confiding in one or two other men in the group is more appropriate.

Many churches facilitate the intimate place through the use of accountability partners or spiritual formation mini-groups. Some churches provide mentors for new or immature Christians where they can share intimate struggles.

In some cases, the formation of smaller groups of three or four is the place to begin as a church develops groups. The pastor might start meeting with three or four others at a coffee shop on a weekly basis to talk about what God is doing in one another's lives and in the neighborhood. This becomes a place of spiritual formation. After six to nine months, those who are a part of this initial formation group branch off and do the same thing with another mini-group. It's not a formal small group or missional community that is open to all to join. It's a way where people learn to be with each other in a more intimate way.

Jesus in Our Four Places

We can think of the four places in two ways. The first applies to the various ways that we group people in churches. The public occurs in weekly worship and through denominational affiliations. The social transpires through classes, age- and gender-based meetings, and times of social interaction that usually involves food. As suggested above, the personal can be experienced in small groups, and the intimate in mini-groups designed for spiritual formation.

However, we are short-sighted if we miss the second way, that of how we move in and out of these four places in secular life. Fostering groups that go beyond into the stories of *Relational Re-vision* and *Missional Re-creation* is not merely about getting sacred groups going for the church. It's also about equipping people to recognize the presence of Christ in all of life.

God is showing up in mysterious and paradoxical ways in all four places we experience, as illustrated by this diagram.

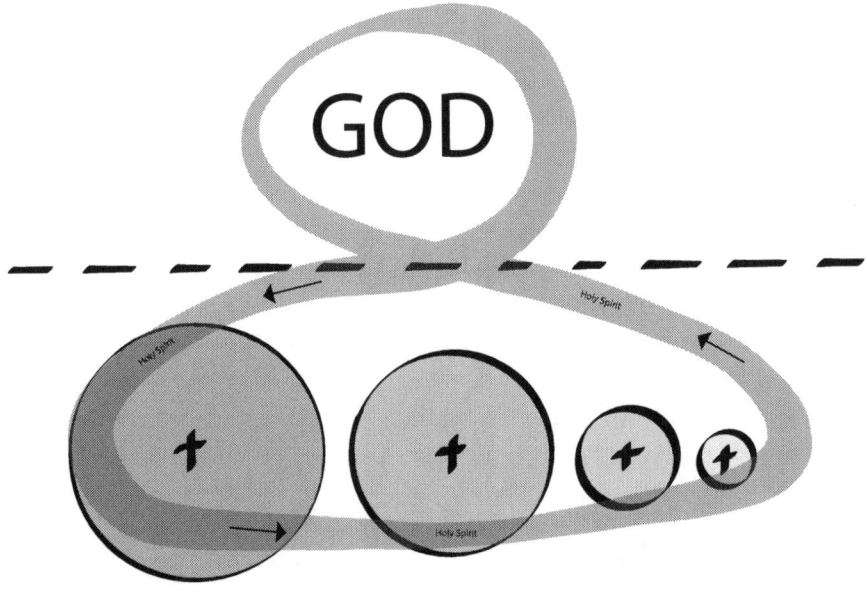

Public connections seem to be the easiest in our over-saturated world. But we also have social connections at work, with other parents at school or at extra-curricular activities, and in third places. We have close friends that at one point we described as personal. And from time-to-time, we are lucky enough to experience refrigerator rights with intimate connections.

Just as Jesus meets us through communion in our worship services and in our small groups—as discussed in the previous chapters—Jesus meets us as we walk through life.

Dietrich Bonhoeffer wrote about the reality of Christ's presence as being between those who are relating. He pointed out that when I love another directly, I am ignoring the reality of Christ's presence and Christ's love as I try to control the other in the name of love. He wrote: "Spiritual love, however, comes from Jesus Christ; it serves him alone. It knows that it has no direct access to other persons. Christ stands between me and others."[6]

I do not know how to relate well to another in these four places without the love of Christ in our midst. The real presence of Christ in our midst is the medium through which we love others, and thereby Christ is freed to love them through me. In so doing, I am giving them room to receive from God what only God can give them because they belong to God through the cross, not to me. My presence is not what they need. My job in these four places is to make room for Christ and to respond in love according to the leading of Christ. Bonhoeffer continues:

[Spiritual love] will respect the other as the boundary that Christ established between us; and it will find full community with the other in the Christ who alone binds us together. This spiritual love will thus speak to Christ about the other Christian [or person in general] more than to the other Christian about Christ.[7]

Our being with Christ in the four places of life depends, in part, on our ability to "speak to Christ about the other more than to the other about Christ." Prayer and presence are tied together so intimately that we cannot differentiate the two. Only as I pray do I have the power to love. Only as I ask God to work in the other will the other be open to what God has. Only as I pray can I see how God is moving. To use the word "only" is somewhat hyperbolic because God is always working beyond my prayers; however, without my prayers, I'm not living into the Presence who is at work. We have the power to offer the presence of being with others as we relate through Christ instead of trying to relate to people directly. Christ in our midst, not me, is that which leads people into true freedom.

Facilitate! Don't Force

Presence in these four places cannot be forced, whether we are organizing them within the church in formal ways or helping people recognize Christ's presence in the four places of their daily life. Relationships that are forced are not actually relationships. We are created to discover connections as friendships arise unexpectedly.

At the same time, we can help facilitate the presence of Christ in these four places. We can do this in a few ways. First, we must acknowledge that people desire the freedom to connect with others who have similar interests, life situations, or areas of expertise. This is one of the reasons helping people connect in social places is so important. "In social space we provide the information that helps others decide whether they connect with us. We get just enough information to decide to keep this person in this space or move them to another space."[8]

However, there is a tension here. If people only join with others because they find those relationships personally beneficial, they will often get stuck in the story of *Personal Improvement*. The groups then become cliques of like-minded people, resembling the high school cafeteria experience. Being with each other while being with Jesus is not about being comfortable. At the same time, if we force people into something they are not prepared for, then they will struggle so much that the connections will fall apart. The most obvious example occurs when white, middle-class people want to "help" people of a different color and socio-economic class. They think that they are relating but often they are projecting their life experiences upon others.

Secondly, when it comes to the development of grouping structures, we need to consider the already-established grouping patterns of the people in our churches. This is woven into the priorities found in Part 4 in the following chapters.

Third, equipping people in the practice of contractual relationships verses the practice of biblical covenanting can help facilitate how we live with Christ and others in the four places. A social contract is the common way that we relate to others, especially to those who are different. It is a way of relating where one party keeps their commitment as long as the other party keeps theirs. If the other person falls short, then I have the right to opt out. A covenant works differently. It means that I commit to you with the full knowledge that you will let me down, and we will fail one another. Through covenant relationships, we learn to love people through the differences, the failures, the misunderstandings and even the judgments. We discover what Jesus meant when he told his disciples that the key to their discipleship was loving one another.

To covenant with others also means that I choose to embrace people who are not like me. Jesus gathered a small group that was comprised of people who were very different. These men possessed no natural inclinations toward connecting with one another as friends except for the fact that Jesus had called them. He did not force them into relationship with one another, but he did invite them into something different than self-sorting.

The four places help us to see that we can enter into covenant relationships with others in different ways. I cannot covenant with 100 people in the intimate place. This is not even possible in the personal place. But I can clarify how I will relate well to ten others in our small group, and we can all come to a clear understanding of what it means to love one another in the presence of Christ.

One of the roles of church leaders is to invite people to live in covenant relationships in the different places, both in our church relationships and in our neighborhoods. Jesus goes before us, and by the Spirit lives between us, whether we see and acknowledge this fact or not. There Jesus invites us to live out cross-like love for the other. He told his disciples, "If anyone would come after me, he must deny himself and take up his cross daily and follow me" (Luke 9:23). As church leaders, we are inviting people to take steps. We cannot force them, nor can we orchestrate connections. However, we can facilitate the move from the broader, safer places into greater levels of risk.

Presence and the Breath of God

Throughout Part 2, I have spoken of the need for the presence of God to bring life to groups. This presence is analogous to the breath of God from the Ezekiel's vision of the Valley of Dry Bones. Only the personal, empowering presence of God can enliven God's bones and body.

The practices that are offered in the next section move us into the discovery of unique ways of gathering in the presence of Jesus as the church, in groups, and in the midst of daily life.

Part 3

Practices

10

What Do Flourishing Groups Practice?

We live the life we practice. The practices that shape us when no one is looking is the life we put on display when others are watching. This is illustrated by a theatrical performance. The key to the success of a stage production is the practice that is done long before the curtains open. The fruit of everything from parenting to accounting, from video production to driving a car, depends upon what is done when no one is looking. As with a plant where the fruit is at the mercy of the roots that lie beneath the surface, so also the fruit of our lives is a manifestation of the practices that feed our roots.

This is also true of group life. It's not enough to commit to a vision for groups and developing a strategy for how they will be organized. That is only a commitment to a belief about groups. We must also train up people in the practices and norms that form the body of Christ in those groups. Parker Palmer observed:

Churches, for example, ask members to affirm certain religious beliefs and the mission those beliefs imply. But rarely are churches intentional about naming—let alone asking members to commit themselves to—the relational norms and practices that would support their beliefs and mission. As a result, the relationships within many churches are shaped more by the norms of secular culture than by those of the religious tradition.[1]

If people are not formed by the Spirit to live out the stories of *Relational Re-vision* and *Missional Re-creation*, your church will be stuck with groups that are practicing the stories of the surrounding secular culture. As proposed in chapter 4, small groups are typically an add-on closet that is unnecessary for real life. The body must be formed, or re-formed, to live out Communion, Relating, and Engagement so that it aligns with the bones that the Spirit has put together.

The image below illustrates how a group might move like a sailboat in the development of Communion, Relating, and Engagement and thus live out the story of *Relational Re-vision* and *Missional Re-creation*. Along the way, we encounter common cultural practices that keep us mired in secular patterns.

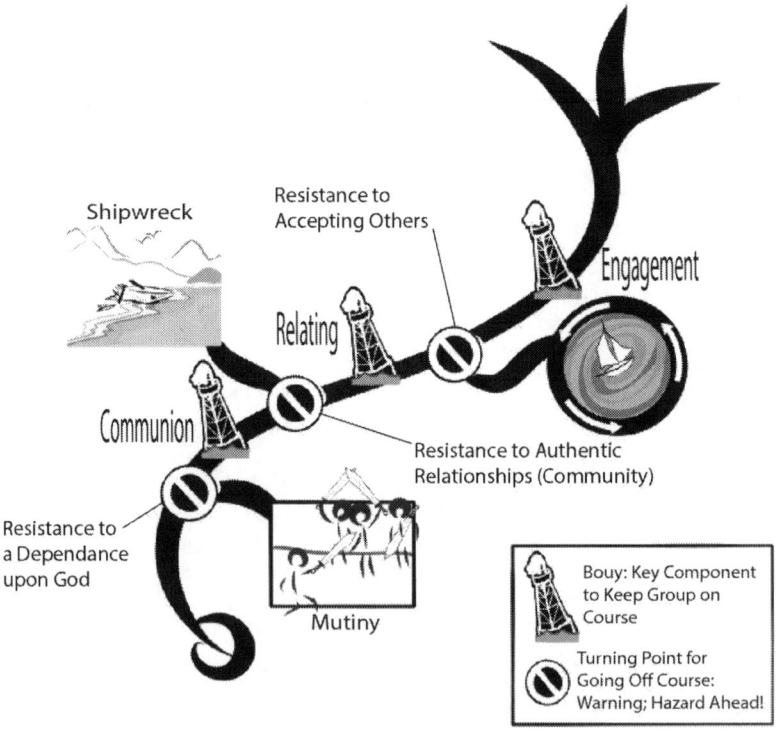

Communion is derailed when the group resists dependence upon God, an issue that is not merely measured by whether or not a group prays. This is about whether the group adopts practices that train people to see God and discern what God is up to in the world. Because the practices of the world train us to operate as if God is not present, we need alternative practices that form us to see Christ's presence in the various places we enter (see previous chapter). Otherwise, things like prayer and worship become nice private options, but they don't invade and reshape our lives.

Movement toward Relating is sidetracked when the group resists authenticity. The world commonly operates according to various practices based in performance, hiding reality, and competition. Relationships are rooted in routines that aim at attaining power, possessions, privilege, and pleasure. Groups move toward God's way of Relating through practices that shape members' ability to be vulnerable with one another.

A group's ability to Engage the world is resisted by practices of enemy-making. The world is shaped by patterns of judgment, condemnation, and boundary building. We have adopted practices that create an us-versus-them world. The way of Jesus's kingdom is a way of loving enemies, of seeing all people as those for whom Jesus gave his life. Therefore, we must embrace counter practices that tear down walls so that we are empowered to love those that the world assumes is an enemy.

How Practices Work

In *After You Believe*, N.T. Wright shares a heroic act from a common life. On January 15, 2009, an act of greatness was reported by news agencies around the world. Captain Charley Sullenberger III safely crash-landed an Airbus A320 in the Hudson River and every passenger survived. After taking off from LaGuardia Airport, a flock of geese moved into the flight pattern and the engines shut down. To land the plane safely, all kinds of things had to happen. Wright records them:

In the two or three minutes they had before landing, Sullenberger and his copilot had to do the following vital things (along with plenty of other tasks that we amateurs wouldn't understand). They had to shut down the engines. They had to set the right speed so that the plane could glide as long as possible without power. (Fortunately, Sullenberger is also a gliding instructor.) They had to get the nose of the plane down to maintain speed. They had to disconnect the autopilot and override the flight management system. They had to activate the 'ditch' system, which seals vents and valves, to make the plane waterproof once it hit the water. Most important of all, they had to fly and then glide the plane in a fast left-hand turn so that it could come down facing south, going with the flow of the river. And—having already turned off the engines—they had to do this using only the battery-operated systems and the emergency generator. They had to straighten the plane up from the tilt of the sharp-left turn so that, on landing, the plane would be exactly level from side to side. Finally, they had to get the nose back up again, but not too far up, and land straight and flat on the water.[1]

What Sullenberger did that day was nothing short of a miracle. Immediately he was called a hero, a wonder, and an example of greatness. This amazing act is similar to the great acts that committed Christians perform at great cost. The way that Sullenberger developed the skills needed to deal with this emergency is the same way we must develop the capacity to live out the love of Christ. He did not develop these skills because he decided to be a great pilot or because the emergency he faced in the moment necessitated them. He, along with the thousands of pilots that fly us around the world, practice such emergency situations routinely. In flight simulators, they have trained their minds and bodies to react quickly—usually failing quite a few times before they get it right—so that when an emergency happens they can respond correctly and avoid disaster.

When we try to build groups only on the level of the bones, as introduced in chapter one, we look for quick fixes and easy answers to difficult questions. We want a magical plan that will make groups work. But there are no quick fixes to becoming the army of God who lives by the breath of the Spirit. The Spirit of God forms the body through practice to live his way as a people. God's breath is inhaled and exhaled as the Spirit works through practices, which only have power when they are adopted as an ongoing part of life. The breath of God is not inhaled as a one-time event. As we make choices about practices, we develop habits and then these habits form our character. We might think of it this way:

Choices lead to actions.
Actions develop into practices.
Practices shape our habits.
Habits form our character.

We don't jump into flourishing groups filled with the breath of God. We start with small choices that might initially look insignificant; however, over time they shape who we are and how we live.

When our son played T-ball, the coach would lead the team in thirty minutes of practice before the games. One night, he traipsed beneath a light rain and tried in vain to climb some playground bars as he waited for the game to start. Then he came back to the car. I suggested that he throw the ball with his team. He said, "It's just practice. I don't need to. I'm already good." This is natural for a young man in kindergarten, however this is often how we treat our development of groups. We assume that we can simply decide what to do with groups and put people in those groups, which will result in their flourishing. The apostle Paul uses the imagery of training for athletic competition to talk about his preparation:

Not that I have already obtained all this, or have already arrived at my goal, but I press on to take hold of that for which Christ Jesus took hold of me. Brothers and sisters, I do not consider myself yet to have taken hold of it. But one thing I do: Forgetting what is behind and straining toward what is ahead, I press on toward the goal to win the prize for which God has called me heavenward in Christ Jesus (Phil 3:12-14).

In sports, games are won or lost on the practice field not in pep rallies, interviews, or celebrations. As we develop groups, things like conferences, seminars, classes, and written resources might get us started, but the real training comes when we practice. We don't develop flourishing groups simply because we decide. They are a result of the Spirit who transforms us from the inside out. For this we need practices. We must develop disciplines that shape us for the journey. Tim Morey writes in his book *Embodying Our Faith*, "A spiritual discipline is any practice that enables a person to do through training what he or she is not able to do simply by trying. They are practices, relationships and experiences that bring our minds and bodies into cooperation with God's work in our lives, making us more capable of receiving more of his life and power."[2]

According to Lyn Dykstra, "Practices are patterns of communal action that create openings in our lives where the grace, mercy and presence of God may be known to us. They are places where the power of God is experienced. In the end, they are not ultimately our practices but forms of participation in the practice of God."[3] Practices train us to move beyond following a small group to-do list as if we are the agents of change so we can participate in God and his action.

Most veterans of the church have been shaped by practices that do not promote flourishing groups. We are experts in these inherited forms of church without even thinking about it because they are part of who we are. That's the way practices work.

New practices are required that align with the bones, body, and breath that promote flourishing groups. These are specific actions that will make space in our souls for the Spirit to work in and through us. They are both a work of the Spirit and things that we do. We are participating in the life of the Spirit as we do them. The balance of this chapter will look at the practices of flourishing groups. The next three chapters explore those of group leaders, group coaches, and pastoral leaders. I break each into bone practices, body practices, and breath practices, based on the vision of the valley of dry bones in Ezekiel 37, which was introduced in chapter 1. Let's consider the practices of flourishing small groups first.

Bone Practices of Small Groups

The most basic practices are external and can be described in concrete terms. First, groups of eight to twelve meet, usually in a space outside the church building. Sometimes, groups aim to be larger, about twenty-five or thirty. Secondly, groups gather at a time and place that works for members; this is not dictated by church staff. Third, meetings usually last about ninety minutes, but they can be as short as an hour or as long as three hours.

Finally, the most fruitful group meetings follow a pattern called the four Ws developed by Ralph W. Neighbour:

- *Welcome*—The first part of the meeting is a time of connecting with each other, usually involving an ice breaker that helps people talk about something safe. How can we expect people to open up and be transparent if we are not willing to listen to one another about something simple about their life? If you don't want to hear what I have to say about baseball or about a book I'm reading, then don't expect me to trust you with something that will make me vulnerable. Or think about it this way: If a person has spent eight hours at work and two hours in traffic before the meeting, how can we expect them to dive immediately into what God wants to do in the meeting?

- *Worship*—This is about recognizing the presence of God in our midst, that God is leading the meeting and wants to speak to us. If there is a guitar player in the group, then you don't have to spend much energy on this. But what's the plan for worship when you don't? Many use video-based worship or a music app, but there are other creative options. The primary point is to focus on the reality of Christ's presence.

- *Word*—This portion of the meeting gets most of our attention. Here the group discusses the topic of the meeting. A simple way to guide a conversation follows the acronym SOIL, developed by Andrew Mason.

S – Scripture reading and focus (this is also the spot for a short video teaching if you're using video curriculum)

O – Observation questions about the passage.

I – Interpretation questions about what is observed.

L – Life application questions about what is interpreted.

Bible study books, sermon study guides, video teaching, and discussion questions serve as resources for the Word. However, the point is not the Bible study, but to hear what the Spirit is saying through the Scriptures and the members of Christ's body.

- *Witness*—This is a time of prayer and planning about what the group will do in order to live in community and mission outside the group meeting.

The following image names various practical activities that can be a part of each of the four W's during any given meeting:

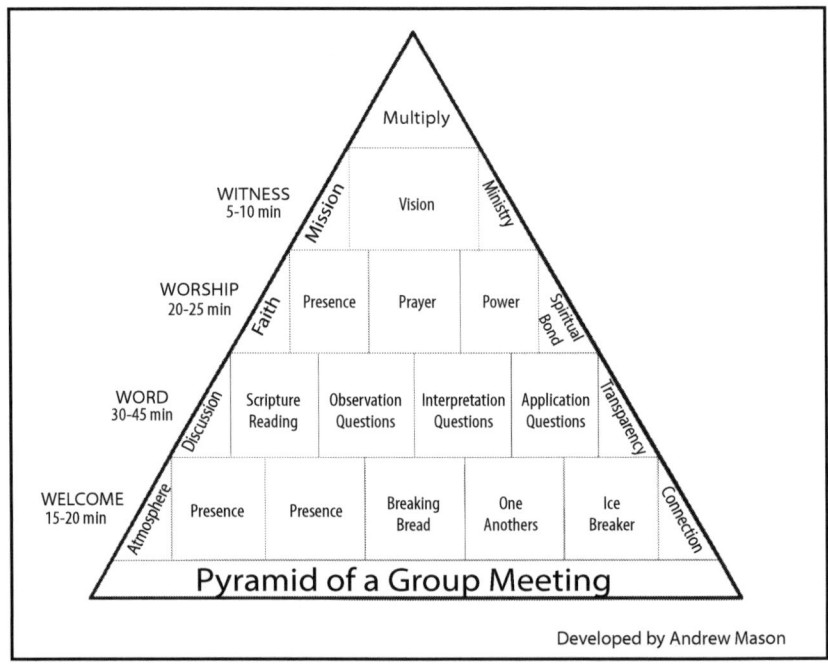

Developed by Andrew Mason

Body Practices of Small Groups

Beyond the surface-level, external practices, Jim Egli and Joel Comiskey have performed extensive research on the factors that contribute to thriving groups. They found eight "surprising discoveries," which are reported in *Groups that Thrive*. These factors provide insight into body practices that makes the bones work. Groups thrive through:[4]

- group members owning the group.
- group members being empowered to minister to the world.
- ordinary people being raised up for extraordinary influence.
- community which influences numerical growth.
- reaching out which increases transparency.
- worship during group meetings.
- focusing on prayer more than studying.
- persistent practice.

This research correlates with the three rhythms of group life introduced in chapter two. In review, they are:

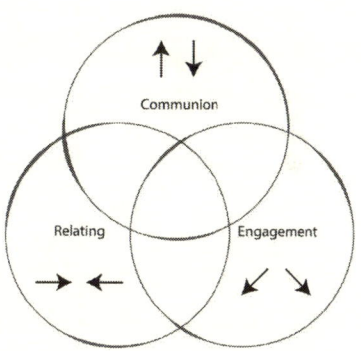

- Communion—A way of connecting with God that forms life patterns with one another so that we are no longer shaped by those of this world but changed from the inside out and thereby can impact people in our neighborhoods.
- Relating—A way of loving one another that stands in contrast to typical relational patterns of the culture, involving mutual service and self-sacrifice that is visible to others and impacts them.
- Engagement—A way of being with people (friends, next door neighbors, family members, co-workers) that displays Christ's love in tangible ways.

Breath Practices of Small Groups

What are the hidden practices that promote these three rhythms along with the surprising discoveries of Comiskey and Egli? These practices foster the breath of God that brings life to the body and bones. I introduce examples of them in my book *Missional Small Groups*. The point isn't to adopt all of these practices simultaneously but to pick three—one for each rhythm—and experiment with how it works in your group. This hidden work generates an organic, serendipitous flourishing. The following offers a brief introduction to these practices.

Practices of Communion

- Worship—The church knows how to do formal worship. But what about worship in a living room? What about worship with friends? Groups must learn how to worship in a circle not just in rows.
- Practicing the Presence—Nothing sets God's people apart like the presence of God. But do we actually expect to meet with God in our groups? If not, why not? What might it look like to meet with God regularly and go beyond the Bible study mentality?
- Alone Together—How do we practice silence and solitude as a private discipline but do it together? Usually we think of this individualistically, but there is a way of being "alone together" before God. How do we practice this?
- Listening Together—How does a group of people practice the art of listening to God together? How might God speak to "you" for "me"? And how do we create space for such an experience?
- Simplicity—The way we spend our time and money relates directly to our worship of God. In our culture we idolize things. If we don't let others in on this part of our lives, we won't change this pattern.
- Jesus's Meal—Traditions usually address this in one of five ways in their formal services. There is an alternative way of doing this around a meal, while at the same time not throwing out any of the current formal traditions of communion.
- Sabbath—Our ability to rest relates to our ability to trust, both God and others. This practice seems to have shaped the Old Tes-

tament people of God as much as any other. What bearing does this have on us as a New Testament people? How can we practice Sabbath today in our 24/7 world?

Practices of Relating
- A Primary Group—Most people have lots of shallow relationships, but they lack a primary group of people who will walk with them and point them toward the kingdom.
- A Safe Place—How do we create relationships that are safe, where there is both honesty and freedom along with accountability and challenge?
- Saying Hello—Greeting one another well is about developing listening skills. Often this simple piece is overlooked by church leadership, and it undermines people's ability to relate to one another.
- Pressing through Conflict—Relationships are messy. Of this there is no doubt. We must learn to work through conflict and refuse to give up on others. This requires some new relationship skills.
- Face-to-Face Contact—Community in our culture must call for face-to-face contact. At the same time we must deal with the reality of how the Internet and cell phones are impacting our ability to interact with one another.
- Build Up Each Other—Encouragement that flows out of the heart of God through his people for others is essential to God's kind of community. What does this look like in practical terms?
- Family Life and Small Groups—Too many times the group is seen as separate from the family connected to each group member. If true relationships are going to be developed, then the group must determine how to connect the two.
- Initiation into the Community—How does a group practice baptism in a way that communicates that new Christians are being initiated into Christ AND into Christ's community?

Practices of Engagement
- Moving into the Neighborhood—One of the keys to engagement is being present in our neighborhoods. This requires the risk of

putting ourselves out there and beginning to engage other people.

- Focus—We need to learn to say "no" to a lot of "good" stuff in order to be involved in God's mission. This may mean saying "no" to some church activities so that we have time to engage the people and needs in our world.
- Speaking Peace—We are present in the neighborhood as agents of peace in the midst of turmoil. What does this look like? What are some ways that work in our specific contexts to take God's peace to people?
- Observe—What is God already doing in and through the people and systems around us? We don't have to generate God's mission. God is already at work. We must see what the Spirit is doing and get involved.
- Hospitality—Opening up our homes to one another is essential to knowing each other. How do we do this in our time-starved world? How do we eat together in our fast-food world? We must address the reality of these questions.
- Righting Wrongs—Ask the question: What does God want to do? There are injustices in our world that are crying out for God's people to show up and offer justice.
- Speaking the Gospel—Instead of a canned approach, we must learn to communicate Christ in relationships with others, viewing them as equals, not as people to be won over to our way.

Getting Started with Breath Practices

In the small group study guide entitled *Cultivating Community in the Way of Jesus*, which is based on my book *Missional Small Groups*, you will find a process for introducing these hidden practices into the life of a group. The following is the introduction for this conversation guide. I include it here to explain why these "breath" practices go beyond studying information about them to discovering and discerning how the Spirit is at work to bring new life into the group.

This is not a Bible study guide, at least not in the sense that you will find at your local bookstore. Be assured that the Bible is a huge part of this study, as I am convinced that entering into the imagination of God's Word to us is crucial to being God's people. However, if you approach this Study Guide with a preconceived imagination of a typical small group Bible study, most likely you will miss its point. Instead, think of this as a practice guidebook.

This is a guidebook for practicing community and mission, a starter kit of sorts. In my book *Missional Small Groups*, I introduce how life in missional community could be compared to learning how to play a guitar. To play a guitar, you learn to play very simple rhythms over and over and then allow them to develop into more complex musical patterns. Missional life might look like radical activism to those looking in from the outside, but really it is comprised of basic rhythms that are played over, and over, and over that make room for the Spirit to lead us in new directions. These rhythms are: Missional Communion, our life together as a community before God; Missional Relating, our life together of loving one another; and Missional Engagement, our life together as we relate to those in our neighborhoods. All three are "missional" because the Spirit of God works through all three to shape our lives to be a sign, witness, and foretaste of God's dream for creation.

Each of these rhythms can be developed by adopting a set of practices as a group. In chapters 6, 7, and 8 of *Missional Small Groups*, I introduce seven practices for each of the three rhythms. In this study, you will walk through a thirteen-step process to help a group experiment with and learn how to be missional by putting three of these practices into action. This expands what I introduced in Appendix A of *Missional Small Groups* in short form.

This is not a list of ideas for you to make happen. Nor is this a preconceived model for you to follow that will make your group "missional." This is a way for your group to enter into the Jesus way as you make room for the Spirit to shape and reshape how you operate and share life as a group. This process depends upon the group listening to the Spirit of God and to the Scriptures. In other words, it is not a process of simply going out and doing something called missional.

Different groups will learn missional rhythms at different speeds. Some will pick them up quickly, while others will develop them slowly. Speed is not the key to effectiveness. The Spirit of God never seems to "get stuff done" as quickly as we would like. The Holy Spirit is shaping us to be a people that demonstrate God's love. And this is cultivated as we choose a practice and repeat it. Even the most gifted and creative musicians practice the basics repeatedly. One professional studio guitarist was asked how he plays with such excellence. He responded, "Every day I repeatedly practice the basic chords that a novice learns." The goal of these studies is to help a group learn the basics and practice them consistently.

These studies work best if the group takes twelve to fifteen weeks to go through the first twelve steps. Then in study thirteen, the group will determine the next steps regarding what it needs to process further. For most groups, it will take intentional focus over a period of six months to a year in order for these rhythms to become second nature.

This guidebook provides rails to get a group started with *Relational Re-vision* and moving toward *Missional Re-creation*. This approach might prove uncomfortable initially for some group members because they depend on Bible study content that is different each week. Instead the point here is to learn how to practice a few things well and see where the Spirit takes the group as they enter into these practices.

11

What Do Flourishing Leaders Practice?

Most of the time, when we think of leading a small group or a missional community, we think in terms of techniques. We live in a world driven by techniques. If you have a problem, someone has a solution they're willing to sell you. If you follow their secret knowledge, then you'll supposedly get the results you want. If you want to make money, there's a plan for that. If you want to be happy, then follow the steps some expert outlines for you. If you want to be a great group leader, there are plenty of ready-made plans that allegedly will get you there.

Bone Practices for Leaders

This technique mindset applies to the bones. For group leadership, these techniques usually sound something like the following:

- Four steps to leading a great small group discussion
- Three keys to building community
- Seven ways to pray for your group members
- Six rules for leading worship in groups
- Five ways to reach the community with the gospel

- How to ask great questions that generate discussion
- How to contact group members between meetings
- A surefire strategy for developing a new leader

However, when we depend solely on techniques, we limit our groups to programmatic experiences. It works like this: if you want a great group, then follow the a + b + c formula. This puts all of the pressure on the group leader to make the group work. We need something more than programs to follow.

Body Practices for Leaders

If we want to move beyond the formulas, we need to understand the basic leadership habits that direct how a leader does his or her work. There are many great resources that name the habits, keys, or principles of great group leaders. For instance, consider the eight habits of small group leaders that are developed by Dave Early:[1]

- Dream of Leading a Healthy, Growing, Multiplying Group
- Pray for Group Members Daily
- Invite People to Visit the Group
- Contact Group Members Regularly
- Prepare for the Group Meeting
- Mentor an Apprentice Leader
- Plan Group Fellowship Activities
- Be Committed to Personal Growth

By identifying priorities like these, leaders can clearly see where to invest their energy. However, if we stop at this point, we continue to place all the pressure on the group leaders to make the group work. Without God's presence and love, we only have man-made steps that produce man-made group meetings. But there is more.

Breath Practices for Leaders

To see this more, we must think briefly about the end or the goal of the group experience. The end we envision for our small groups will dictate the kinds of practices we adopt as leaders. Over the years there have been many different "ends" offered for small groups or missional communities. They include things like evangelism, discipleship, getting people connected, Bible study, multiplication of groups, or creating a Jesus movement. Those with the goal of evangelistic growth will focus on practices to reach the lost. Those that seek Bible study will spend great effort honing their Bible study skills. And if these are the "end" of your group, you can find a technique that will get you there. Just search the web and find a resource.

While the "ends" often promoted are good, they are secondary. They are not the ultimate end that God has in mind. As I've suggested throughout this book, the ultimate end is to lead others into the flourishing of God's life. With this end in mind, we are simply talking about becoming the kind of leaders who live in the love of God demonstrated on the cross, allowing God's love to move through us. The end is God's love, and since God loves the world (John 3:16), we are simply joining him in the continuing work of the Spirit to love the world with cross-like love. Therefore, we need leadership practices that will align us with how God's Spirit is moving. We are creating environments in our groups so that people can grow in this cross-like love. This is the end, the goal.

Over the years I've observed that leaders who grow in this cross-like love engage in a common set of practices. They include:

- Hear the Rhythms of Beyond—Leaders who empower groups to flourish have ears to hear and eyes to see what God is doing in their groups and through their groups. They listen for God's ways, even if they stand against the rising tides of the world.
- Gather in the Presence—Groups flourish when they take Jesus at his promise that he will be present when they meet in his name. The leader then is not primarily focused on leading a great Bible discussion but upon encountering the presence of God together.
- Lead Collaboratively—The best small group leaders have learned that they do not have to lead the group by themselves. They instead gather a team within the group whose members work together to guide the group.

- Be Yourself—Group leaders do not need to pretend. Great groups are safe places where group members can share about the realities of their lives. If leaders pretend to have it all together or if they lead in a religiously pretentious way, then the group will not flourish.
- Hang Out—Great groups are not merely about having great group meetings. The kind of life that God wants to foster is the kind that happens when people learn to live in community in the informal down times of normal life.
- Make a Difference—Leaders of flourishing groups do not merely focus on what is happening inside the group. They seek to participate in what God wants to do in the world around them.
- Fight Well—Leaders understand that God works through conflict, not around it. The Spirit uses our differences to lead groups into new spaces of group life.
- Point the Way to the Cross—Group leaders are not at the center of the group. They do not have the ability to fix the community or the people in it. The job of the leader is to point people to Christ and allow the work of the cross to bring transformation.

I write about these practices in my book *Leading Small Groups in the Way of Jesus*. Instead of a list of things that leaders do to make the group work, they are activities for investing in the hidden ways that open up space for the Spirit to work in the unexpected. These practices open our eyes to see what God is doing by training our imagination to move with the Spirit. After all, this is what really brings life change.

12

What Do Flourishing Coaches Practice?

Jim Egli has completed extensive statistical research to determine the factors that result in group health and growth. In the questions he asked of small group leaders, one was about the support they receive from a coach or a pastor. The statistical evidence is overwhelming. Egli reports, "When leaders are personally encouraged by supervisors or pastors the group leaders have stronger prayer lives, the groups engage in more outreach to others, and new leaders are more actively identified and utilized."[1] The quality and quantity of coaching that a group leader receives directly impacts the life of the group.

Statistical evidence that proves the importance of coaching is not surprising. What was surprising is that this one factor proved to be the most important, more than small group leader training, monthly support meetings, or promoting small groups publicly. Good coaching promotes flourishing groups. Good coaching stimulates group growth. Good coaching positively impacts the prayer life of small group leaders. Good coaching develops new small group leaders which results in new groups. Good coaching produces small group momentum.

However often pastors tell me, "My group leaders don't want the input of a coach or a pastor. They find the extra meetings a waste of time. They lead groups quite well on their own."

Leaders don't want oversight. They don't want a big brother telling them what to do. And they don't want extra meetings to explain lots of theory about what should be happening in their small groups. But there is something that impacts groups far more than conventional coaching. Groups move into the way of Jesus by "eldering."

Eldering might very well involve coaching and encouraging the leader, but the role of coaching does not necessarily involve the ministry of an elder. The elder invests in the people that belong to the various groups under his or her care. The common imagination of a coach—at least in the most popular books on the topic—is that the ministry is to and through the small group leaders. I use the word elder to point to the role of a leader who cares for the groups as a whole, not just the leaders.

The term elder has been used in many different ways in the history of the church. Some traditions have a board of elders. Some talk about a teaching elder. These are official roles within established structures. Still others speak of elders as those who should be respected for their life-long commitment and walk of faithfulness in the church.

Basically, the New Testament term for elder (*presbutas*) denotes someone who is older and more experienced. It was a common practice in the wider culture for elders to serve the Jewish religion or a city. This practice was carried over into the church. Paul established churches, and then appointed elders to lead the church when he left.

There is a desperate need within the church for experienced people to guide and lead others. Age is one contributing factor, but experience in walking with the Lord is even more important. Elders have been shaped to be people who can guide others.

Eldership with this understanding will include coaching and mentoring of small group leaders, but it also means the care of and investment in the life of the groups. With this understanding of leadership, I propose that the elders are those leaders in the church who invest in, care for, and walk with groups under their care. The small group leader can certainly help with this goal, but elders are those with the life experience and spiritual maturity who can walk ahead and lead. When applying this to missional small group development, elders might be the leaders of a house church of 20-50 people with small group leaders within the house church. They might oversee three to five small groups and lead periodic gatherings or help those small groups network and work together in mission.

Bone Practices for Coaches

Jim Egli offers four basic actions that coaches adopt to serve the group leaders and groups under their care. These are the visible actions required to put the bones together. The first is one-on-one meetings. There are two questions that drive these meetings:

- How is your ministry going?
- How are you doing personally?

The second activity is praying for the leaders. Daily intercession for the leaders, their families, and their groups is crucial. The coach should know the needs in their leaders' lives and ministry so that they can pray specifically, having faith that God is at work.

The third thing a coach does is to meet with all the leaders. The two-meeting monthly pattern has proven to be effective. One meeting gathers all small group leaders within a church and includes a break-out time for the coach to interact with his or her leaders. In the second meeting, coaches meet as a small group only with their leaders at a time convenient to the leaders. Some churches facilitate these coaching meetings through group phone sessions or online video chat.

The final activity is to visit the small groups under the coaches' care. This gives the coach insight into the way that the group is operating and to the needs of the group members. The coach can also model ministry for the group.

Body Practices for Coaches

Here I offer an introduction to seven basic practices that shape the work of small group coaches. These practices are derived and adapted from the book *How To Be a Great Cell Group Coach* by Joel Comiskey:

- Receive—Coaches are called to empower the group leaders that they are walking alongside. They can do this best when they receive God's life and then offer it to group leaders. Coaches have nothing better to offer than their prayers.
- Listen—One of the key practices of the coach is that of listening to what God is doing in the leader and in the group. Many assume that the primary job of the coach is to give direction or advice. However, in most cases, what the leader needs is someone who will prove to be a faithful listener who will walk with them through the ups and downs of leadership.
- Encourage—Leaders need someone in their lives who will be a voice of God's encouragement. Paul spoke of this as edification or building up. Leaders often feel alone and lost as they faithfully serve their groups. They need someone who is going to listen to what the Spirit is saying and build them up.
- Care—The coach does not merely work with the leader regarding issues of the small group; he or she also cares about the life of the leader. The hope is the coach will build a relationship with group leaders so that he or she can minister to their needs. Sometimes sin sneaks in the back door which requires confrontation. The coach is there to care enough to confront.
- Develop—Group leaders lead out of vision. This is what will give them the passion to pursue God and serve others. Coaches can help leaders articulate this vision and develop it in such a way that others can gather around it.
- Strategize—Group leaders need support in addressing challenges, especially in times of conflict. They also need someone who can think through the vision of the group, the recruitment of new leaders, and to develop a process for group multiplication.
- Challenge—Paul says in Ephesians 4:15, "Instead, speaking the truth in love, we will in all things grow up into him who is the Head, that is, Christ." Any good athletic coach will push their players to stretch them and tap into their potential. Love for the leader will compel the coach to see the leader's gifts and strengths and challenge them to move into God's calling.

Breath Practices for Coaches

Jim Egli compares the work of the small group coach with the work of a coach of a sporting team. Consider how the work of a coach relates to a player on the field. A player usually has a limited, short-range point of view that focuses their attention on the next play, doing their job in the moment, for the purpose of winning the game now. A coach on the other hand looks at the entire game, the big picture of how the entire team works together for the sake of winning in the long run. Therefore, the coach must step back and look at the bigger picture of what God is doing. He or she will do this in the following ways:

- Envision—The small group leader is focused on the group. Usually they are focused on the week-to-week challenges that arise. It is the job of the coach to look at the big picture and see where God is leading the group. Even more, a vision is needed for the area of care. For instance, if the coach works with groups in a specific geographic zone, they seek God's vision for future group development and pray that God would raise up ministers for that vision.
- Recruit—In accordance with this vision for their area of care, the coach is looking to see what God is doing in people's lives and investing there. Who is heeding the call to lead? Who has the potential, but does not yet have the confidence? Who needs training?
- Encourage—All leaders need encouragement. The Apostle Paul called it edification, or building up. The words of the coach to the leader can be filled by the Spirit to strengthen them in their gifts so that they can guide their groups.
- Communicate—The coach is a conduit between the pastoral leadership of the church and the group. One of the most important aspects of serving as a conduit is that of securing help for groups when situations arise that are beyond the skills or gifting of the leaders. It's not necessary for the coach to provide this ministry, as the needs could require extensive time and effort of a pastor, counselor, or other specialized support.

To Know God

The point of these practices is to "know" God, just as Paul wrote:

What is more, I consider everything a loss because of the surpassing worth of knowing Christ Jesus my Lord, for whose sake I have lost all things. I consider them garbage, that I may gain Christ and be found in him, not having a righteousness of my own that comes from the law, but that which is through faith in Christ—the righteousness that comes from God on the basis of faith. I want to know Christ—yes, to know the power of his resurrection and participation in his sufferings, becoming like him in his death, and so, somehow, attaining to the resurrection from the dead.
—Philippians 3:8-10

We use the word "know" in many different ways. For instance, someone might ask you if you know a person named Jerry. With this question, you are being asked if you have been introduced to that particular person and thereby have a knowledge of identity. Another use can be imagined if your pastor uses the word "eschatological" in his sermon and you have recently attended a class where he provided an extensive understanding of what that word means. This gives you a knowledge of information. A third use is illustrated by your overhearing a conversation in Spanish and you took a few classes and you actually paid attention and worked at it. As a result of putting the language to use, you are able to understand what they are saying. This is about having a knowledge of practice.

When we hear Paul talking about the "surpassing worth of knowing Christ Jesus my Lord," we must ask what kind of knowledge he is talking about. Is he talking about knowing the identity of Jesus? Was he referring to information about Jesus? Was his meaning about having a knowledge based on the practice of the faith?

The answer to each question is both yes and no. Knowing Jesus of course referred to knowledge of his identity, of specific information, and of an understanding formed by specific practices. However, the knowing Paul wrote about here went beyond this. This is the kind of knowing that we might refer to as knowledge of union. This kind of knowledge is personal because it affects us at the core of our being. We can experience this kind of union in a variety of ways. For instance, when asking my grandmother how to make one of her dishes, she would say something like, "Well you turn on the oven to medium heat. Then you mix a bunch of flour with some milk, a bit of water, add a few shakes of salt ..." At that point, it became clear that there was no way that someone could do what she did in the kitchen. She was not working from a technical knowledge of the information about cooking. She was working from a knowledge of cooking that had shaped who she was.

Information builds upon identity, as we cannot know something that we are not acquainted with. Practice builds upon information. My grandmother did not arrive at that point of knowledge of cooking without practice. However, knowledge of union takes us beyond all three. This is the kind of knowledge that coaches of flourishing groups offer to leaders.

13

What Do Flourishing Pastors Practice?

A basic rule of life is that people reproduce life patterns that they have learned from other people. More specifically, authority figures in our lives serve as models for how we lead others. We learn to lead through relationships.

Group leaders lead in the way they have been led because the leadership pattern trickles down. For instance, if small group leaders experience a formal, mechanistic relationship with their pastors, then they will lead their groups in a similar way. Or consider the model of a pastor who leads meetings by talking for eighty percent of the time; this inadvertently socializes others to repeat that pattern. I once heard a story of a young Christian in Southeast Asia who dressed in suits to lead a house church in his rural village; he preached for forty minutes, often yelling at the people sitting the circle. When asked where he learned to do this, he explained how he had watched tons of videos of great preachers from America. He was only leading in the way that he had been led.

Pastoral leadership of group leaders is as much, if not more, unspoken than spoken. Consider a small group pastor that focuses most of his or her energy on the mechanics of the bones from their offices—managing group tracking software, organizing curriculum, and designing promotional brochures. The way that they lead the groups is driven by the leadership metaphor of a middle manager. Their job is to lead the program, get it organized, and make sure that people have what they need in order to lead the groups. All of their time is spent in meetings, addressing administrative issues, planning services and events, studying, and putting out fires.

This middle manager metaphor shapes the imagination of how many see their pastoral oversight of groups, and, as a result, it shapes their pastoral practices. In this chapter, I want to propose an alternative metaphor along with a corresponding set of practices.

The Metaphor of Shepherding

The metaphor of sheep and shepherding offers an alternative imagination for pastoring a group system that flourishes. This imagination is based in a story, a narrative of Jesus. God has not called us to pastor in order to produce lots of groups. God has called us to pastor in a way that lives into Jesus' way of pastoring.

The Bible describes Jesus as the good shepherd (John 10:11). Matthew 9:36-38 reads, "When he saw the crowds, he had compassion on them, because they were harassed and helpless, like sheep without a shepherd. Then he said to his disciples, 'The harvest is plentiful but the workers are few. Ask the Lord of the harvest, therefore, to send out workers into his harvest field.'" The interesting thing is that this passage immediately follows a verse that reads, "Jesus went through all the towns and villages, teaching in their synagogues, proclaiming the good news of the kingdom and healing every disease and sickness" (Mark 9:35).

During the time of Jesus' ministry on earth, he could not shepherd everyone by himself because shepherding is not something that can be done with the masses. He needed others to help him care for the scattered sheep. He needed shepherds who would be with the sheep and guide them in his way. Likewise, Peter wrote, "Be shepherds of God's flock that is under your care, watching over them—not because you must, but because you are willing, as God wants you to be; not pursuing dishonest gain, but eager to serve; not lording it over those entrusted to you, but being examples to the flock" (1 Peter 5:2-3).

I grew up tending a flock on my dad's farm; therefore I've had many conversations in response to the question, "What does it mean for leaders to be shepherds?" The original audiences of the Scriptures would have had a thorough knowledge of sheep and shepherding. Even if they did not have firsthand experience, they knew others who did or they had observed the life of sheep and shepherds in their villages. After all, sheep were as common then as smart phones are today. The last conversation between Jesus and Peter reads:

> When they had finished eating, Jesus said to Simon Peter, "Simon son of John, do you love me more than these?"
> "Yes, Lord," he said, "you know that I love you."
> Jesus said, "Feed my lambs."
> Again Jesus said, "Simon son of John, do you love me?"
> He answered, "Yes, Lord, you know that I love you."
> Jesus said, "Take care of my sheep."
> The third time he said to him, "Simon son of John, do you love me?"
> Peter was hurt because Jesus asked him the third time, "Do you love me?" He said, "Lord, you know all things; you know that I love you."
> Jesus said, "Feed my sheep" (John 21:15-17).

Leading groups into the stories of *Relational Re-vision* and *Missional Re-creation* is a call to feed sheep. If we do this, the sheep will naturally and organically grow and move toward a life that fulfills the Great Commission and the Great Commandment. Feeding the sheep well is the outcome of the leadership practices we develop. If we are going to do this, then we need to understand a bit more about sheep.

Sheep require up-close-and-personal care. For instance, sheep lack the ability to regulate how much they eat. If food is available, they will eat it. If they eat too much, they will die. In addition, they have sensitive stomachs, which requires a shepherd to feed them the right amount of the right food. Also, sheep have no ability to protect themselves. They are frail and slow, and they cannot kick, claw or bite. They are easily spooked. They will scatter in panic and, once cornered, sit petrified while staring at their predator.

Therefore sheep must be penned at night and watched over by day. Sheep are loud, they are intellectually challenged (scientific fact), they are prone to wander off, and they stink. Oh my, do they stink. Just imagine four inches of wool at the end of a long rainy winter. Sheep are the only farm animal that requires annual shearing. This can be a good thing because it provides income, but it also illustrates the kind of special care a shepherd provides that is not required by other animals. This one biological characteristic demonstrates how sheep cannot live on their own. If somehow sheep got smarter and developed the ability to protect themselves, they still could not survive in the wild. If the wool were not shorn, it would grow so long that it would get top heavy. Then when it got wet, they would fall over, legs flailing. They would die helplessly waiting for a shepherd to come and turn them over.

Finally, experience with sheep has taught me that they cannot be driven. In his book *They Smell Like Sheep*, Lynn Anderson tells a story about what the story of shepherding might mean:

> Several years ago in Palestine, Carolyn and I rode a tour bus through Israel's countryside nearly mesmerized as the tour guide explained the scenery, the history, and the lifestyle. In his description, he included a heart-warming portrayal of the ancient shepherd/sheep relationship. He expounded on how the shepherd builds a relationship with his sheep—how he feeds them and gently cares for them. He pointed out that the shepherd doesn't drive the sheep but leads them, and that the shepherd does not need to be harsh with them, because they hear his voice and follow. And so on …
>
> He then explained how on a previous tour things had backfired for him as he was giving this same speech about sheep and shepherds. In the midst of spinning his pastoral tale, he suddenly realized he had lost his audience. They were all staring out of the

bus window at a guy chasing a 'herd' of sheep. He was throwing rocks at them, whacking them with sticks, and siccing the sheep dog on them. The sheep-driving man in the field had torpedoed the guide's enchanting narrative.

The guide told us that he had been so agitated that he jumped off the bus, ran into the field, and accosted the man, "Do you understand what you have just done to me?" he asked. "I was spinning a charming story about the gentle ways of shepherds, and here you are mistreating, hazing, and assaulting these sheep! What is going on?" For a moment, a bewildered look froze on the face of the poor sheepchaser, then the light dawned and he blurted out, "Man. You've got me all wrong. I'm not a shepherd. I'm a butcher!" This poor, unwitting fellow had just provided the tour guide and all of us with a perfect example of what a 'good shepherd' is not.[1]

Another place that points out what God's shepherds are not to do is found in Ezekiel, in a prophetic confrontation of Israel's leaders:

The word of the Lord came to me: "Son of man, prophesy against the shepherds of Israel; prophesy and say to them: 'This is what the Sovereign Lord says: Woe to you shepherds of Israel who only take care of yourselves! Should not shepherds take care of the flock? You eat the curds, clothe yourselves with the wool and slaughter the choice animals, but you do not take care of the flock. You have not strengthened the weak or healed the sick or bound up the injured. You have not brought back the strays or searched for the lost. You have ruled them harshly and brutally. So they were scattered because there was no shepherd, and when they were scattered they became food for all the wild animals. My sheep wandered over all the mountains and on every high hill. They were scattered over the whole earth, and no one searched or looked for them" (Ezekiel 34:1-6).

The shepherds of Israel did not do these things; therefore we can turn this confrontation into constructive statements about what it means to be God's shepherds. They care for the flock, strengthen the weak, heal the sick, and bring back the strays, which contrasted with leaders who only care for themselves. This prophesy is a challenge to God's leaders to lead not for the sake of vocational advancement or leadership glory, but they are called to lead for the sake of those being led.

Group leaders will shepherd the flocks under their care in the same way that their shepherds care for them. They will reproduce what they receive. The following introduces shepherding practices that will foster leaders with the capacity to shepherd their groups.

Bone Practices

Plan the Strategy and Develop the Supportive Systems

There are many moving parts that are needed to support the life of groups, including things like new leader training, curriculum resources, coaching development, group member discipleship processes, group multiplication strategies, etc. These are addressed further in chapters 21 and 22.

Champion the Journey

There must be one person who owns the process of leading groups along a path toward flourishing. This person serves as an architect who carries the responsibility for this development more than others. This process is comprised of the eight priorities introduced in Part 4.

Oversee the Administration

The key here is "oversee." Those on the pastoral team must not be required to focus on the administration of groups. The gift set of an effective groups pastor that enjoys shepherding is not the same gift set needed to effectively administer the details of the system. Therefore, pastors must not spend inordinate amounts of time on tasks like brochure development, organizing events, or all the other minutia that so often eats up days upon days of work. A key for effectively putting this practice into motion involves finding a gifted administrator who can do this work. Also, identify a user-friendly group management software program that can track the development of groups. Finally, keep the administration as simple as possible. The point is people, not events. People suffer because pastors across America are consumed with tasks that keep pastors from being with people.

Body Practices

Train

Training is not the same thing as teaching. Teaching depends upon an expert who disperses information that the student absorbs but cannot necessarily practice. Trainers provide experiences that can be repeated by those they are training. People repeat what they experience, not what they are told. If you teach them about the importance of facilitating discussion and explain how to ask good questions, they will be impressed by your knowledge as a teacher. But they will only have information about the theories of facilitating. If you train them by giving them a living exercise of facilitation, they will experience something in the training that they can repeat in their groups. In other words, leading people in an exercise of group facilitation that they can repeat in their own group meetings is much more effective than thirty minutes of teaching on the topic of facilitation. The principle is this: whatever I do with the leaders it must be done in such a way that it can be replicated in a home with a few friends. Will people walk away from the training and be able to repeat what they experienced in that training with their small group or even a few friends while drinking coffee?

Another thing to consider in your training is the use of social media. Today people learn in short snippets, not elongated classes. Short video recordings on how to lead an ice breaker, how to facilitate worship, or the importance of listening that are posted on YouTube are a great way to train leaders. They need not be high quality productions. They only need to be three to five minutes in length and encourage leaders in practical skills that they can experience and repeat.

Mentor

Identify three to five leaders in whom you will invest. You can train many, but you can only mentor a few. This is often overlooked by busy pastors because they feel guilty when they don't treat everyone equally. One way of doing this is found in the section entitled "Strategy #3: Triads" in chapter 19.

Get Out of the Office

Do as much of your ministry out of the office as you possibly can. Groups happen in the real world. The more small group pastors get out of the office and personally minister to leaders and members, the more effective the small groups are.

When you meet with leaders, meet them at a coffee shop. In fact, you could set up shop at a coffee shop and get to know the employees and other regular customers.

Another way to do this is to minister in the homes and businesses of the people. Make home visits to pray for needs and encourage people in their walks with God. Visit businesses to pray God's blessings over the work done there. Eat breakfast and lunch with people to speak life into small group members and minister to needs. Some might argue that this has been a practice of the traditional pastoral leadership for years, but the difference lies in the fact that the staff pastor does not wait until there is a crisis, an extended absence from church attendance, or a request on the part of a church member. Instead, the pastor takes the proactive approach and sets up appointments to minister to different people during the week.

Recruit New Leaders

The staff small group pastor is in charge of the future growth of the small groups under his or her care. Small group leaders need support in the recruitment and training of future small group leaders. Small group pastors should make it a regular practice to sit down over lunch with potential leaders and say, "I see God's hand upon your life. He is raising you up into leadership. Have you ever thought about going through the small group leader training?" When a pastor says this, it carries much more weight than when a small group leader says it.

Breath Practices

Pray

Build time into the daily work schedule for prayer and intercession for those in groups. I would suggest at least thirty minutes per work day. This prayer can be done individually or as groups. Suggestions about prayer as it relates to the role of a group pastor is further explored in chapter 23.

Cast Vision

In reality, this section should be entitled "over-communicate." Communicate with group leaders, with the congregation, with other staff teams, with the senior pastor, and the executive pastor. Group ministry is not a silo alongside other ministries because groups infiltrate every aspect of the life of the church. The only way to make this work is to communicate. One key way to do this is to tell stories of what is happening in groups. The vision will be cast through stories more than through theoretical abstractions.

Ask Questions and Listen

Breathing involves two parts, inhaling and exhaling. We breathe in God's presence, and we exhale our response to God. The Spirit comes to us today in dialogue, not in unilateral force, as was reflected in the revelation of Christ. Jesus came into the world with kingdom words and works, as he exhaled God's breath. However, Jesus also allowed others to influence him, even to the point of allowing others to kill him. He did not force his agenda upon the world. He put the kingdom on display in circles of conversation, not unilateral announcements. God wants leaders to develop the character that reflects his dialogical nature.

God wants relationship, not robotic alignment. This practice applies to the pastor's relationship with God as well as their relationships with those they lead. Too often, pastors have treated coaches, group leaders, and members like worker drones who are expected to fulfill their vision that they received in isolation. They treat the breath that is working through them unilaterally, as a one-way conversation—which actually is not a conversation at all. As a result, there are no feedback loops. The vision and strategy are fixed and there is an absence of adaptation that comes through open dialogue. (The topic of dialogue is covered further in chapter 16.)

Conclusion

The Bible opens with "In the beginning, God …" God is the subject who acts in the course of history. God creates. God talks. God walks. God interjects. God intervenes. God protects. God leads. God corrects. God disciplines. God comes. God heals. God turns water into wine. God teaches. God eats. God raises another from the dead. God loves. God dies. God rises. God ascends. God empowers. God works.

We know who God is by God's action.

The Bible starts out with God as the subject. With the turning of each page, we read how the story unfolds with God as the primary actor. If we don't get this about the Bible's way of talking about God, it would be like watching *Hamlet* without a Hamlet, or *Forest Gump* without anyone actually playing Forest Gump. There would be no story.

The leadership practices introduced here are meant to provide a path for pastors to lead in a way that aligns with God's action. This is a challenge today as the leadership practices that are commonly promoted work as if God is not active, as if leadership goals depend upon us to make them happen. We go through our days as if each of us is the lead actor on the stage of life. While the choices we make each day definitively matter, none of us are the lead actor in the story of creation. God is at work in the world, creating and recreating life, doing far more than what we can do in our a + b + c perspective of trying to make groups work. God still acts. God still comes. God still intervenes. God still works miracles. These practices train our eyes to see what God is up to and get involved according to the Spirit's leading.

In the midst of our world where the sense of divine presence has been squeezed out, we need pastors who have the active patience to let the lead actor of the Bible's story shape their imaginations. "In the beginning, God …" This begins the story of God in our world and this continues as we walk through God's creation.

Part 4

Pilgrimage

14

What Does the Pilgrimage Look Like?

Churches do not change because leaders merely choose to do so. We need a process that will lead us into a different way of thinking and acting. Otherwise we will continue to get the same results. Einstein once said, "The definition of insanity is to keep doing the same thing, while expecting different results." If we want different results, we need to embrace a different process. This chapter introduces this different process, which will be further detailed in the remaining chapters.

Three Levels of Change on the Pilgrimage

When people enter a change process, they must wrestle with many different levels of change at the same time. Imagine a suburban church of 200 people that has been doing Sunday school since its inception twenty years ago. There are three levels of change that correspond with the bones, body, and breath that are introduced in chapter one.

Changing Structures (Bones)

Changing the structure stands out the most when a church begins small groups, because the structure is what people can see. For many churches, small group ministry is radically different from the ministry of the traditional church. The change to a small group strategy involves reorganization of leadership, development of new training, meeting outside the church building, and refocusing the vision. These are the visible trappings.

Changing the Culture (Body)

Culture can be described as the set of beliefs, feelings, and character that a group of people shares. The culture of a group of people is so much a part of who they are that it is impossible for them to define it. It is like asking a fish to explain water to a mammal. It cannot understand water because water is its culture. Likewise, Christians are a part of a church culture. Some share a culture that understands church as programs, committee meetings, and congregational voting. Others share a culture that views the church as a building where people come for weekly spiritual feeding and entertainment. Still others share a culture where people get saved and walk the aisle, but the relationships within the church end when the pastor says, "Amen." Many small group initiatives have stalled because pastors failed to address the beliefs, feelings, and character that hide beneath the surface. This is why Part 3 on Practices is so important. As we adopt practices, people develop new habits, and those new habits shape character. From that character, culture is shaped.

Changing Individuals' Desires (Breath)

Without the third level of change, that of changing individuals' desires related to their passions and loves, neither the strategy nor the culture will ever change to be what God is calling it to be. Imagine the small group leader who has been an elder for twenty years but has blocked every leadership initiative that pastors has suggested. Imagine the former seminarian who is leading a new group but talks for two hours because he is the only one who knows Greek. Imagine the Sunday school superintendent who does not know where she fits into the new system, the music minister who does not want to pastor people, or the children's minister who does not want to change what she is doing.

Picture the deacon who is judgmental of "sinners" and has no desire to build relationships with the lost and invite them to a small group.

These people have passions, dreams, and loves that motivate them to do the things that they do. These passions do not change merely because they are supposed to change. Change in what one loves or desires requires a deep work of the Spirit in our lives. To facilitate this work of the Spirit, people first need information about what God is doing in and through the community that is fostered through groups. Second, they need practical steps to get started on a different path. A third thing that is required to change desires is to provide opportunities for people to talk about their passions because people need safe places to express their deep desires and their hopes for the church, along with their frustrations. Passions change not because we shut down people in order to get them to "line up" with the body and bones. They only change when we create safe places for people to name what they feel, even when it is misguided. Then the Spirit is able to take that honesty and redeem it, even change it, so that God's breath might flow in and through God's body.

Pilgrimage Strategy Options

The journey churches have taken in the development of groups typically fall into one of four categories, the last of which introduces the strategy outlined in the following chapters. The first three are offered as a contrast.

Instant Groups Strategy

In this strategy, innovative leaders get the vision and run with it. One of the characteristics of this strategy is that small groups are legislated by the pastor. I heard the story of one pastor who stood before his church on a Sunday morning and held up a book on small groups and told church members that the book represented the new direction of the church. Then he said, "Either you are going with me or I am leaving to lead another church in this vision." The good news is that this pastor had served this church for over twenty years and had enough credibility with the people to make such a statement. The bad news is that most people did not understand what the vision entailed, and consequently the church unnecessarily struggled to get small groups on the right track. Another pastor used a similar tactic and was fired by his deacon board the same day. He works at a secular job today.

Legislating change in a church rarely works, even if a pastor has the power of the Pope. There are two reasons this is true. First, persuasive arguments cannot convince someone that one way of life is better than another. No matter how much data you give people that small groups are a better form of ministry, those who have ties to other styles of ministry will still resist the change. Human persuasion alone will not get people to give up the stability of what they have today to change to something that is unknown.

Secondly, even if people are persuaded of the value of small groups, enforcement will not lead to changed character and desires. When groups are legislated and people are assigned to join groups, people become a part of a programmatic small group system. It might have all the trappings of a working small group system, but it has little life because the people see small groups as a different way of doing the same kind of church.

The Blueprint Strategy

This strategy happens when one church tries to replicate the strategy of a model church. People read a book on small groups or go to a conference. Then they return to their churches and try to mimic the strategy of the church they have observed.

To illustrate the weakness of this strategy, imagine an owner of a small manufacturing company visiting General Electric to learn how they run their operation. He purchases all of its manuals, interviews key leaders, and reads every book available on this great "model" business. He returns home to implement everything that GE does. But he soon discovers that it is impossible. First, GE does business on such a grand scale that no small business owner could copy all of its methods. Second, GE has refined its methods over a period of decades. The small business owner needs time to learn how the methods work. He cannot force them to work overnight.

Because most churches are small and model churches are large, the model cannot be replicated. In addition, these large model churches have refined their ministry methods over years. Other churches need the space to do likewise. Any church that develops a flourishing group system will do so in its own way. It is crucial for small churches to learn from these large model churches. Even seeing what they do with small groups and adapting that strategy to one's own setting will prove vital. However, to mimic or impersonate another's small group strategy is often a recipe for disaster.

The Road Map Strategy

This strategy assumes that leading people into small groups is a linear process of going from A to B to C to D .... With this assumption, people look to books and churches for a logical place to start. They offer a uniform set of steps that supposedly lead to success. However, in my research of churches, those who have developed flourishing groups have not started in the same way nor have they progressed in straight lines. Some began with one group, others with a few, and others with many. Some moved very quickly, while others moved slowly. And still others took more than a year to prepare themselves for the initial small group start-up.

Pastors often adopt the Road Map Strategy because they see it as a way to control the change process. They do not want people to get out of hand or get too creative. Therefore they take charge of everything and make sure that the entire small group system lines up with preconceived ideas about what it should look like.

Another reason for adopting this strategy is that pastors see the process of changing to group ministry as a simple shift from what they have been doing in previous ministry. In other words, if a church plans to transform its Sunday school classes and committees by using small group principles, the leadership can see this kind of change as progressive and linear. However, the change process that leads to flourishing is not linear and map-like. This kind of change is too fluid to fit on a map.

The Charting Strategy

This strategy draws from life on a ship. When a captain determines that he needs to change course in order to arrive at a new set of coordinates, he uses a nautical chart that shows water depths, surface obstacles, common sea lanes, and navigational aids. The captain charts a course that is unique to the position, destination, and the particular capabilities of his vessel. On the sea there are an infinite number of courses to take and each is unique to each trip, not just to each ship. In other words, no two trips will be the same, even if they begin at the same starting point and end at the same destination.

Weather, water currents, prevailing winds, and other factors will constantly impact the course a ship steers. As the voyage progresses, the crew will regularly re-evaluate the course and make adjustments as necessary to ensure that they arrive at the proper destination. Leonard Sweet states, "Maps and blueprints are useless on water, never the same. The sea knows no boundaries. The only way one gets anywhere on the water is not through marked-off routes one follows but through navigational skills and nautical trajectories."[1]

One of the navigational skills serving ship captains over the centuries has been the ability to read the charts of the captains who have gone before them. They listened to the explorers who charted unknown islands. The pilgrimage introduced in this chapter is based on the reading of such charts of pioneers.

The Both/And Journey

Previously, I introduced the need for both Connecting Community and Missional Community. Some in your church will be ready to respond to the leading of the Spirit by the sailing that Missional Community calls for. They will be prepared to venture out in new ways to explore how to live in community and engage their context with the gospel. Others—if not many—are only ready to explore the waters through Connecting Community. They need something programmatic and controlled, with the hopes that this will prepare them to make the shift into Missional Community at some point in the future. Previously, I used this illustration to demonstrate how both run alongside one an-

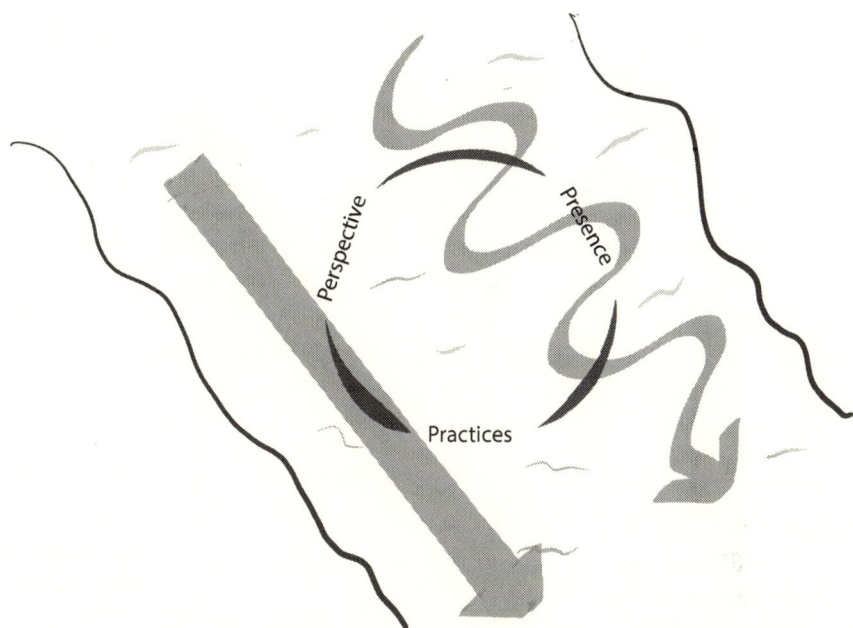

other in the river.

This process guides the development of both Connecting Community that cuts like a straight path and Missional Community that works according to the unpredictable winds of the Spirit.

The Connecting Community system helps get people started with group life. Admittedly this track is programmatic, even technical, in nature and it has the goal to get people started in group life by living out the stories of *Personal Improvement* and *Lifestyle Adjustment*. The goal is to move people and prepare them to want to move into the third and fourth stories, as illustrated by the arrow on the top of the next page.

As groups respond to the leading of the Spirit, they move into the second arrow on the next page. The Missional Community strategy will facilitate the stories of *Relational Re-vision* and *Missional Re-creation*. The different shapes to the far right depicts how groups living out the *Missional Re-creation* story will take on forms that are creative because they respond to the needs of specific contexts.

The specific way that a Missional Community strategy will work with a Connecting Community strategy will be different in different churches. The emphases will vary depending upon the tradition of the

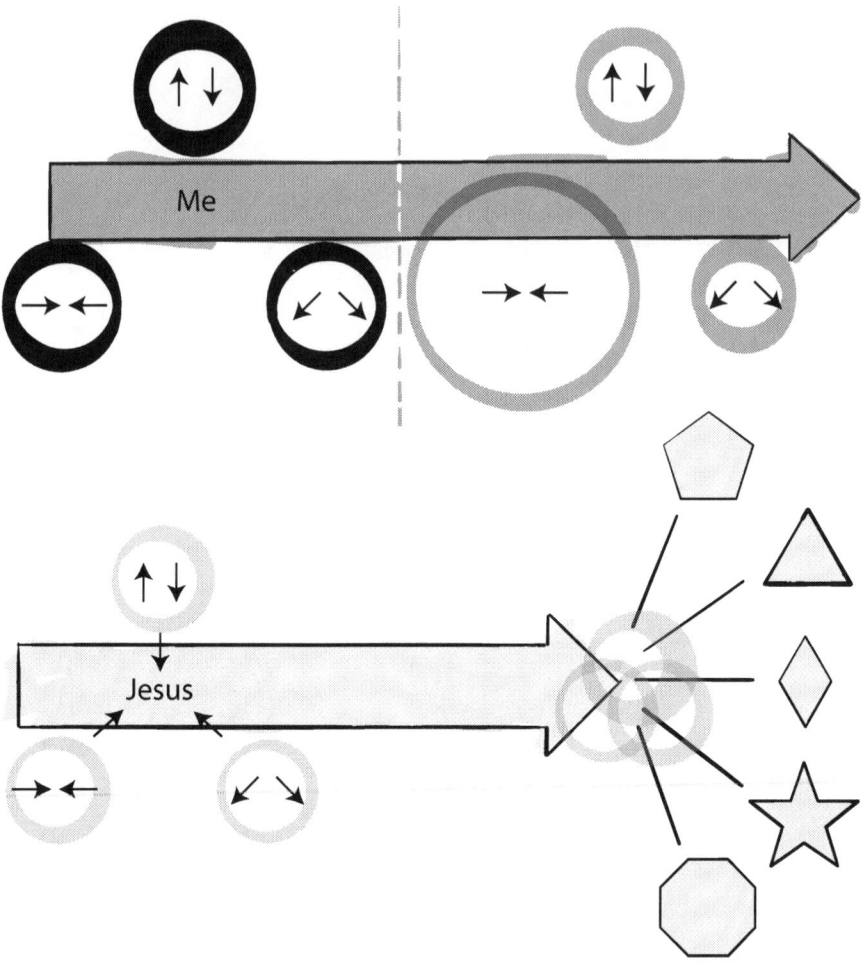

church and its context. For instance, if your church has a big front door, then at first there will be more emphasis on Connecting Community. In an established church that does not have many new people attending, then the current ministries remain in place while a team focuses on Missional Community experiments. In a church that starts out totally focused on reaching people through organic Missional Community, it will focus almost all of the energy there, while recognizing that those who come from a traditional church background might need some kind of simple initiation that will look more like Connecting Community.

Leadership Priorities

This journey calls for a set of leadership and pastoral priorities that make space in our lives for the work of the Spirit, training us to respond to the winds and the waters of the Spirit's leading and drawing us up into the participation in the divine nature. The eight priorities include:

1. *Work from reality*, not from where you wish you were. God works with us where we are, not where we think we ought to be.
2. *Lead as a team of dialogical learners*, not as experts. Groups will be developed by a team who work together to creatively think and pray about the journey.
3. *Think systems*. Groups are developed as a part of an inter-connected whole in an open system. They are never successful if groups are viewed as an independent silo alongside the other ministry silos of the church.
4. *Provide subversive connecting experiences*. The Spirit leads people into "aha" moments where they discover unexpected truths of what it means to live in community. Instead of attacking the challenge of community and mission directly, we provide environments for people to discover the truth for themselves
5. *Foster missional community experiments*. Within a local church there are some (maybe as few as five to seven) who are ready for more than a connecting group. They sense God's call to live in community and participate in God's mission. Missional Community experiments serve as a seedbed or a foretaste of what groups might look like in the future. This cannot be done with the entire church at the same time because experiments are organic in nature, not programmatic. After a season, others can be included in the experiments.
6. *Develop a spiritual formation environment*. Your small group journey as a church will ride the back of spiritual formation. Group life and discipleship go hand in hand. Woven into the two previous priorities will be tools and experiences that integrate spiritual formation on a personal level, however this priority focuses on the integration of spiritual formation into the culture of the church. More than offering some classes or hosting some retreats, this is about creating a pro-

cess that will move immature believers along a path toward maturity. The goal is to integrate this spiritual formation process into the life of the groups, thereby establishing a discipleship culture, not just a discipleship program.

7. *Establish the hidden support systems.* Beneath the surface of every great group ministry you will find that there is much more than groups going on. There are hidden systems that support the life of the groups. Most miss this because they only see the obvious, what actually occurs in the groups themselves. The unseen is what keeps the groups on the journey. These include things like vision communication from the senior leadership, relational investment into groups by pastors, on-going leadership training, coaching of leaders, and prayer.

8. *Invest in the indirect work of the Spirit.* The future church will be developed by plodders who pour their lives into the Spirit's indirect movement, not the overtly direct action of control. For instance, hospitality is a counter-cultural, unspectacular practice of being with each other and being present in the local for the common good in the mundane stuff of life. This practice is about putting down roots, continuing the work when things get tough, and pressing through when the results are not spectacular.

Now let's explore each.

15

What Is the
First Step?

God meets us and works with us where we are, not where we think we should be. You must actually work from your present reality, which is always different for different churches.

First Church Middle City, USA still meets in the building that the founders built in 1946. The remodeling project in 1975 and the expansion in 1987 to build a gymnasium both resulted in new excitement and growth. Jerry assumed the role of senior pastor three years ago, and he has become frustrated with what he perceives as a lack of passion for God or others within the church. The people are content attending on weekends, but it feels like church is just a spiritual product that people consume so they can get back to their normal lives. Jerry looks at the big, new church a few miles away with their new building and their great small groups. He wonders if small groups could work like that in his church.

Just down the road sits Second Church. It is about the same size and age as First Church. The leadership has realized that its buildings are dated, but they cannot afford to renovate or build a new building. Giving has decreased over the last five years and attendance has started to drop. Sam, the pastor, has been leading the church for about fifteen years and key leaders are starting to express concern over the church's direction. Many express how they want to get back to the roots of their tradition, which means that they want to return to the old programs of their heyday. Sam sees how this is not possible and how small groups might help.

Both of these churches have a lot in common, at least on the surface. It's a bit like making a list of commonalities between two people of the same age. Take two eighth-grade boys that go to the same school in Kansas. While they share much in common when compared to a eighth-grade boy from China or a 45-year old woman from Germany, the list of differences between these two boys from Kansas is endless.

Nothing in creation has been produced off an assembly line. Every human is a unique creation of God. The same is true of churches, being that churches are comprised of people.

Your church is currently experiencing a unique reality that is not shared by any other church in the world. That reality is where God works with you. The Spirit does not come to you with the assumption that you are like another church. Your church is distinct in three ways.

First, it's unique in its history, and that history has shaped who you are and how you operate. Things like the tradition of the church, its growth and decline over time, how conflict has been resolved (or left unresolved), and the previous experience with small groups all impact who you are today.

Second, the reality of where you are is shaped by how the people in the church do life. For instance, in more traditional church settings, the church plays a more significant role, at least for those who have been and continue to be committed to Christ. For those where the church has developed more recently, church (and God) is more of an add-on, (as discussed in chapter 3). Where the church is in its current reality is not simply about the church as an organization. It's about the kind of life the people of the church lead.

A third way that your church is distinct relates to the local context where the church is set. Is the neighborhood of the church suburban, exurban, urban, rural? If you were to move to India to be a missionary, you would spend a significant amount of time trying to understand the context where you are ministering. This is the kind of mindset needed with regard to group development. This means that the first step for developing groups is not directly about groups; it is about seeing the reality of your current situation. The following provides practical handles for you to discern your reality.

Seeing Reality

In most cases, group strategies do not provide any direction on this practice. Instead, they focus on the group principles and what is needed in order to get groups going to accomplish a specific strategy. It's as if every church is a blank slate. This is one of the reasons why we get what we get from our groups, as proposed in chapter 3.

As stated previously, groups are about people. The story of how we relate to God and others will shape the story we tell in our groups. In order for a church's relationships to work differently, we have to understand the way the relationships work now. We cannot lead people to a new place if we don't understand their current relational reality.

For instance, if a church has been shaped by decades of programmatic church life that requires clergy direction, fixed events, and printed curriculum, it does not matter how much you talk about relationships and community. Those old church patterns are part of the unspoken way that church works. If the leadership does not understand this fact, how can they lead the church into something new?

Or consider a church where the majority say that they are committed to live in community with one another and that they want to reach their community with the Gospel, but the reality is that people just want things to return to the way things were when the church was growing in the 1970s. And they want the pastor to fix it. Bringing in a new strategy might brighten things up for a short while, but it won't result in great groups.

Exegesis

To see reality rightly, we need to develop the skill of exegesis. When preachers attend seminary, they take classes on biblical exegesis, a technical skill that provides deep understanding or critical interpretation. When we preach or teach Bible classes, we aim to do so with a sound knowledge of what the Bible means. We start from where the Bible is coming from and then move those truths into our life today.

In a similar way we need to do exegetical work to understand our current reality. This will develop a deep understanding in the three domains introduced above:

- The church
- The life of the people in the church
- The local context

Exegesis of the Church

When I work with a church as a leadership coach or a strategy consultant, one of the first things I do is listen. Through a series of interviews and surveys, I gather their stories. I want to hear where they have been, what led them to this point in the journey, and how they feel about it. How can we understand where God is leading a church if we don't understand how God has been leading it? How can we see where we might be off right now, if we don't understand how we have been off in the past.

One of the hardest things for church leaders to do is to have an accurate view of its own journey. I find that they either think things are far better than reality or that they are much worse. This is the reason you need to ask questions about the church that you would not normally ask. For instance:

- What are the highs and lows of the church's life?
- Where have the main transitions occurred?
- What are the unique strengths?
- What are the weaknesses?
- What has occurred in the last three years that we should celebrate?
- What has occurred in the last three years that we should mourn?
- How are people expressing a sense of urgency?
- How are people stuck in complacency?

From a strategic point of view, the last two questions are especially crucial. Without a sense of urgency, at least within a pocket of people, it is hard to move a church into a new reality. People do not change because you have a great new idea. Change is an emotional issue, and people refuse to change not because they don't like your new idea but because they don't want to give up what they have. Therefore, exegeting the church is a way to help people develop a sense of urgency about what God is already doing and what God wants to do in your church. (Note: it is often helpful to get someone from the outside to help you see this reality accurately.)

Also, it is helpful to exegete the past experience of the church with small groups. Here are some questions to consider:

• What kind of group system has your church promoted in the past?
• What has worked? What are the positives that you can build upon?
• What has failed? How have the failures created resistance regarding group participation?
• What were the results?
• How do people perceive their experience in groups? (The perception by the participants could be very different from that of the pastors and leaders who organized the groups.)
• Describe the common patterns of life experienced in those groups. For instance, if the experience has been dominated by Bible study curriculum or lectures by a teacher, think through how these patterns and habits have shaped the life of the groups.

Exegeting the Life of People in the Church

The deep understanding that comes as a result of this work is not directly about how churched people relate to the church vision or programming. Nor is it about moral issues. This is about understanding how people do life. Questions here might include:

• What is the standard of living? Blue collar? White Collar?
• What is the ethnic makeup?
• What is the average commute to work?

- Describe work patterns of individuals.
- How do people spend their free time?
- Describe the involvement of kids in extracurricular activities.
- Where do people live in relationship to the church building? How has this changed in the last two decades?
- How do people relate to others? Are friendships established or are they transitory connections? Is there consistent contact or limited interaction.
- What is the nature of the relationships and connectivity within the membership of the church? To what degree are friendships dependent upon church programming? To what level do people feel connected to others in the church?

Exegeting the Context

Awareness of what is going on in the local context is something missionaries have developed for generations when they went overseas. It is not necessarily something that comes to mind when we think of leading ministry in our own context. However, this is crucial for two reasons. First, the church is called to be salt and light in our local context, and the context of the Western world is vastly different than it once was when churches were thriving. Second, it is helpful to understand how the relationship patterns of those within the church compare to the relationship patterns of those outside the church.

Therefore the questions provided in the previous section for people inside the church should be asked of the local context. Additional questions might include:

- How has the neighborhood changed in the past decade?
- How does the neighborhood perceive the local church?
- What are the opportunities that we have as a result of what's going on in the context?
- What are any challenges that we face in this context?

In addition, an exegetical walk can open people's eyes to what's going on in the context. This is an exercise you can do by yourself or with a group. It's a way to see what you don't normally see, to pay attention to what is unspoken. First, draw a simple map of your neighborhood so you can visualize how it is laid out. Focus on the area where you live that is actually walkable. Set the boundaries of an area that you can walk in a two-hour time frame. Then take a notebook, a pen, and a few of the following questions to help you see what is not obvious.[1]

- As you stand outside your residence, look both ways. What do you see? What do you hear or sense? What activities do you notice?
- As you walk, notice the architecture of the residences. What is the average age of the buildings? Is there any renovation going on?
- What do you notice about the exterior and yards of the residences? Are they cared for? How many residences are for sale?
- What indicators of transience do you notice?
- Is there a major highway nearby? Imagine how the introduction of this highway changed the neighborhood.
- Stop in a quiet spot. Then stop by a busy intersection. What are the smells and sounds of the different places?
- How many community or civic buildings are there? What are their purposes? Do they look inviting? Well used?
- Is there a local park? What do you notice about it?
- What do the design and appearance of the churches in the area communicate to you?
- What kinds of commercial buildings are there? Who makes up the clientele?
- Are there places where you wouldn't go? Why?
- Where are the places of life, hope, and beauty?
- What evidence of struggle, despair, neglect, and alienation do you see?

My suggestion is to do this exegetical walk in a series of rounds. First, if you are a pastor on a church staff, do this by yourself in two locations. Do it where the church building is located and then in your own neighborhood. If you are part of pastoral staff, I would suggest doing this with other pastors and talking about it. Secondly, do this with your Groups Team, which will be introduced in the next chapter. Start by doing this near your church building and then identify an area of town that has the highest concentration of people who attend the church; do an exegetical walk there and compare the two. On a third level, this exercise can help groups of all kinds—both Connecting Community groups and Missional Community groups—see what's going on in their context. (See my book *Difference Makers* or my *Cultivating Community in the Way of Jesus* for how this can be introduced to a group.)

Processing this Information

Part of the work of the small groups point leader is to make sure that this information is gathered and held up before the leaders of the Groups Team. The groups point leader need not be the one doing all of this work as there may be someone else on the team who is better suited for it. My suggestion is to develop a shared file where the information gathered can be added over time.

After you work through each type of exegesis, write a summary paragraph that describes how you see the information you have gathered. Then revisit this paragraph once per year. Put it on your calendar so that you will come back to it one year from now.

As with biblical exegesis, we do not develop a deep understanding of a topic and then move on to the next step. Instead this understanding grows along a path that is shaped like a spiral. With each pass (for instance if you work through these questions once per year), we go deeper in our understanding. At first, we might attain a surface understanding of the pressures that people feel in our culture regarding how much they have to work, for instance. This might give you some clues about how people need to learn about the need for simplicity and learning to waste time with friends. Through small experiments you will engage a deeper understanding of this pressure as it relates to finances or how parents feel the need to make sure that their kids get in the right kinds of schools.

This is not a practice that you do up front and then move beyond. That's just not possible. Instead, start off with a basic understanding of the above questions, develop a simple document that provides a rough hypothesis of what you see as answers to those questions, and then move forward. Revisit it on a regular basis.

Conclusion

This practice is not about action, if you define action as getting groups going. This may be frustrating for some. In most cases, pastors are held accountable for bottom-line results that are measured in terms of concrete numbers. If your job is to get groups started or to take groups to the next level, then you are expected to do something to make that happen. While you can opt for the make-something-happen approach, we must be honest about the fact that we have taken this approach for far too long. We assume we are heading toward the right vision, but because we don't see the church's unique reality, our sense of direction is misaligned. This practice helps you assess where you are so that you can better see where the Spirit is leading.

16
Who Guides the Pilgrimage?

Priority: Lead as a Team of Dialogical Learners

God is the God of eternal conversation. The Father, Son, and Spirit live the story of who God is through dialogue. Life and love are found in the midst of such interaction, which results in mutual understanding and self-sacrifice for the other.

Small groups do not work just because ten people gather once each week for a meeting. The story of the way of Jesus in small groups is a result of the flow of the dialogue of God into and through the people in the groups. We could use words like community, shared leadership, collaboration, family, and teamwork to describe this life. This life is a mutual experience where individuals tear down the walls that divide them and make space for the Spirit together to live into the divine life.

In many cases, the stories told by our groups are limited by the stories told by the leaders who oversee those groups. For instance, if the groups point person works in isolation and does not collaborate with others, the small group leaders will do the same because that pattern of leadership trickles down. If the pastor works with a team to lead the church, practicing shared leadership, transparency, and delegation, then small group leaders will be more likely to lead their groups in community because they are being formed by that way of leading.

The difficulty is that most pastors have been trained to lead from isolation. A pastor learns of small groups through a conference or book. He or she feels God leading him to move in that direction. He enters his study to develop a strategy, which he subsequently presents to his leaders. Much to his surprise, they respond less than favorably.

Even when church leaders consent to the small group vision presented by an individualistic pastor, the vision rarely works. The issues related to leading people into small group life are too complex for one person to recognize and evaluate. Different kinds of leaders with different kinds of giftings are required to make sure the right factors are recognized, spiritually discerned, and acted upon in order to guide the pilgrimage. In addition, most pastors do not have the time to give to group development because they are called to lead the entire church, prepare sermons, and provide direction for people not yet in small groups.

Also, when multiple people contribute to a vision and strategy, the rest of the church will be more likely to trust its validity. The churches that have developed the most effective small group systems have developed teams to work on small groups. In some churches, the team effort was deliberate, while in many it was an informal accident.

The Right Kind of Team

The team should be no smaller than three people because any fewer would not make a team, and it should be no larger than seven because any more and it would be difficult to manage. Those selected should be people who enjoy working "on" a project, as opposed to "in" a project.

The difference is significant. "On" people like to discover possibilities and search out boundaries of what could be. They see the whole perspective of the project and are good at providing the guidance to the entire system. "In" people like to work within the project. They are hands-on and enjoy the action. "In" people get frustrated when the "on" people begin to discuss ideas, concepts, and vision. They only want to know what the finished project will look like and what they are supposed to do. If "in" people are recruited for the Groups Team, the process will prove very frustrating.

During a presentation on grouping strategy, I noticed the dismay of an older couple named Ned and Nancy. They expressed frustration because they couldn't catch the vision in the way their pastor had hoped. Even though he'd presented the vision for over three years, they couldn't get their minds around it.

At the same time, this couple led a very effective small group. They practiced all the ministry habits of good group leaders. They were happy to lead at that level, but they didn't concern themselves with big-picture questions of theology, vision, training, or strategy. They were much more concerned about actually caring for the people and doing the work of ministry.

On the other hand, during that same training, there were four others who couldn't get enough information about the intricacies of the group strategy development. Even after the conference, they bombarded me with questions.

Even though people like Ned and Nancy have served as faithful leaders in the church for years, it doesn't mean they have the ability or desire to strategize and lead the charge into the future. During the seminar with Ned and Nancy, I explained how people who don't thrive on big-picture questions of vision and strategy need not concern themselves with trying to understand it. They only need to see their role in the strategy and follow God in it. Immediately, Ned and Nancy breathed sighs of relief.

Ned and Nancy were frustrated because they were being asked to participate in the Groups Team, even though they don't think like "on" persons. They're leaders in their church, respected ministers who love people, pray for people, and serve as pillars of faith for others to follow. People like Ned and Nancy are "in" people, because they like to focus their energy working inside the vision, not on the vision.

Church leaders need to determine if they're an "in" or an "on" person. Here are some factors to consider:

• Broad knowledge about, or a desire to learn about, what's happening in the church in Western culture.
• Credibility, connections, and stature within the church.

• An understanding of the internal workings of the church.
• Formal authority and managerial skills needed to plan, organize, and oversee the process of implementing groups.
• Leadership skills for developing vision, communicating that vision, and motivating people to enter that vision.
• A commitment to daily prayer and hearing God's direction.
• A hunger to see biblical community developed in the church through groups.
• The availability to work on the team.

Team Composition

Groups Point Person
Let's get practical by addressing some of the issues regarding the composition of this team. First of all, let's consider the role of the small groups point leader, the vision champion for group life. In larger churches, this role will be taken on by a staff pastor. In smaller congregations, this will be fulfilled by either the senior pastor or by a volunteer. The larger the church, the larger percentage of time will be invested in this aspect of the work.

The role of the groups champion calls for three perspectives. First is that of overseeing the development of the group system. This is about vision and strategy. In other words, the champion oversees the journey of leading the group through these eight priorities.

The second perspective is that of a shepherd who does the mundane, repetitive work of caring for the sheep.

The third is that of administering the details. Too many times, the point person's job turns into that of a program administrator, i.e. tracking growth, running budgets, organizing curriculum, managing the small group calendar, and reading reports. They know how to administer the details involved in running the group program, but they don't have the time to invest in group life, develop new leaders, share life with multiple groups in an area, deal with group conflict, or eat meals with people under their care. They don't feed the sheep.

A great way to determine if this is happening is to evaluate how much time the groups champion is doing his or her job from the church office. The work of shepherding groups and leaders of groups happens out in life, not in the church building.

We tend to hire program administrators to run the small group ministry, much like we hired Sunday school administrators to run the adult education programs of past decades. Instead, we need to empower pastors who are gifted shepherds who will do the mundane, repetitive work of caring for sheep. Effective group pastors possess strengths that allow them to focus their energies on caring for people, developing leaders, and gathering people around a vision.

For the administrative things that need to be done, enlist help. Don't get focused on all those details at the expense of vision and shepherding. I've seen the champion spend hours sitting in the office trying to figure out group management software, ordering curriculum, attending endless meetings, and typesetting brochures. Those are all necessary things, but if the passion of the champion is that of vision and shepherding—as it should be—then most likely these things that are more detailed in nature are not things that he or she does well.

Senior Pastor

In some cases, the senior pastor will play the role of the groups champion. However, when this is the case, he or she can only take on the vision part of this role. There is just not enough time in the week for the senior pastor to do the work of the senior pastor while at the same time doing the shepherding and administration. He or she will need help from the team to fulfill those roles.

The skills needed to preach, lead the various aspects of church life, and work with the different departments of a church are different than the skills needed to shepherd groups. Most senior pastors don't have the gift set for recruiting and training leaders to oversee groups and develop group leaders. In fact, many times the best small group champions who pastor the groups are not great preachers.

In the situations where groups have been the most effective, the senior pastor does not assume the role of the groups point leader. At the same time, the relationship between the senior pastor and the groups point person is crucial. The senior pastor and the groups champion work together and as a result the senior pastor carries the vision, talks about groups, and teaches about group principles.

Let's briefly look at a few marks of lead pastors who are compelled by this vision:

1. They own the vision for groups. Most likely they are not the primary point persons of the small group ministry, but they promote it more than anyone else.
2. They participate in group life and speak from their experience.
3. They understand the strategy of the group life team. They participate in that team at appropriate times so that they are doing more than just serving as the promoter.
4. They lead relationally. They are involved in the lives of the leaders with whom they directly work. They know them beyond their jobs and minister to them as a shepherd.
5. They work with other leaders as a team. They have shed the expectation that they have to be the super-star leader who has all the gifts. Instead they have found leaders who have other strengths and gifts that compliment their own. In this setting, they have learned to defer to others who have insight and gifting in areas that they do not.

Executive Pastor

As churches grow, the role of the executive pastor within the system is crucial. Therefore the importance of the relationship between the groups champion and the executive pastor cannot be overstated. Simply put, the executive pastor and the groups champion must be working from the same page and set of expectations. Otherwise it is doomed to fail. This is difficult and requires extensive conversations. Because the executive pastor is often pulled in so many directions as he or she oversees various ministries in the system, the strategic nature of group life as it impacts the overall life of the church often gets treated as simply one ministry alongside others. As we will see in the next practice, this mode of operation will undermine the development of groups.

Volunteers

When considering those who would be effective members of this team, consider the following:[1]

Position Power: Are enough key players on board, especially key leaders, so that those left out cannot easily block progress?

Expertise: Are the various points of view—in terms of discipline, work experience, nationality, etc. represented so that informed, intelligent decisions will be made?

Credibility: Does the group have enough people with good reputations so that its proposals will be taken seriously by others?

Leadership: Does the group include enough proven leaders to be able to facilitate the change process?

Humility: Do the group members demonstrate the ability to submit to one another?

Availability: Do the members have the available time to commit to this process?

Aptitude: Do the members have a propensity to work on the small group ministry and think critically about the big picture strategy and future development?

Prayer Life: Do the members have a passionate prayer life and love for God?

The Practice of Dialogue

An essential tool for doing this practice well is dialogue. Dialogue is the process by which a team accesses a pool of common learning that cannot be accessed individually. A team practices dialogue when the members contribute to a free flow of thought, resulting in team learning. This concept has been developed for team leadership by MIT business professor Peter Senge.

Senge contrasts dialogue with discussion. "In a discussion, different views are presented and defended, and ... may provide useful analysis of the whole situation. In dialogue different views are presented as a means toward discovering a new view. In discussion, decisions are made. In a dialogue, complex issues are explored."[2] Most leaders, including pastors, are comfortable with discussion because they want to argue and defend their points of view. This is a form of monologue where one person has a plan and aims to convince others of that plan. Dialogue can prove threatening because "the purpose of dialogue is to go beyond one individual's understanding."[3] Its goal is not to win, but to discover.

Senge outlines the three basic conditions necessary for dialogue:

1. All participants must "suspend" their assumptions while at the same time communicating their assumptions about the topic. In other words, team members disclose the logic behind their opinions and hold them up for examination.
2. All participants must regard one another as colleagues and friends on an equal plane. Dialogue does not occur when some team members feel that their opinions are less important than the opinions of others. Every team member must be granted permission to share honestly, even if it means sharing concerns about an idea from the pastor or a senior elder.
3. There must be a facilitator who guides the context of dialogue. Most people do not know how to dialogue. They know how to discuss, arguing their point. For the team members to practice dialogue, there must be someone who opens the door to dialogue and keeps that door open.

Monologue is not evil, but it limits discovery. The Groups Team will quickly stagnate if members get caught up in arguing one point against another. Dialogue will allow each team member to verbalize assumptions, deal with nagging questions, express concerns, and articulate points of view. This will establish a foundation for the vision and set the stage for each person to share how he or she sees the issue.

Dialogical Questions

Asking good questions as a team is more important than finding the right answers. There are many "right" answers when it comes to how we develop groups. But if we are asking the wrong questions then we can very easily be led down a fruitless path.

In his book, *Community*, Peter Block writes about the kind of life that brings transformation to neighborhoods. He writes, "The small group is the unit of transformation and the container for the experience of belonging."[4] This transformation is both personal and societal. Throughout his book, he consistently makes a strong argument proving "authentic transformation does not occur by focusing on changing individuals" but by creating environments where small groups of people can generate an alternative future for the social fabric of a neighborhood. To put it in the language of Jesus, the kingdom of God comes through a group of people who are willing to embody the good news and manifest that good news in the everyday life of local neighborhoods.

Block states: "Social fabric is created one room at a time. It is formed from small steps that ask, 'Who do we want in the room?' and, 'What is the new conversation that we want to occur?'"[5] These questions generate conversations about creating an alternative future or a group of people who live in a distinctively different way compared to one's cultural norms. They are questions that require little communities to come up with their own answers instead of implementing a program that has been orchestrated from the top down or borrowed from a book from a mega church. In other words, these questions make space for discovering what the Spirit is saying to the church. This kind of work begins in the Groups Team as it learns to ask great questions and thus creates a culture where groups are naturally asking these questions.

The kinds of questions that we need to ask fall into two categories. The first are the common questions that focus on hard data of external factors. The second set of questions are much harder to ask because they focus on soft data that relates to the life that is going on in groups.

Hard Data Questions:
Questions about the entire group system might include:
- How many groups does your church have?
- How many people are in groups?
- What percentage of your church is in groups?

- How many of your groups multiplied in the last year?
- How many new groups have formed in the last year?

Individual groups or group leaders ask questions like:
- How many people are in your group?
- How many people attended your meeting this week?
- How many people have you reached for Jesus?
- What is your plan for group multiplication?
- Who are you mentoring to be a future group leader?

Soft Data Questions:

Theses questions fall into three categories, Communion with God, Relating in Love to One Another, and Engagement with our Neighborhoods.

Communion
- To what degree are our groups experiencing God's presence when they gather together?
- What specific actions are individuals taking to simplify their lives so that they have time to share in community life with others?
- What kinds of sacrifices are people making to be shaped by God for leadership?
- How are people who are not Jesus followers experiencing the presence of God through the group?

Relating
- How are groups working through conflict and difficult relational situations?
- How frequently are people within groups sharing meals together outside of official meetings?
- How are group members sacrificing their personal priorities for the sake of other people in the group?
- How are people who are not Jesus followers experiencing the relationships that are distinct from the world through the group?

Engagement
- How are groups being led to minister outside of predetermined expectations, and meet needs spontaneously?
- How are people using their money in unique ways to invest in redemption?
- How are groups and individuals investing in relationships in their neighborhoods?
- How are groups and individuals embracing the poor and seeking to bring redemption to the social outcasts?
- How are people who are not Jesus followers encouraged to participate in the process of serving the world together?

The Value of Conflict

When a Groups Team is assembled and it begins its work of dialogue, conflict will be a part of the journey. Different people bring different perspectives, and those different perspectives will generate energy. At some point, the energy will produce friction. It's just inevitable. If the team assumes that the point of the team is to produce quick results, then this conflict will be perceived as an obstacle to the work of God. Then members will either withhold their contributions or someone will take over and try to shape the group through monologue.

Often the members of a Groups Team will shut down and look for someone to take over through monologue because they don't like the feeling that conflict brings. Friction that arises in the team pulls people from their comfort zone. When this occurs, their immediate fight or flight responses kick in. We do this to protect ourselves, without even overtly thinking about it, hoping that we can quickly return to our comfort zone.

When we do this, we miss out on the reality that conflict is one of the ways that the Spirit uses to draw us out of our comfort zones and discover something new together. Instead of an obstacle to progress, conflict generates the environment where the Spirit's leading becomes a possibility. While we naturally want to snap back to our comfort zone, the team members will only see how the Spirit is at work by pressing through the stress to see what might arise on the other side of conflict.

I expound upon the value of conflict in *Leading Small Groups in the Way of Jesus*. Suffice it to say, working through the conflict that arises through dialogue is especially crucial when dealing with adaptive challenges. When we face them, the solutions most likely will not come as quickly as we would prefer, but the differences between one another create space in the midst of the team to wait for an alternative to arise. Therefore, solutions do not come directly from books or conferences but through the gifts of those in the room.

17

How Do You Prepare the Church for Groups?

God created the world as an interactive system of systems. The word system denotes the reality of an interconnected whole where each part "hangs together" because those various parts impact other parts, many times in unexpected ways. Our bodies are a system of sub-systems that all influence one another. Weather systems are studied to predict how the rise in temperatures on one continent might influence storm patterns halfway around the world.

Everything is connected as we are part of and influenced by systems every day. The economy is a system. An increase in the price of oil, for instance, has a far reaching impact on things that might look unrelated. There are also local systems, like your local neighborhood. Imagine the complex impact that removing a system like trash collection would have. Our lives are full of parts that are endlessly connected to other parts.

In the same way, every local church operates as a system, which is part of a larger system like a denomination or the local neighborhood. There are things that are done simply because that's the way things are done in your church, and we don't even think about how they are done. It is quite common for writers about the church to make this observation and then conclude that such realities point to church institutionalization and the need for church renewal. But such an argument is naive because it fails to see that they are simply trying to replace an old system with a new one.

And this is impossible. If you change one part, it changes everything else too.

Groups are Not Developed Independently

While it is easy to confess that there is an interconnected relationship between various parts of church life, the common approach is to treat the development of groups as a closed system. In other words, each ministry within the church only needs to develop its sub-parts in order to work effectively. As a result, preaching, children, youth, welcome, outreach, education, and small group ministries are all treated like individual silos. If the parts within each closed system is working rightly, we assume the church will be effective.

An established church in Texas set a course to develop effective groups. However, all of their more faithful members were already involved in a wide array of ministries. The choir ministry had been an established mainstay of the church for decades, but no one wanted to have the conversation about how adding small group leadership might impact their involvement in the choir. Because some of the best small group leaders were also leaders in the choir, they felt pulled in multiple directions. The leadership of the church set groups at a high value, but the established patterns of choir participation created system stress. We could say the same about any number of ministries in the church.

This in no way is meant as a judgment of churches that have choirs, as if that is part of the church of yesterday and the church of today needs groups. If only it were that simple. The point of this illustration is to help us see how groups are developed as a part of an open system, not a closed system of independent silos.

How Systems Impact Group Development

We often fail to understand the various systems that directly im-

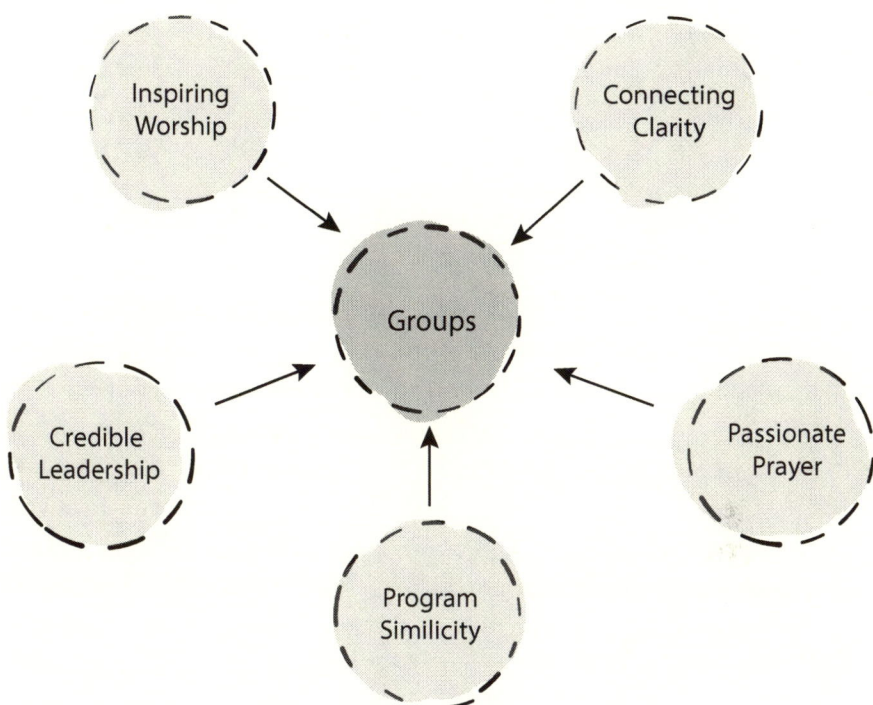

pact the development of groups, especially in the early stages. In other words, in many cases, the fact that groups struggle has more to do with factors that are not directly related to the specific grouping strategy. Instead, they fall short of our hopes because of other factors. The five identified in the diagram above are the most common.

Credible Leadership

Participating in groups is a risk because it requires people to change. If people don't trust the leadership to lead them into that change, then they will resist. It matters not how much you preach about the importance of community. Some of the things to consider that undermine credibility when it comes to groups include:

• Previous small group launches that fell short of expectations
• Disunity in the church leadership
• Controlling pastoral oversight

- Program hopping, where new ideas are promoted and changed with high frequency
- Traumatic experiences (i.e. leadership immorality, financial scandal, etc.)

These issues put stress on the culture of the church as a whole and therefore they will influence the environment in groups. As such, they are like debits counted against the balance of trust. Church leaders accrue debits through things like initiating new programs with little follow-through, making promises that are not kept, scolding the people for not being committed, excluding church members from participating in ministry, high turnover of pastoral staff members, and always asking for money. If previous pastors have had contemptuous relationships, didn't stay long enough to carry out the vision, or had been involved in something immoral, the position of the "pastor" carries a debt load that subsequent pastors must pay off.

Credits are accrued when pastors lead the church into positive results: financial debts are paid off, new ministry ideas are developed and produce fruit, the pastor shows a commitment to stay longer than five years, people feel encouraged while at the same time challenged through the sermons, and people sense the presence of God upon his or her leadership.

Pastors must observe their leadership bank account as they lead people into transformation. Pastors with a high leadership debt load need to not only transform the life of the church but also to transform the view of leadership.

An important note, but one that I cannot address in depth: Essential to credible leadership is the well-being of the pastor and other leaders who guide the church. If leaders are exhausted and their souls are empty, then it is hard to provide leadership that is trustworthy. Spiritual leadership is leadership submitted to the leading of the Spirit and this requires us to make space in our lives for the Spirit to guide us. Much could be stated about this, but it goes beyond the purpose of this book. There are many great resources that serve as helpful guides for pastors on this journey.

Inspiring Worship Services

In most cases, the churches that have been the most effective at starting effective small groups already had vibrant corporate gatherings where people experienced the presence of God. The large group experience feeds life into the small group start up. When first starting groups, so much energy is required because the learning curve is so high. If corporate worship is boring and people do not expect to meet God, people will not have the energy to invest in small groups. Group members and leaders draw life from corporate worship so that they can minister in the groups.

The key to a life-flowing experience in worship services is not found in the style of music, as the styles are many. The key is found in the answer to this question: do people experience the presence of God to the point that they leave corporate gatherings inspired?

In addition, the large group worship services should be a place where the people hear the Word of God taught. I have yet to find a church that developed strong small groups who did not place a high value on teaching and preaching.

Connecting Clarity

When I work with a church to help them develop a grouping process, I start with something very simple. I ask my host to park the car in the parking lot just like a fringe person might on a Sunday morning. (If I'm present for a Sunday service, all the better.) Then I take the walk into their building and follow the path, as closely as possible, just like a fringe person might follow to enter the building. Being that I have the eyes of an outsider, I can see how easy or difficult it is to get connected.

By in large—unless the church is relatively new—I find that the communication is designed for church insiders, not fringe people. For instance, I often find that it's not clear where I am to enter the building on a Sunday morning or that the signs are hidden behind a bush. When I walk into the building the place to check in the kids is not clear and the welcome center is filled with information that is written for insiders.

My comments here are not new. In fact, church growth trainers have been addressing this issue for over forty years. Therefore I will not belabor this point. I will only provide two observations: First, if you want to connect people into groups, do your homework with regard to how people experience the welcome area of your church.

Secondly, make your communication about getting into groups as simple as one, two, three. If you want people in a culture that is chronically disconnected (as stated in chapter 4) to trust you enough that they will take the risk and get connected, then you have to make it easy and clear. If it's too complicated, then they will pass.

Passion for God Expressed Through Prayer

The most effective small-group-based churches around the world are praying churches. Small groups without prayer are like water bottles with no water. After Joel Comiskey traveled the globe to understand the basic principles that make holistic small groups work, he wrote:

> Cell group churches contain the power, the current of the Holy Spirit. They don't automatically produce that current. If your church is choking the life of the Spirit of God, don't expect cells to remedy your problem. You must first invite God to fix the basic problem and clean the rusty pipes that impede His flow. He uses the small group system, but He winces at being used by it.[1]

Churches that have seen the most success with groups had already developed a seedbed of prayer before they started groups. It is much easier to lead people into change when they have a deep hunger for more of God.

The stronger the prayer effort, the more quickly a church can develop small groups. If the key leaders in the church do not have established patterns of prayer, then as you develop groups also consider how this will be woven into the church leadership culture.

Groups and Church Program Simplicity

You cannot do everything. There are more needs than any one church can meet. And there are more good ideas than any one church can do. The enemy of the best comes in the cloak of not being willing to say "no" to good ideas.

In our busy world, we cannot ask people to participate in groups if they are already participating in other ministries or volunteering in various capacities.

Many established churches have been doing so many good things through the years (sometimes decades) that they can only think in terms of adding new stuff on top of that which is already running. This is just unrealistic. An important skill for leaders is to regularly evaluate the existing programs in the church. This would include every committee, ministry, outreach, singing group, even things like Vacation Bible School, and missions trips. Some leadership groups should be charged to think and reflect about how these various programs and ministries align with what God is doing. To help facilitate this evaluation, these leaders can use the following categories:

- dead
- wean now
- wean eventually
- simplify
- keep and refocus
- keep as is

The dead programs are those that can be eliminated now, as they serve no purpose—a fact that's obvious to almost everyone.

There are other programs that still have some life, but it's clear that they don't fit with the new vision. These fit into the category of "wean now," and the church leaders can begin the process of de-emphasizing their importance.

A third category would include those programs that still have some life, but they conflict with the new vision. However, many people feel deeply attached to them. To eliminate them or de-emphasize them at this point would be detrimental, so leaders would wean these programs down the road.

The category called "simplify" includes those programs the leaders sense are necessary to keep, but they need to be retooled so they don't take up so much time and energy.

In the category of "keep and refocus" are those programs that are essential, but they need to be focused on the new vision of the church rather than the disparate visions of the past.

The guiding rule is "Never take something away until it can be replaced with something else." If you terminate something people value, they will feel frustrated and lost, resulting in a temptation to leave. They won't understand the reason for the sudden change. Therefore the move from the old to the new would look something like this:

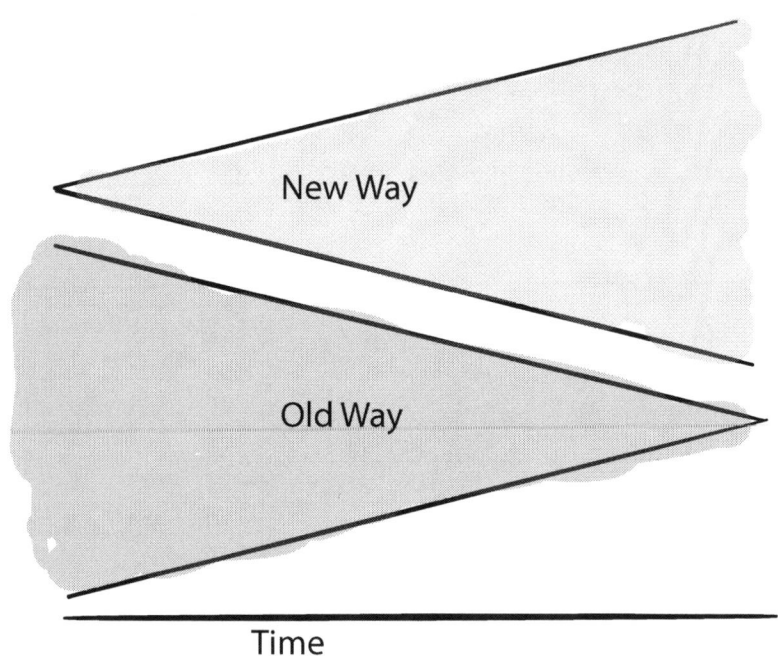

The hope of this is to bring various ministries into unity. In many churches, members have become so accustomed to the reality of competing visions that it has become the *modus operandi*. Most don't even see them as a problem because they have defined the way the system operates. For instance, the outreach team has met for the last twenty years on Wednesday night. Also on Wednesday night, the youth meet for a youth worship service, the pastor leads an adult Bible study, and various children's programs are held.

Each of these has an individual vision, but no one quite knows what that vision is. These activities just happen, whether or not they fit into a larger vision. Eventually the vision becomes: "to keep the activity going." In order to understand what is going on, it can prove helpful to determine the current (most often unstated) vision for each activity in the church. Here are some key areas where the visions must be identified:

- What's the youth pastor's vision? Is it to create a biblical community of young people? Is it to entertain young people so growth can occur and he can eventually get a job at a bigger church? Is it to serve faithfully, using youth ministry as a stepping stone to become a senior pastor?
- What's the vision for children? Is this an effective ministry that's attracting young families? Is it stuck doing the same form of ministry developed fifty years ago? Is there anyone who has a vision for the children, or are people just filling positions?
- What's the vision for Sunday school? Has anyone articulated the vision of Sunday School in the last five years? If so, who carries this vision? Or are people just going through the motions of doing what they've always done? If so, what's the unstated vision?
- What's the vision for worship? Is there a stated vision for worship? Is the church fulfilling this vision? Or is it just singing songs and listening to the choir perform beautiful medleys?
- What's the vision for the primary weekly service? The answer to this question might seem obvious at first, but most churches haven't articulated the vision of their Sunday morning service. They're stuck doing the same thing in their services, because they've done those things for the last fifty years.
- What's the vision for secondary services (i.e. Sunday night and Wednesday night)? It's interesting to learn that the original intent of the Sunday night service was to serve as an evangelistic meeting to reach farmers who worked all day. In many traditions, Wednesday night was designed to be a prayer service. Do your secondary services have a vision? Or are they just repetitions of the Sunday morning service, done for a smaller crowd? What's

the vision for women's programs and men's programs? Many denominations have programs for women and men. If these are used, what's their vision?

Through the identification of visions, the people who carry these visions will become obvious. The volunteer music minister puts much energy into what he does with the choir every week. The Sunday school director has served the church in this capacity for the last fifteen years. The youth pastor is young and brought in a vision he saw working at the church in which he grew up. People like these are the vision carriers. Each has an investment in their visions.

Evaluate each vision carrier and determine which ones are the most open to a new vision. Ask questions like:

• Who thinks outside the box?
• Who's frustrated with the status quo?
• Who leads with a constant desire to follow God's new direction and is stretching the boundaries?

Many pastors or group champions try to force the change of established ministries. This is where adaptive leadership is appropriate (see chapter 5). Trying to control the agenda won't get you where you want to go. And if your leadership credits are low, it will put you further in the negative. You will have to work together to discover how to proceed.

Conclusion

Groups are woven through every aspect of a church's life. How those connections work in your church will be unique to your local situation. Take the time to think through those connections and develop a plan to move forward.

18

How Do You Get People Connected?

> *Priority: Provide Subversive Connecting Experiences*

In the Gospel of Mark, Jesus begins his ministry by proclaiming, "The kingdom of God has come near. Repent and believe the good news" (Mark 1:15). Mark's Gospel progresses without providing a clear definition of what Jesus meant by the kingdom of God. Jesus did not explain his mission to his audience. He used terms that any first century Jew would understand, but he did not refute their understanding of the kingdom with propositional statements. When he calls the first disciples immediately after making this proclamation about the kingdom, Jesus does not lay out a ten-page proposal of what it meant to be a disciple. He just said, "Come, follow me."

Does this mean that Jesus did not have a clear vision for the kingdom of God or that he was discovering it along the way? Doubtful. He knew his vision was so radical that it would lead to the cross, yet he did not reveal these things up front. Instead, Mark tells us that Jesus repeatedly talked about the mystery of the kingdom. R. T. France states that:

[The use of the Greek word *musterion*] can easily mislead English readers who naturally think of a 'mystery' as something which is inherently hard to understand, and which can be unraveled only by unusual cleverness—if it is not totally incomprehensible. But the true sense of *musterion* is better captured by the English 'secret', which denotes not incomprehensibility but hiddenness. A secret is that which is not divulged—but once known it need not be hard to grasp. It is privileged information rather than a puzzle.[1]

Jesus cloaked the meaning of the Messianic kingdom in a secret. After the Parable of the Four Soils (Sower), Jesus told the disciples and a few others close to him, "The secret of the kingdom of God has been given to you. But to those on the outside everything is said in parables" (Mark 4:11). Jesus purposely revealed the meaning of the kingdom through the use of encrypted language or parables. He hid what he was up to. This hiding was not done through covering up the vision, but through the creative display of actions and parables that would redefine the meaning of the kingdom without the use of propositions.

The Parable of the Four Soils highlights how people respond to the kingdom message in different ways. Jesus explained to those close to him that the secret of the kingdom has been made available to those who have ears to understand. To those who cannot understand it, he was just telling interesting stories. If he were to take a propositional approach, they would understand the meaning of the kingdom too quickly, forcing them into a premature decision about Jesus. If he had defined the meaning of the vision to the masses in propositional terms, he would have had too many followers and too many enemies. Eugene Peterson writes of Jesus' use of parables:

> Jesus continually threw odd stories down alongside ordinary lives (para, "alongside"; bole, "thrown') and walked away without explanation or altar call. Then listeners started seeing connections: God connections, life connections, eternity connections. The very lack of obviousness, the unlikeness, was the stimulus to perceiving likeness: God likeness, life likeness, eternity likeness. But the parables didn't do the work—it put the listener's imagination to work. Parables aren't illustrations that make things easier; they make things

harder by requiring the exercise of our imaginations, which if we aren't careful becomes the exercise of our faith.[2]

The artistic use of parables allowed Jesus to share the vision with everyone who was willing to listen, without giving the masses too much information about the mission. He needed time for those close to him to understand and embody the mission of the kingdom. He had to demonstrate his radical vision through his actions. He had to teach them over and over the meaning of what he was doing. He had to provide experiences for them so that they might be able to touch and see how the kingdom worked. The use of subversive parables provided an alternative to propositional teaching, thereby providing people with the space to process the meaning of the kingdom without requiring premature discontinuous change.

This priority is about creating safe places where people can connect and hear the truth in parabolic ways to help them discover truth. This invites people to talk about what the Spirit is stirring up in them so that they might own the way of Jesus for themselves.

Leading People Through Subversion

Eugene Peterson comments about the need for subversion when leading people into the kingdom:

As a pastor, I don't like being viewed as nice but insignificant. I bristle when a high-energy executive leaves the place of worship with the comment, "This was wonderful, Pastor, but now we have to get back to the real world, don't we?" I had thought we were in the most-real world, the world revealed as God's, a world believed to be invaded by God grace and turning on the pivot of Christ's crucifixion and resurrection. The executive's comment brings me up short: he isn't taking this seriously. Worshiping God is marginal to making money. Prayer is marginal to the bottom line. Christian salvation is a brand preference.

I bristle and want to assert my importance. I want to force the recognition of the key position I hold in the economy of God and in his economy if only he knew it.

Then I remember that I am a subversive. My long-term effectiveness depends on my not being recognized for who I really am. If he realized that I actually believe the American way of life is doomed to destruction, and that another kingdom is right now being formed in secret to take its place, he wouldn't be at all pleased. If he knew what I was really doing and the difference it was making, he would fire me. ...

The methods that make the kingdom of America strong—economic, military, technological, informational—are not suited to making the kingdom of God strong. ...

But America and suburbia and the ego compose my parish. Most of the individuals in this amalgam suppose that the goals they have for themselves and the goals God has for them are the same. It is the oldest religious mistake: refusing to countenance any real difference between God and us, imaging God to be a vague extrapolation of our own desires, ...

I am being subversive. I am undermining the kingdom of self and establishing the kingdom of God. I am helping them to become what God wants them to be, using the methods of subversion.[3]

When we consider leading individualistic, isolated, overly-busy Americans into the way of Jesus, we must recognize that the direct, propositional approach will not clear the path for grouping people in the way of Jesus. We have to provide opportunities for people to discover the truth about how they live and thereby see the need for an alternative. The following are some practical aspects of this subversive leadership:

1. The larger the group, the more cryptic and secretive the message about the way of Jesus should be. The vision must be communicated to the church-at-large, but it should be done through the telling of stories, dropping hints of alternative approaches, and the sharing of testimonies. Propositional presentations that define the vision explicitly will force the crowd into a decision they are not ready to make.

Repetition and creativity is crucial for vision casting to the crowd. The kingdom life will not be embraced through one sermon series. It will take years to get this into the imaginations of the crowd. Concrete calls to action come in the form of the "next step" that people can take that will move them toward the ultimate vision of community and mission.

2. Use a variety of non-propositional teaching methods with those in leadership. Jesus told more parables to his disciples than he proclaimed to the crowds. Understanding requires experiences and mentoring. Repetition is crucial for leaders to redefine what church means. Leaders need time to process the vision and dialogue around its meaning. Share books and point them to videos and blog posts. Hold discussion groups around what they are learning. Take them to conferences. More than anything, enter into relationship with them so that you build enough trust with one another to process what you are learning together.

3. If your church has multiple levels of leadership, there must be a different communication strategy for each level. For instance, those who are the core leaders of the church (three to seven) will need to come to a place of understanding that demonstrates absolute commitment and lifestyle embodiment of the vision. Communication at this level will be much more prophetic and intense and it will require less time. For each level of leadership out from the core, the strategy will be more cryptic and more experiential.

4. Helping people at different levels of leadership see the way requires time—lots of time. Taking the long view is essential. The further out people are from the core of leadership, the longer it will take for people to understand what the way of Jesus means.

5. Facilitate dialogue around the scriptures. Create space in leadership team meetings to reflect on key scriptures that define what it means to be the church. For instance, some have used Luke 10:1-12, Matthew 9:35-38, and Ephesians 4:7-16 to help people see the vision for the kingdom. Read one of these scriptures aloud, sit in silence for a few minutes and then share what you see. Do this with the same scriptures in every meeting, allowing the Spirit to reshape your imag-

ination. It's a subversive way for people to "see" the kingdom without having to have a leader tell them.

6. Pray. The mission of God is mysterious stuff. We cannot expect to control it or own it. As we seek God, the Holy Spirit will include us in this mystery and the mission will take hold of us. It will consume God's church. As his mission consumes us, the holy fire of God will consume everything that does not fit with that mission.

7. Create spaces for self-discovery. This is the purpose of connecting community explicated in the next section.

The goal of this subversive leadership is to provide a holding environment. This is a space where people have an opportunity to discover that there is more. Instead of these connecting groups merely playing the role of "closing the back door" or helping people to find friends, these connections create space for the Spirit to stir up a hunger for the kind of community that lives on mission (see the next chapter).

Principles of Connecting Community Strategies

Be realistic. Most are not ready for more than some kind of Bible study that tries to live out the stories of *Personal Improvement* or *Lifestyle Adjustment*. In fact, at least 90% of the people within a church are only ready for these first two stories on the path as depicted below. They are simply too busy or they are not equipped for more.

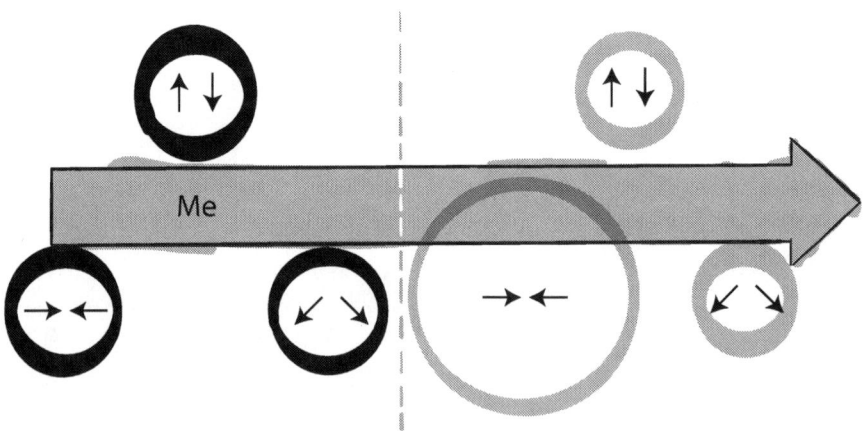

Here are four principles of subversive Connecting Community:

1. Make connecting community easy-in, easy-out. People are more likely to change when there is an easy way to begin. If the change requires huge up-front investments before people can try it out, they will not likely change. Likewise, if people feel that the connecting experience is a long-term commitment, they will resist it.

2. Promote a starting point and an ending point. A basic rule for connecting community groups is "Nothing is open ended." They can go six weeks, three months, six months, or nine months. The point is to give people a good experience so that they will want more. By giving an ending point to groups it gives people permission to explore other group experiences.

3. Refuse to judge small group consumers. As stated many times, God works with us where we are, not where we think we should be. We may not like that people want to find a different group or that a leader wants to step down for a season, but forcing people into relationships doesn't work. And making people feel guilty for where they are might change their actions, but it won't change their hearts.

4. Prepare people for more. Connecting Community is a good thing, but it's not the goal. In other words, you can learn a lot from books that lay out a program for getting 100% of your people in groups, but these strategies can be used for the sake of a greater end. Use Connecting Community experiences to subvert their expectations. Provide information and environments that will prepare them to move into Missional Community and stir up a hunger for more.

Connecting Strategy Options

On the landscape of connecting group strategies there are a few approaches that stand out:

The Semester Sermon Study Strategy—With this approach, all groups meet for thirteen weeks, and the groups cycle over again two or three times per year. There are no permanent groups, except for those that continue from one semester to the next. The focus of all groups is to study the sermon. Key Resource: *Sticky Church* by Larry Osborne.

The Semester Multi-Option Strategy—This strategy is very similar to the first one above, but the difference is that groups vary in what they do or study. Usually each semester opens with some form of small group fair where leaders educate interested people in the kind of group they will form. Key Resource: *Activate* by Nelson Searcy.

The 40-day Campaign Strategy—With these groups, people sign up for a six to seven week commitment to a short-term group with no expectations that the group will continue. The group content is tied to weekly sermons, a study guide for personal reflection, and some sort of activity, whether a service project or an equipping event. Key Resources: *Small Groups with Purpose* by Steve Gladen and *Exponential Groups* by Allen White.

The 9-month Closed Group Strategy—Groups in this system last from September to May and all are closed. The expectation is that a new leader will be raised up within each group to start a new group during the following September launch. The content of such groups can be sermon studies, allowing groups to choose their own, or a specific discipleship program. Key Resource: *Creating Community* by Andy Stanley and Bill Willits.

The "Let's Throw People Together" Strategy—This might not sound strategic, but it actually works. Gather all those interested and form small groups that meet at the church building for four weeks. Each on-campus group is formed by the geographical location in which the members live. Identify a host within each group who can facilitate simple questions. During the initial four weeks, the groups are led through some basic curriculum to help the members bond and to help them better understand the parameters of what it means to meet together. After four weeks they move the meetings into the host home.

The "Quick Let's Throw People Together" Strategy—A variation of the previous strategy is to invite interested potential group members to a large group gathering. Then these people are sorted according to interests or geography and they begin meeting in the host home. In such cases the curriculum is usually video-based so the group can form around a program that carries the weight while relationships and leadership are being developed.

The Mid-Sized Program-Driven Strategy—With this approach, people gather around a topic or a need in a programmatically-driven mid-sized group and then they break out into small groups for the balance of the evening. Examples of this are recovery group programs, Alpha, spiritual formation classes, and so forth.

Some Churches Need to Work with What They Have

One option for creating connecting community is to consider how your current programs can serve this purpose as they stand. Instead of developing a new program for connecting groups, established programmatic ministries could be employed to serve this purpose. They would simply need to be re-organized to emphasize circles as opposed to rows. This would mean shifting the emphasis in those ministries from stage ministry which depend upon an expert teacher or worship leader to conversations around table.

This approach can prove especially appropriate in established churches that do not have a lot of new people streaming in on Sundays. Instead of developing a programmatic approach to groups that reorganizes the people you already have, the group development energy can be placed on experiments that move people into organic, missional group life that is introduced in the following chapter.

A Process for Developing Effective Connecting Experiences

To develop a connecting plan that best fits your context, here is a process that fosters movement through the stories of *Personal Improvement* and *Lifestyle Adjustment* and prepares people to go beyond them. Again, these kinds of groups help people group as if they were in small motor boats who are learning how to get in the water, as depicted by the strait line in the image on the next page. They are not like groups that are fully sailing in response to the winds to the Spirit thereby living out *Relational Re-vision* and *Missional Re-creation* (which is the subject of the next chapter). But these kinds of Connecting Groups meet people where they are and prepare them for more.

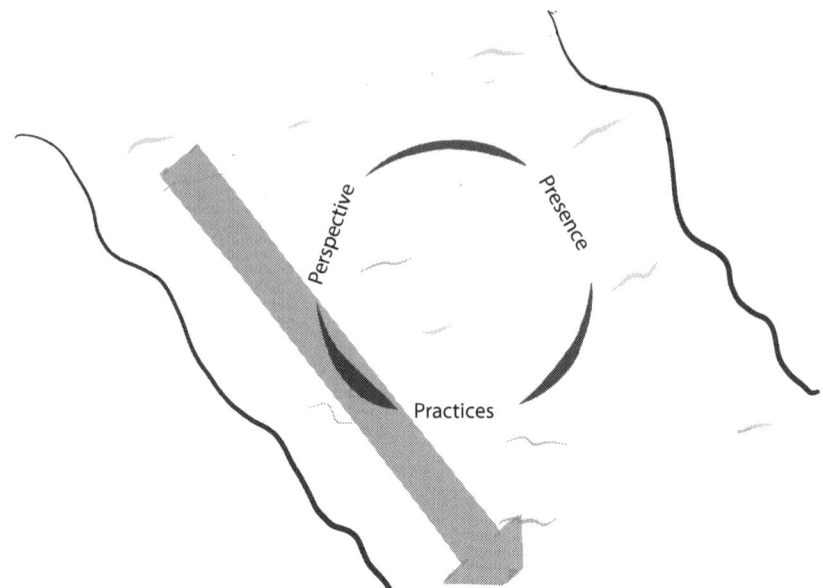

Step 1: Be clear about the purpose of Connecting Community experiences.

This step is meant to help leadership get realistic about the expectations of these kinds of groups. This is where the four stories can help a church clarify what one can expect from these kinds of groups.

Step 2: Identify connecting experiences that are already in place.

As stated in the previous section, not all churches need to develop new kinds of connecting groups. In many cases, people are already connected and living the story of *Lifestyle Adjustment*. Consider a church of 70. Social belonging is quite natural. Even in a church of 250, almost every gathering provides an opportunity for people to connect in social ways. The question then becomes, How can these already-established connecting experiences be used in a more strategic way?

Connecting group strategies are needed most in churches where there is a big front door. They know how to attract people through the weekend event. If a church is not attracting a good number of people through the weekend services, then the development of a new connecting strategy may not be necessary. Most likely it is already in place.

Determine if there are already small groups in place that are living out *Lifestyle Adjustment*. In many cases, the members of those groups are content with what they have. Let them be, but ask them to participate in the new beginning and ending cycle. While many of them will want to continue as they have been at the end of the cycle, it gives them an opportunity to get in the habit of asking what's next. And for people with the desire to move into a Missional Community experience as expressed in the next chapter, they have permission to do so.

Step 3: Don't re-create the wheel.

You don't have to figure out a connecting strategy on your own. There are numerous books and Internet resources on this subject. Novelty is not needed here. Almost any imaginable strategy has been developed and most of the good ones have been perfected. Save yourself the time and money and learn as much as you can from others. It will prove cheaper in the long run.

At the same time, don't maintain a "lock, stock, and barrel" attitude. No strategy will transfer from one local church set in a unique context into another in its exact form. We can learn from others, but we need not emulate another church as if the Spirit of God speaks and leads one church and not others that choose to copy it.

Step 4: Analyze the culture of your church.

Think through the cultural questions related to the people you are trying to connect. Important questions might include:

- What is the socioeconomic situation of those we seek to connect?
- What is the level of education among these people?
- How much church background do these people possess?
- What is the level of cultural uniformity within our church?

When a church is more culturally diverse, including those who are in lower socioeconomic brackets or have less education and less church background, then connecting people in small groups that meet in homes will prove to be more of a challenge. A struggling single mom with four kids and two jobs who makes it to church three out of four weeks a month is probably not interested in opening up her home to host a group. It matters very little how easy we make it with video curriculum. The challenge is simply too much for some. In addition, if there is significant cultural diversity, the communication skills required to connect on a social level make it a challenge to empower people quickly enough to lead groups that meet in homes.

As a result, the connecting strategies listed above seem to work better in homogeneous, suburban churches comprised of people who have transferred from other churches. The last strategy, called The Mid-Sized Program-Driven Strategy, tends to be a bit more flexible where there is socioeconomic diversity.

Step 5: Make connecting easy.

In order for people to get on the Connecting Community path, there must be easy entry points. Questions to consider here:

- What are the natural seasons that people look to connect? Usually these begin when school starts in the Fall and after the new year.
- Where are the places that people find out about connecting? Think through the use of the welcome center, the way things are communicated on the website, the information meetings, and how announcements are made about connecting groups.
- Is the process as simple as 1, 2, 3?
- How will people sign up for groups? This is a question of what kind of computer software to use. I find that the system developed by Church Teams to be the most user friendly (www.churchteams. com).

Step 6: Be clear about your primary ways of connecting

Communicate, communicate, communicate. If the primary verbal communicator does not talk about getting connected, then it won't be valued. Whatever approach you take, the primary communicator must proclaim it.

Try This Connecting Strategy

This connecting group strategy is an adaptation of the 40-day campaign option has been developed by Andrew Mason, the founder of smallgroupchurches.com. It is illustrated in this way:

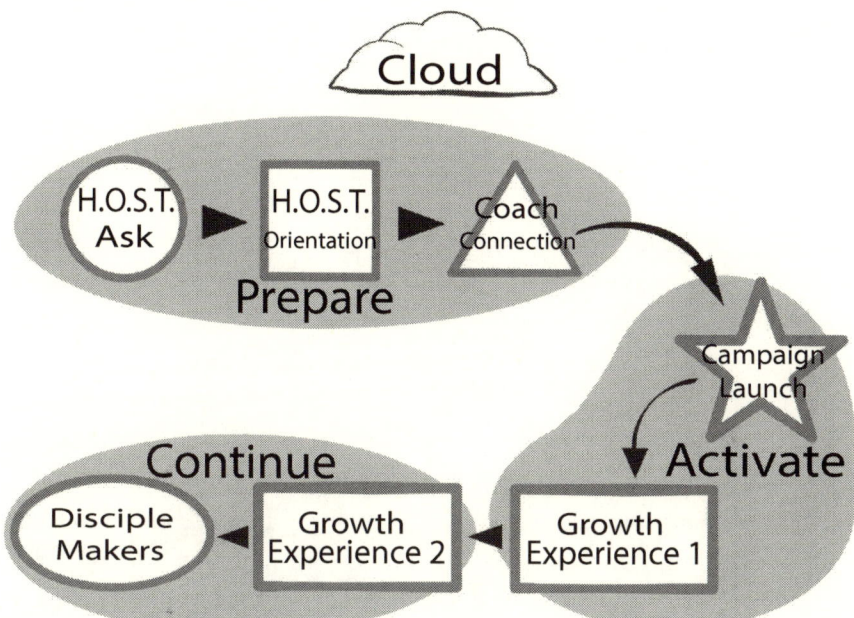

This pathway is broken up into three parts. First, there is the preparation, which begins at least three months before the campaign. It is crucial that the pastoral leadership and the primary speaking pastor have buy-in to the content that will be taught during the campaign. The second part is activation. This is the period of the campaign itself, during which the H.O.S.T. serves the group. The third part, called continuation, is the period when the H.O.S.T. and the members seek God's leading about the future of the group.

The *cloud* represents various online resources that are needed to support the church-wide campaign. These include the following:

- Video curriculum for the small group meetings
- Daily devotions for the entire church
- Equipping Videos for H.O.S.T.s (5 minutes in length)
- Group Ministry Articles
- Podcasts on Keys to Group Success

A group leader in this approach is called a H.O.S.T., which is an acronym for:

- **H**eart For People
- **O**pen your home or a space
- **S**erve a few snacks
- **T**urn on a Video

The process for actively developing groups starts about six weeks before the beginning of the campaign with the *ask* for people to serve as a H.O.S.T. This leads to a one-hour H.O.S.T. orientation, in which they receive an introduction to the nature of the campaign along with training in the basic skills of serving as a H.O.S.T. for six weeks.

The next step involves a *connection* with a *coach* who will serve them through the campaign and walk with them as the group starts.

The *campaign launch* begins with group sign-ups, which entails the promotion of the campaign and the process for people to join a group. It is important to give people at least two weeks to sign up. There are two basic ways to do this. One is through an online program where potential members can choose from a list of open groups and sign up through the online program. When the H.O.S.T. is notified of a person who has joined, they can send an email or extend a phone call to welcome them. (Note: inviting people to submit their names in order for staff to assign potential members to groups is extremely time consuming and it is impossible to make everyone happy. It is much more effective to allow group members to interact directly with H.O.S.T.s to see what group will work best.)

The second approach entails providing a directory of the groups with contact information so that people can select a group and reach out to the H.O.S.T. personally instead of through electronic communication. In addition, hold a Connection Event with free food, music, and a small group mixer. At the Connection Event, potential group members can talk to H.O.S.T.s and determine which one will work best. There are seven keys to this Connection Event:

1. Be Creative—Do something different. For one event, Andrew rented a 30×30 tent and set it up in front of our church building. It created a practical place to hang out and talk. Even more, it stood out because people passed it as they were entering and leaving the church building. If your church has a fellowship hall or lobby area that can be used in this way, do something unique with it so people will stop and take notice.

2. Promote—Andrew promoted the launch of his small group ministry heavily on Sundays for three weeks leading up to the Connection Event. They had a video ad campaign, shared testimonies, and distributed almost 1000 Small Group Directories over the three-week span.

3. Create Atmosphere—Andrew provided a free breakfast (for the 8:30 am service) and BBQ chicken, pork, and beef brisket that was smoked in the parking lot. They set up a sound system that played upbeat music.

4. Identify H.O.S.T.s—Andrew's church released the H.O.S.T.s five minutes early from each service. They had name tags and a small notepad with a pen for recording names, emails, and phone numbers to follow-up on the contacts they made. Several times during the mixer a pastor jumped on the microphone and asked all of the H.O.S.T.s to raise their notepads in the air to identify themselves.

5. Be Enthusiastic—Encourage H.O.S.T.s to show up with passion and enthusiasm. People want to be a part of something exciting. If a leader looks bored, nobody is going to be interested.

6. Collaborate—There are too many details involved in launching a small group campaign to lead such an event alone. Andrew added a fund raiser for the student ministry as a part of the mixer. The youth pastor and his team prepared and served the "free" food, and they accepted donations to raise money for teens to go to camp. They raised over $900 for the youth ministry while people connected with H.O.S.T.s. When you're leading an activity with different dimensions to it, see if there are opportunities to partner with other departments within your church in order to

bring more value to the event.

7. Align—Make it clear how joining a group at the event is crucial to the life of the church. The senior pastor must promote this vision.

Growth Experience 1 is a ninety-minute H.O.S.T rally that occurs during week four of the six-week campaign. At this meeting, the H.O.S.T.s learn about the option of continuing with a four-week follow-up study, which is also video based.

Group Experience 2 is a one-day group retreat to which H.O.S.T.s and members are invited. The content of this retreat focuses on key elements of what it means to live in community, with the hope that groups will take the next step on the journey. Essential to this teaching is equipping for how to build a core team and multiplying a group.

Finally, the *Disciple Makers* part of this process is initiated through a curriculum map that provides options of studies from which H.O.S.T.s can choose. The curriculum map is organized by themes and offers suggestions based on the length of time the group has been together. For instance, you might suggest studies for "rookie groups" that have been together for six months or less, for "seasoned groups" that have gathered for six to twelve months, and for "maturing groups" of more than twelve months. This map provides direction for a longer journey of discipleship and group multiplication.

Conclusion

Most small group programs focus on helping groups get to this point. This priority helps people get connected, to close the "back door" of the church, with the hopes of moving people from the story of *Personal Improvement* to that of *Lifestyle Adjustment*. The goal is not merely to set up a good program but to design environments that cause people to be open to the Spirit so that they might long for more. Grouping people at this level is not an end. It is a zone of preparation that will create desire for *Relational Re-vision* and *Missional Re-creation*, which is the topic of the next chapter.

19

How Will You Initiate Organic Missional Experiments?

Priority: Foster Missional Community Experiments

The Bible shows us that God is a God of revelation, as God pulls back the curtain of who he is and we discover that he is not what we expect him to be. Because I grew up going to church, often hearing sermons and attending Bible studies four of five times per week, I became so familiar with stories of the Bible that they lost their surprise factor. It is a bit like having watched a suspense thriller for the twentieth time. The unexpected twists were no longer unexpected.

Periodically, I will read a book of the Bible while putting myself in the imagination of someone from 95 A.D. living in a city like Ephesus, with the goal of letting it surprise me. Honestly, this is not easy, but from time to time, it hits me how absurd the story of the New Testament sounds. Three things in particular startle my imagination. First, the fact that God would become a man is shocking, and to those who heard this for the first time, it would have been jaw-dropping. Even more, the fact that this man was an Israelite—a part of a no-name country occupied by Rome—an illegitimate son conceived out of wedlock, lacked a formal education, and never held any formal leadership role makes the claim that God came in this man Jesus even more far-fetched.

Secondly, this story claims that this God came and died the most horrible kind of death imaginable. While claiming all authority in heaven and earth, he did not manifest that power in a way that protected himself. Instead he suffered and died as an infamous criminal.

The third surprise comes in the stories about him rising from the dead. What a claim!

Not even someone as imaginative as Stephen King could have come up with the surprising twists to the story that the early church preached. It's so foolish that no one would tell it unless it were true.

Yet this is the way that great stories work. Whether in the movies, written works of fiction, or historical accounts, stories work because they have surprising twists. The story of God contains the greatest twist of all.

In the stories of *Personal Improvement* and *Lifestyle Adjustment*, the twists are minimal. In most cases, the plot line of such groups is relatively predictable, a bit like a detective television show from the 1980s. We might not know the details of who killed whom, but the pattern is predictable. For many, that's all they are ready to embrace.

The stories of *Relational Re-vision* and *Missional Re-creation* follow a different pattern, one that is shaped by surprises.

Four Surprises

In my own journey, I discovered *Relational Re-vision* and *Missional Re-creation* as I listened to unexpected, surprising stories that did not fit into the small group structure that we had developed in our church. Let me share four of them:

Story #1

Kent and I met for lunch. He had been a group leader in the past at our church but not at this point. Before joining our church, he served as the volunteer small group point person at another congregation. He was well-versed in small groups from extensive reading, and he had even traveled oversees to observe what some of the most creative churches were doing with groups. As I listened to his story, I wondered why we were not tapping into his expertise. Then he told me about where he was investing his energies. He was leading a team who facilitated the Alpha course every Wednesday night at the Salvation Army in Minneapolis. Most of the men at the "Sali" (his abbreviation) were in a transitional situation as they had recently been released from the county jail. Some of the men that "graduated" from the Sali would participate in a house owned by a non-profit ministry where Kent led a weekly house church meeting. My immediate thought was, "This does not fit our group structure, but shouldn't it? Why is it the case when someone experiments with something new that they have to go and start a new organization to do it?"

Story #2

Sandra launched the small groups ministry at the church where I served over a decade before my arrival. She had subsequently been on the staff of two of the largest churches in North America and then began work in the inner city in an economically under-resourced neighborhood. As a part of her ministry, she began a small group with women from her neighborhood, individuals who would most likely never attend our weekend services. Again, I asked, "Why is it that someone who belongs to our church has to operate outside the church system to accomplish the kingdom vision?"

Story #3

Tim was a leader in the church who had a passion for the geographic area where he lived. After moving into his home, he adopted his street and befriended those who lived nearby. When we first met and spoke about his connections to his neighbors, he was not participating in one of our official groups, which I naturally questioned. As I listened, I found that I needed to wait and see what God would do on Tim's street. After many long conversations with Tim, a retired couple caught a vision to live more simply. So they sold their large, suburban home and moved two houses away from Tim and his wife. The four of them have established a ministry core to those who live on their block. The members of his small group live within walking distance, even though none of them attend Tim's church or any other church for that matter.

I wondered. "How is God working through this unique situation and how can we learn from this so that our groups can capture this 'out-of-the-box' imagination?"

Story #4

The last story is about a guy named Ken. He would talk about his house church that met every Saturday night, often going into the wee hours of the morning. This group had been living in community, praying for each other, and his house church members were connected to ministries in Haiti. When asked why he or another one of the group's leaders were not coming to the various support meetings that we were providing, his response was "Why would that help us do what God is calling us to do?" At first, I judged what seemed like arrogance, but as I listened more to what they were doing, I realized that his honest response was dead on. Again, it made me think about why we had no room in our small group imagination for one of our best and most creative leaders.

Responding to These Stories

These four stories came as a surprise to me. They were not following the plans and procedures that we had developed from the "center" of the church's leadership. They were operating on the fringes, and there they were living out stories full of surprising twists that could not be controlled or manufactured. After hearing their stories, I had three options:

- Promote a high control system and require all groups to fit the official pattern and structure that the church had established.
- Opt for a low control system and embrace everything people wanted to do in group form.
- Develop a wiki-control system, one which continues to promote unexpected, surprising self-initiated experiments on the fringes, while offering checks and balances that provide guidance.

It has become clear to me that God wants to move through groups in unexpected, out-of-the-box ways if the leaders who oversee that system don't force the groups to look, act, and feel like all the other groups in their system.

The Spirit is Ahead of Us

The Spirit resides in and amongst us in our groups, even when we don't fully see or understand what the Spirit is doing. When we accept this truth, group life then moves far beyond meetings, studying curriculum, or fulfilling the expectations established by church leaders. The Spirit fills the group with life. Peter tells us that we are "participants in the divine nature" (2 Peter 1:4). God's nature is love. As the Spirit enlivens a group to move beyond a Connecting Community experience, the life and love of a group will move into the unpredictability of love, which means that the group will take on new ways of existing and operating.

As we participate in the Holy Spirit with others, we are participants in his love. Love is not something that can be prescribed in a book or through a teaching session. Love is creative in nature. Each situation where love comes to life will be unique. The Spirit carries the love of God out beyond the bounds of Connecting Community structures, into our neighborhoods, inside our families, at the workplace, and among friends.

Therefore, it is impossible to prescribe a form for Missional Community. Instead it is a creative expression of practices that have shaped a group to move beyond Connecting Community and into God's mission. (These practices are introduced in chapter 10.) These practices form group members in the ways of the Spirit that moves in the life of the community. Then, as these practices become regular group patterns, the Spirit leads them to the creative fringes, to the unexpected, to experiment. The diagram on the next page illustrates the new life that is birthed through experiments.

The story of *Relational Re-vision* arises from the lives of those who want more. In many cases, this arises out of frustration with group life that might fit into the normal patterns of Connecting Community. They have a hunger for something other and a passion to learn how to

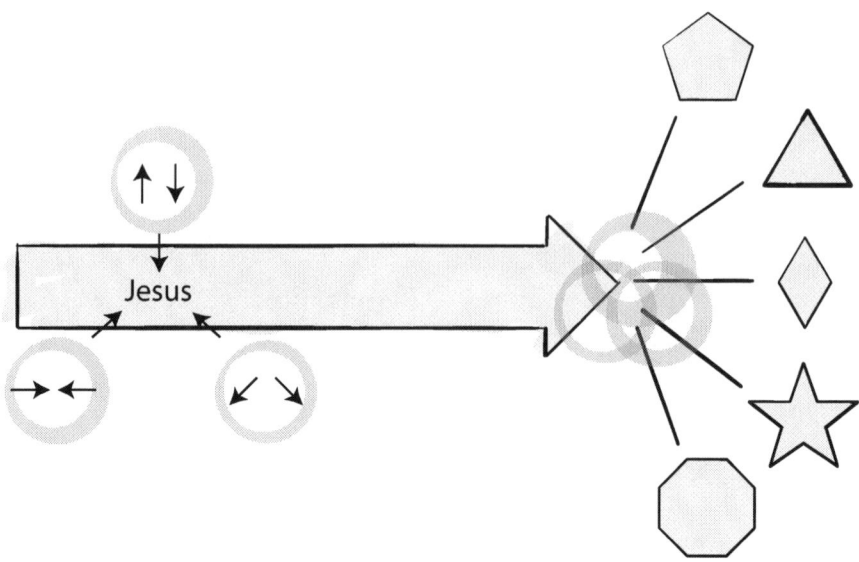

do it. It is something that the Spirit of God stirs up in their hearts, not something that can be mandated from the top. In fact, I've found that when church leaders try to enforce a vision for Missional Community, people either refuse or, even worse, they give verbal ascent but continue to do what they have always done. Missional Community must be generated on the fringes, hence the use of the word "experiments." These experiments train up those who are ready, and over time these experiments serve as living parables that draw or woo others to follow down the road. This after all is how most people learn. They need to see it in action before they can experiment with something new themselves.

Who Experiments?

Most people are not naturally the kind of people who like to experiment with new ideas because they are prone to predictability. They prefer to know what to expect from their group experiences. The following population bell curve is commonly used to describe how new ideas are disseminated.[1] This illustrates different responses people have to experiments. A few respond well to new ideas and change, while most need time and information before they embrace new ideas. Let's consider these five basic responses to experimentation.

Innovators love experiments because they tend to be obsessed with

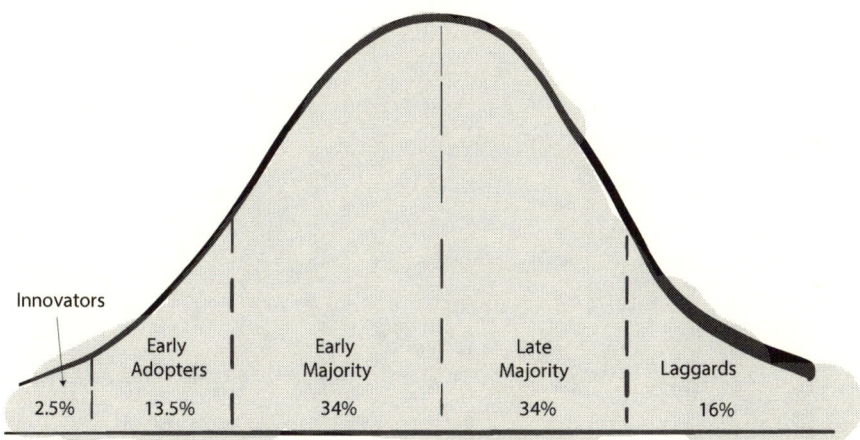

being venturesome. They challenge the status quo and expand the current boundaries by introducing new ideas. While not all of their ideas are practical or workable, their concern is to explore new territory. Innovators make many mistakes because they will adopt new ideas simply because they are new.

Innovators are able to visualize a new idea without ever seeing it. They do not need to increase their dissatisfaction with current reality, because they are always dissatisfied with the old. They continually feel a sense of urgency and embrace change just because it is change. To introduce a new idea to an innovator, a simple meeting, followed up with some reading material, is often sufficient.

Early Adopters are characterized by respectability. They are ahead of the pack, but not too far ahead. Therefore, they have the greatest degree of influence upon others in the church, and an experiment cannot survive without the early adopters. These are the people who learn how an experiment works and then turn it into action.

Those in the *Early Majority* are deliberate individuals who make up one third of the population. They adhere to the motto, "Be not the first by which the new is tried, nor the last to lay the old aside." They will follow with deliberate willingness, but they will seldom lead. As such, they are not prime suspects for the early stages of experimentation.

It takes longer for members of the early majority to see the value of a new idea. They need time to process current reality and a leader who will make them feel safe in this process. They have a limited ability to understand a new vision by reading about it or seeing it at another church. Primarily, they need to experience it after someone else has worked out a few of the kinks. They will follow people they trust into a new vision and then they will take it on as their own.

Late Majority. Making up another third of the population, these people view new ideas with skepticism and caution. The pressure of peers and obvious circumstantial pointers must lead them to see the necessity of change before they will change.

Because those in the late majority category only adopt a new idea after other people are doing it and thereby proving it successful, you cannot expect this group to put any value on experiments until they are actually no longer classified as experiments.

Laggards. These are the last to adopt new ideas, as they are traditional and their reference point is in the past. They tend to be suspicious of the new and those who promote new ideas. This group rarely feels an urgency to change until they realize that they are being left behind. They will change only because everyone else has.

In most cases it is not hard to identify those who fall into the innovator or early adopter categories. They are often those who are never satisfied even when things are going good. They are reading books that talk about things differently and seeking new ways to do things. These are the people who need to lead through experimentation.

These people are usually not the stakeholders who sit in positions of power in a church. The stakeholders are typically stable, centered people who usually fall into the middle adopter categories. If that is the case, those people don't particularly like experimenting with new ideas. It is crucial to establish clear communication and a working relationship between those doing the experimentation and the stakeholders on the church board, but to force the board to commit to figuring out new ideas is counterproductive. And to change the board so that experimenters can have the power is equally frustrating. No innovative company puts those good at research and development in charge of the daily decisions. However, if the research is going to be productive, the two groups must learn how to communicate with one another.

Learning from Experiments on the Fringe

The innovators and early adopters embrace what is happening at the edges or fringes. They meet in creative ways and in creative places, in pubs or coffee houses with unique interactive Bible discussion that does not fit with traditional forms of sermon discussion meetings or Bible studies. They respond to the creative ways of the Spirit's leading like those aboard a small sailboat. They move forward as if sailing, tacking back and forth.

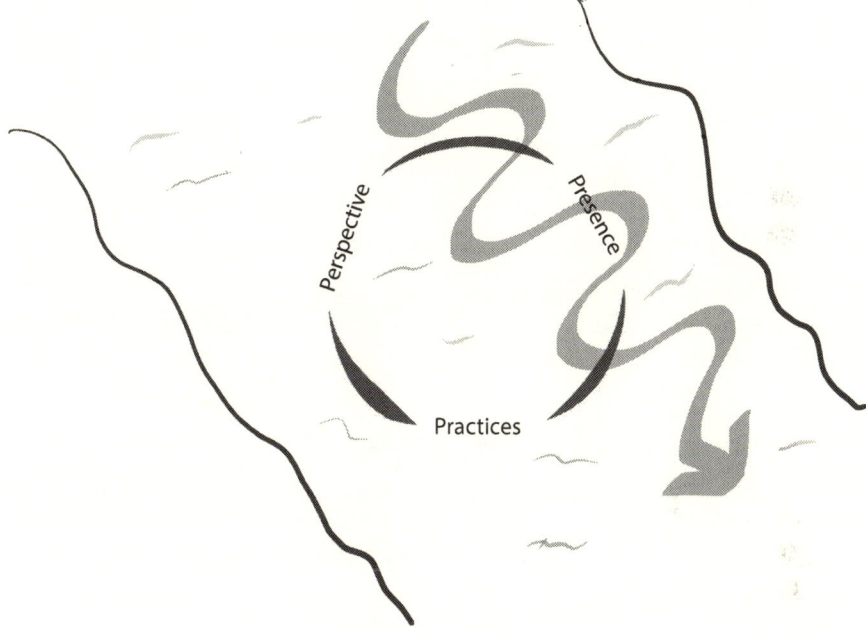

Middle adopters usually focus on doing groups as they have been taught, seeking to connect with those who attend their traditional church services. Often people assume that we need to choose between the two. Therefore some churches focus on developing fringe groups, while most focus on centrally-controlled groups. By doing this, we separate those who are creative from those who have the ability to take creative ideas and work them out over the long haul.

Typically innovators and early adopters who like experimentation are disconnected from those at the center, people who have the ability to carry out successful experiments to completion.

Those at the center need those on the fringes to open up new paths and test new perspectives. Those on the fringes need those at the center to keep them grounded and accountable so that we are no longer just creating new ideas for the sake of new ideas.

No church can embrace a single way to successfully promote Missional Community. Our context is always changing and new experiments are always needed. And we need those who are more stable to carry out the experiments to fruitful life.

When presenting this concept to a group of pastors, a church leader from Ireland told me about a group that had been a challenge for him. He shared that they were very innovative and their creativity and zeal had resulted in some radical experiments. They regularly shared meals, sacrificially supported one another, and invested in the people of a specific apartment building. Before my presentation, he thought that they no longer fit the norms of the church and assumed they would spin off as a separate church. Within this new paradigm, he saw how this missional group could serve as a lived experiment from which others could learn.

The Purposes of Experiments

The experiment process allows innovators and early adopters to explore new ways of grouping and thereby set a model for others to follow. The best way to lead people into something new is to model the possibility that something new can be done. This general purpose is worked out in three sub-purposes.

First, experiments serve as learning workshops, seeking to answer the questions "Is missional community possible?", "How well does it meet needs?", and "What must be adapted to make it work?" The biggest question that they answer is, "What do the group leaders and members do differently to live out Missional Community as opposed to groups that only experience Connecting Community?" Such questions can only be answered through experience in your local context.

Second, the experiments model the stories of *Relational Re-vision* and *Missional Re-creation* to others. Most people (middle adopters) have to see a new idea in action before they understand what it looks like, how it works, or if they even like it. Experiments help people see answers to practical questions like:

- What should happen among small group members?
- What should be going on in group meetings?
- What are some of the ways groups will pray?
- What does community look like?
- What does evangelism look like and how are new people incorporated into group life?
- How do groups practice edification?
- What are some ways that individuals practice personal spiritual formation?
- How are new leaders developed?

Third, Missional Community experiments provide space for the Spirit to shape us to live out the hope we have for Communion, Relating, and Engagement in the midst of a world shaped by individualism and secularism. When a group commits to living the story of *Relational Re-vision*, it needs to adopt a set of practices that will move group members from where they are now toward the vision of Communion, Relating, and Engagement.

How people experiment will vary from church to church and from context to context. There is not a set formula. However there are some general patterns, which can be described by these four specific experiment strategies.

Strategy #1: The Simple Experiment Process

The first strategy is a simple and intentional process where one experimental group is initiated. One leader works with eight to twelve early adopters to learn how to live out Communion, Relating, and Engagement by adopting a distinctive set of practices that will form their life together. Then after six to nine months, these members work together to lead three other experiments. These groups work under the radar screen, not as an official public ministry. After two or three generations of experiments, then Missional Community will become public.

Strategy #2: The Complex Group Experiment

The second approach is a bit more complex. Consider a church that has ten groups that are living out the stories of *Personal Improvement* and *Lifestyle Adjustment*, with three or four of these groups that are hungry to go deeper. These three or four groups can serve as Missional Community experiments that are working out the practices of Communion, Relating, and Engagement in their local contexts.

In this approach, the three or four groups will possess different strengths and weaknesses. One small group holds really good small group meetings. Another discovers how to do relationship evangelism. And still another group practices incredible body life. When this occurs, the pastors should facilitate cross-pollination so that all the groups can share their strengths with one another.

The pastors who oversee groups should focus on supporting these three or four small groups, instead of spreading out their energy over all of the groups. It is tempting to focus energy on the groups that are struggling while allowing the groups that have potential for Missional Community to develop on their own. But pastors should focus their mentoring on their best groups so that they can make a way for others to follow. The way into Missional Community cannot be discovered by trying to bring all groups up to the same level.

Material for both Strategy #1 and #2 should focus on making space for open conversations about what the Spirit is doing to form the group into the story of *Relational Re-vision*. Don't do a typical Bible study. An example of such a resource is my *Cultivating Community in the Way of Jesus*, which serves as a study guide for *Missional Small Groups*.

Strategy #3: Triads

This approach is the simplest because it only requires two people to get started.[2] These two people of the same gender begin meeting with the goal of moving into the story of *Relational Re-vision*. They could meet at any place that is convenient, because the focus lies on the relationship shared between them, not the specific formula they adopt. As they share life with each other, the hope is that they can add a third person to their group, and together they can explore what it means to live out Communion, Relating, and Engagement.

It often helps to read through some kind of spiritual formation material together. For instance, those in the triads could work through the content found in *Cultivating Community in the Way of Jesus*, but it need not be followed in a formal way as it would in a group of ten or twelve. The point of this triad is to talk about what the Spirit is doing to move each person forward on the journey and to move forward together on that journey.

After a period of six to nine months, the hope is that a fourth person might be added to the group, and then a new triad could birth, each one seeking to add a third. The development of the triads could be depicted in this way:

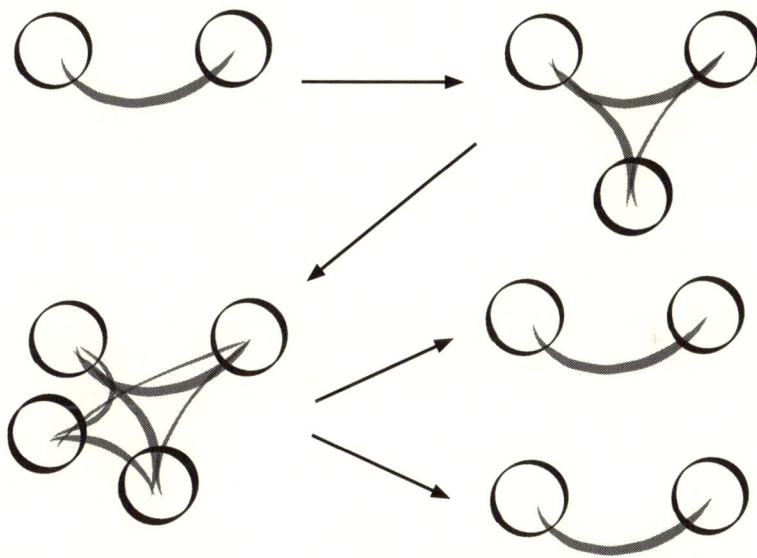

The person being added to a triad could be an established Christian, someone who has been recently baptized, a person returning to Christ, or a seeker. The key is that the person is hungry to know God and to live out God's mission in the world.

After three or four of these triads have been formed, each of the members of the triads then will join together to form a Missional Community. The triads would continue to meet in the same pattern that has been previously practiced; it's just at this point, the group of ten to fifteen would also gather to experiment with how they are moving into the story of *Missional Re-creation*.

Strategy #4: Neighborhood Experiments

A final suggestion to consider is a strategy of following God into the neighborhood to see where the Spirit is at work in unexpected ways. This approach is based on the work of Alan Roxburgh and his various writings on the subject. The book *Joining God, Remaking Church, Changing the World* introduces this process. The objective is to release people to experiment with new expressions of gathering and to talk about where they see God at work. A few examples of this approach include:

Table Experiments

The basic pattern is a regular (weekly or biweekly) gathering around the meal of a group living in proximity to one another. Over meals they can share their lives, pray for one another, and intercede for the neighborhood. Also, this is the place where people talk about ways God is leading them to practice hospitality in the neighborhood.

Parish Experiments

The most mission-shaped, counter-cultural move a local church can make is to structure its life in specific neighborhoods. The church moves from being a building where people gather to a center where people are empowered to see their neighborhood as their parish— the place where they belong, connect, live, eat, love, and welcome the stranger for the sake of the kingdom.

Such local churches see the neighborhoods where its people live as the centers of mission and life. What a local church would do, therefore, is reintroduce the idea of the parish for a neighborhood, four or five streets in urban areas, or an actual suburb in suburbia. These people would meet in table or mission groups in the name and for the sake of being God's people in that area. The local church, with its staff and building, would become a training, resourcing, and equipping center for its parishes and their ministries.

Felt-need Experiments

This kind of group is comprised of people who have come together around a specific need in their neighborhood. Examples might include: caring for latch-key kids; running a drop in-center or after-school education program; developing a child/parent program; working with unemployed youth in the area; launching programs and resources for the homeless and poor in the area; embracing a specific ethnic group in an area, and so forth. Such groups are supported by a covenant that spells out what it means to belong and participate. It will shape itself around a basic rule of life and a set of practices, while always keeping focused on its mission covenant.

Interest-based Experiments

This might include things like book clubs, gatherings at a local park for young families, a community garden, or just adopting a third-place to be present and get to know the people who frequent it. Many times, interest-based experiments arise from simply observing the patterns of life in a local neighborhood and entering into one of those patterns alongside others.

A Simple Process for Neighborhood Experiments

According to Roxburgh, the process for entering into these experiments involves five basic steps. First, the group listens in order to become aware of what is happening in a specific neighborhood. This involves an exegesis process that is introduced in chapter nine. The second step is to discern what the Spirit is leading the group to do in response to what has been observed. This entails a discernment process where the group listens to one another through the sharing of stories about what they are experiencing as they engage the neighborhood.

The third step focuses on the experiments themselves. These work best when they are simple, do not require extensive organization and planning, and they do not depend upon the input of experts. They could even be collaborative efforts with people in the neighborhood.[3]

The fourth step is shaped by reflection on the group's experience with the experiments so that the group becomes clear about what they have done, what they have learned, and what this might mean for the future of the church. This is the time to identify what needs to be communicated with the church board and with the congregation as a whole.

Step five involves making decisions about how the church will progress toward movement into the neighborhood. Here reports are given to board members and to the congregation. Stories are shared and testimonies about how God has been present are given. From this will arise next steps about how others can participate in these experiments, drawing people into the same five-step process.

Church, Not Just Meetings

When Paul wrote the word "church" or *ecclesia* in Greek, he was envisioning small groups of people who gathered in homes. His mental images of church and ours are vastly different after 2000 years of development. Because the modern definition of church emphasizes the organization, the building, and large group worship, we impose these mental models onto Paul's use of the word *ecclesia*.

Ecclesia was a word that the followers of Christ used to define themselves. It simply meant "an assembly" or "a gathering." It was used in the Septuagint to translate the Hebrew word *quhol* which means "assembly," often used to describe the "assemblies of the Lord." New Testament theologian James Dunn writes, "There can be little doubt that Paul intended to depict the little assemblies of Christian believers as equally manifestations of and in direct continuity with 'the assembly of Yahweh,' 'the assembly of Israel.'"[4] At the same time, his use of the word includes the gathering of large groups. For instance, in Corinth, he refers to the gathering of all the Christians in the city as *ecclesia* (1 Cor. 1:1). As a result, Paul could freely envision both small groups of believers meeting in homes and periodic gatherings of Christians of one city meeting in a larger venue as the *ecclesia*. One did not compete with the status of the other because both were gatherings or assemblies.

Due to our modern definition of "church," most of the time small groups are viewed as sub-units of the "real" church. This is appropriate for groups that are only living the stories of *Personal Improvement* or *Lifestyle Adjustment*. However, when groups begin to manifest the stories of *Relational Re-vision* and *Missional Re-creation*, this is an experience of *ecclesia*, not merely a second-rate version of the real thing. When this occurs, the corporate meeting becomes a gathering of the churches, the little bodies of Christ. When enough groups move into these stories, the nature of the weekend worship becomes an opportunity to celebrate the life that God is doing in and through the groups, as well as an equipping venue to empower them to press on.

Inviting Middle Adopters to Shift from Connecting Community to Missional Community

After five to seven groups are living out the stories of *Relational Re-vision* and *Missional Re-creation*, then it is important to help clear a path for others—who tend to be less creative in nature—to follow suit. They need more direction in the beginning, as this will give them the tools to be creative and follow the leading of the Spirit. In other words, this path helps move people from Connecting Community into Missional Community. Moving people along this path will look different for different churches. Consider the diagram on the next page. The diagonal arrow that moves from the bottom horizontal line to the top illustrates the purpose of the shift embodied by this strategy. Consider the following examples.

Attractional Church

For instance, for a church that has been established on a pattern of providing great weekend services for spectators and groups that close the back door through Connecting Community, there might be a series of four to six classes on a Sunday morning for people who want more out of group life. One church that has written a 26-week process to help equip people for Missional Community life. They don't want people embarking upon Missional Community without a full understanding of the cost and thereby inadvertently watering down Missional Community into another Connecting Community experience.

Established Traditional Church

One traditional church in the suburbs of San Fransisco went all out

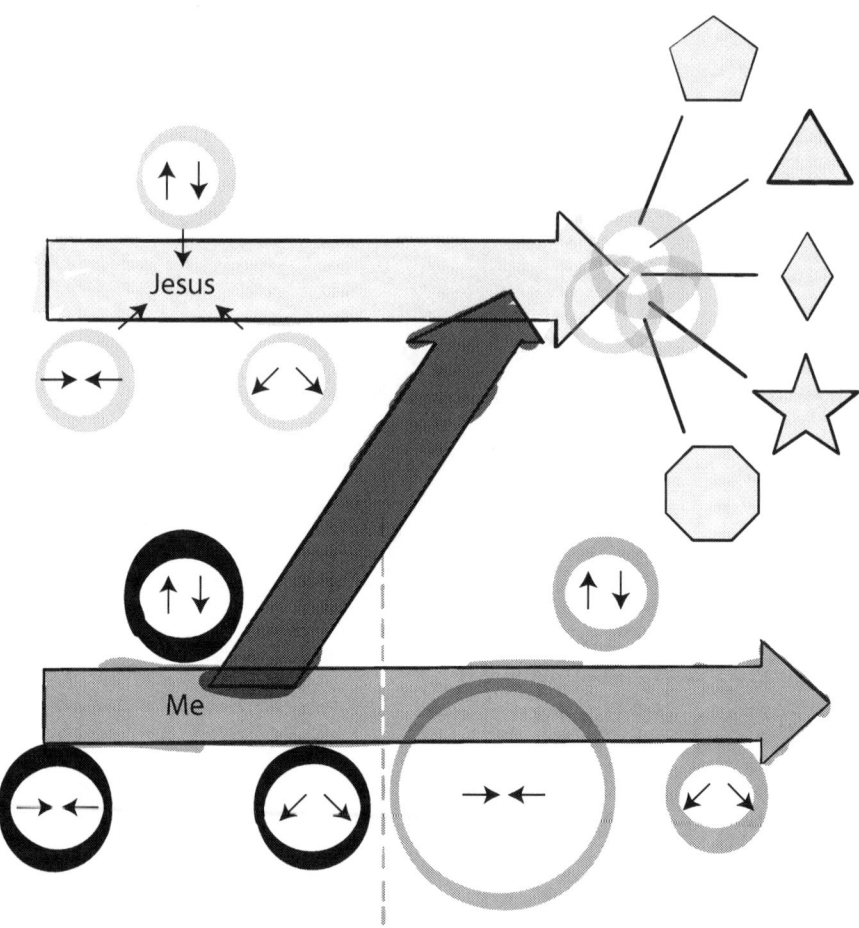

for Missional Community. The church voted to go this direction and the board was fully behind it. Traditional Christians even participated in the groups. But then they started reaching people with painted hair and tattoos, and they started coming to worship services. That's when it became clear that the established people were not ready for missional life. They had not been formed for mission. Even though the established members of this church had been followers of Jesus for many years, they were not equipped to be the kind of church that makes missional communities flourish. They needed time to process the changes without it being a threat to everything they knew about church. Something like a regular town hall meeting where those who were inquiring about Missional Community might have the freedom to process the differences without it being forced on them often works quite well. Even more important are the informal conversations between the leadership of the church and those who are traditional church members.

New Experimental Church

In many cases, a new church will be solely focused on the development of Missional Community. In a previously shared story, I introduced how I was a part of such a church. While we did not fit the normal patterns of church life as we tested new ways of living in community, many joined us from other churches who needed an introduction into the what we were doing. They needed a clear path that would move them from traditional ways of doing small groups so that they could move into the stories of *Relational Re-vision* and *Missional Re-creation*.

Even new churches that are solely focused on Missional Community need a process that will equip people who have been shaped by traditional church expectations so that they can flourish in a missional environment. Be very clear up front, in black and white terms, about the nature of the vision and ask them to join an intense discipleship process that will re-shape their imagination and form them for mission.

When To Experiment

Some churches will focus most of their energy on the development of experimental, organic groups that live on mission. This is especially appropriate for new churches that have a clear vision not to conform to traditional church expectations. Established churches may not need to focus on developing programmatic groups but instead they will put their energy in group experimentation. When a church has a large flow of new people attending worship, programmatic groups—introduced in the previous chapter—will be the initial priority. In whatever situation you find yourself, start with the people who are hungry for more out of their group life and work with them. It will most likely begin small, like a mustard seed, but it has the potential to burgeon and grow beyond your wildest dreams.

20

How Will You Form People for Flourishing Community?

Priority: Develop a Spiritual Formation Environment

Jesus modeled a way for others to follow. Through the years, many have made this argument, claiming that the key to Jesus' ministry was that he mentored a small group of twelve people and equipped them to do the same with others. However, the way that Jesus came demonstrates something much more fundamental to the Jesus way than the fact that he led a small group. The most basic aspect of his life and ministry was the fact that he lived in absolute union with the Father by the Spirit.

To develop groups that flourish is to live into this fundamental union by the Spirit. We need to be formed as God's people in a way that fits the movement into Communion, Relating, and Engagement. In other words, we make room for the Spirit to form in us the character that fits the hopes and dreams for community and mission. Just implementing a good strategy—while helpful—won't make that happen.

We are formed by the Spirit to live in community, which shapes the story told by groups. We experience this formation as a journey, as illustrated by the claim of the Apostle Paul when he said that he sought "to know Christ and the power of his resurrection and the fellowship of sharing in his sufferings, becoming like him in his death, and so, somehow to attain the resurrection from the dead" (Philippians 3:10-11). Paul follows this verse by stating that he has not obtained this goal, but that he is pressing on to "win the prize for which God has called me heavenward in Christ Jesus."

For a church or a small group to move forward on a journey together, individuals must also make space in their lives for the formation by the Spirit. This practice is about providing opportunities for individuals to experience this formation by helping people along a journey toward maturity in Christ.

The Journey of Formation

The ultimate goal of the people of God is to participate in communion with the Father, by the Son through the Holy Spirit. The gift of the Spirit draws us along a journey of formation whereby we are trained to experience this reality of participation in God in greater ways.

There is no one-size-fits-all formation process for everyone in the church. We cannot expect to run everyone through a series of classes or ask everyone to complete a discipleship book and assume them to be mature.

At the same time, neither can a church set up a customized spiritual formation process for every person. That's just unrealistic. Instead, in order to generate a spiritual formation culture, we need to think in terms of four basic levels of formation.

Connecting Formation is needed for anyone, whether a committed believer or not, to help them learn how to belong in the community. This will come through worship services, small group activities, events, classes, church-wide study campaigns, conferences, and retreats.

New Christian Formation is provided for those who are new to the faith to help them establish a strong foundation. This might come in a course like Alpha, a book, or through curriculum that guides a conversation between a mentor and the new Christian.

Missional Community Formation helps those who are moving forward in missional experiments to grow in their faith. The best way to experience this is through sub-groups of three or four who share with and challenge one another.

Leadership Formation provides a clear set of spiritual disciplines so that leaders grow in their faith as they lead.

Let's explore each of these levels of formation further.

Connecting Community Formation

It's not enough to announce that people need to get in a group and start practicing the "one anothers" (love one another, encourage one another, bless one another, serve one another, and so forth). Telling them what they should be doing without equipping them for the task is like sending a student home with homework without teaching them how to complete it. So many small group experiences begin with great hopes and dreams of how the community could be empowered to impact others, but they too often fall short because they do not know how to do some of the basic things to make relational connections within groups work. Consider the following examples.

Level 1: Simplicity

God is calling God's people to live simply so that there is room in our lives to love and be loved. As we stated in chapter 1, the complexity and chaos that rules life today subtly erodes love. While we were made for more than work, stress, and church activities, people need basic equipping in how to live differently. How can we be God's witnesses when the way we do life really does not look that much different than the average moral American citizen? We might have a different message, but if that message has no tangible, practical impact on the here and now of our lives, we should not be surprised when our groups remain banal.

Level 2: Relationship Skills Training

Paul instructed the churches at Rome and Corinth to greet one another with a holy kiss. This kind of greeting was not especially spiritual. It was simply the social way of seeing another person. How we interact socially has ramifications upon how we love one another as a community. If we greet well, the doors will open to deeper connections.

If you stop to ponder it, many of the "one another" passages are reminders about how we should treat each other socially. However, many people do not possess the skills to honor others in a social way that is a blessing. Specifically, people in our churches and groups need to process:

- How to greet another person when they come into a room.
- How to ask questions of a person to get to know them.
- How to listen to another person.
- How to invite a few people to your home for a meal and make them feel welcome.
- How to share life with people who are significantly different in personality and interest.
- How to relate to people from different ethnic backgrounds.

In previous generations, the development of these social skills was not as crucial as they are at this point in history because people learned social skills as a part of growing up in their culture.

In addition, relational conflict training is often helpful because many in our culture today do not possess the basic skills for working through conflict. We have become so accustomed to running from conflict because it's so easy to do so in our world that when it arises in group life, often it leads to group shut down. By the time a group enters into conflict, it's too late to equip members to effectively deal with it. When someone is frustrated or even angry at another group member, they don't want to hear something like, "You know what you are experiencing is normal. This is called the 'conflict stage of group life.'"

New Christian Formation

Discipleship for the sake of discipleship is akin to a dog chasing its tail. Discipleship must be for the sake of something else, not an end in itself. The goal of discipleship is to know Christ (Phil 3:8). Or we might say it's to more fully participate in the divine nature (2 Pet 2:4). Or to put it in another way, we could say that it means to grow in love. Paul put it this way:

I pray that out of his glorious riches he may strengthen you with power through his Spirit in your inner being, so that Christ may dwell in your hearts through faith. And I pray that you, being rooted and established in love, may have power, together with all the Lord's holy people, to grasp how wide and long and high and deep is the love of Christ, and to know this love that surpasses knowledge— that you may be filled to the measure of all the fullness of God (Ephesians 3:16-19).

In this passage, Paul prayed that the Ephesians would grasp the vastness of the God of love and be rooted and established in love. The goal is for new believers to be set on this course toward taking on God's character of self-sacrificial, other-oriented, choice-based love. This is a journey from what Henri Nouwen called the house of fear into the house of love. Here we discover the roots that lie behind the fear and keep us bound up within ourselves and hinder us from risking love.

Such equipping begins as people learn the basics of who Jesus is and how to cultivate the space in their lives to know him more each day.

Missional Community Formation

Elizabeth O'Connor writes of the missional experience of The Church of the Savior in Washington D.C. She states, "This deepening of the spiritual life is not spontaneous. People do not just become great Christians. They grow as they make certain purposeful responses to life and to the grace of God. We call these ordered responses 'disciplines.'"[1]

In the monastic tradition, these ordered responses were shaped by what they call a "rule." Hence, Saint Benedict created a rule of life for all those who chose to enter into a Benedictine community. While I am not advocating a certain monastic tradition for small groups, we should learn from Benedict's specificity. We need to develop a "rule," or what I call rhythms. These rhythms, which were introduced in the previous chapter, identify specific patterns for living as God's people during this time, therefore causing us to stand in contrast to the surrounding culture. O'Connor again helps us see the importance of this:

As members of a mission group we need to be disciplined and we need to be willing to require a discipline of those who would be on mission with us. No person or group or movement has vigor and power unless it is disciplined. Are we willing to be disciplined ourselves and to require it of others when it means that we will be the target of the hostilities and the pressures of many who do not see the necessity? The chances are that we will give in unless we know that this "giving in" means that our mission group will have no hard sharp cutting edge and will in time peter out.[2]

Few would be so blunt today. This book was written in 1963. One might discount the writings due to its age. However, it is based on timeless wisdom. She continues with:

This does not mean that we exclude a person from the Christian community. It simply means that we define his [or her] participation in the mission. We do not ask him to articulate what he does not know, or subject him to pressures for which he is not ready. The army does not take a man, put a gun in his hand, and march him to the front when he has never held a gun and does not know how to load it.[3]

In their book, *Organic Disciplemaking*, Dennis McCallum and Jessica Lowery write about how their church has been built upon the truths that O'Connor wrote about 50 years ago:

Xenos is a local church that grew up spontaneously beginning in 1970, during the Jesus Movement. ... Leaders are not recognized unless they are truly making disciples. With over 250 student and adult home churches, each led by a team of three to six leaders, the church has over 500 recognized leaders and around 900 "servant team" members. All servant team members must show they are working with disciples before being accepted to the team. Throughout the church, most people are either being discipled or are discipling others.[4]

Another example is Antioch Church in Waco, Texas. Their small groups are not just places for people to get connected and study the Bible. They have set an expectation that people will be shaped to live radical, sacrificial lives, which they see as the genuine "normal Christian life." The founding leader, Jimmy Seibert, writes, "Discipleship was the foundation for everything we had started in 1987 and continues to be a major part of everything we do today."[5]

The first question we need to ask is not "What kind of small group can be missional?" or "What can we do to be missional?" Instead we must ask, "How are we going to create a culture of conversations of the way of Jesus?"

One of the primary ways that this is addressed is through micro groups where people can share their journey with each other in transparent ways. Neil Cole writes about Life Transformation Groups, which he uses to form people within the organic churches that he oversees.[6] A group of three meets together weekly for the sake of personal conversations about their life and their walk in Christ. It can grow to four but no bigger. And once it does grow to four, the members of the group look to include two others and create two groups of three.

John Wesley understood the importance of spiritual formation and conversations more than anyone. He developed bands of three or four, which were sub-groupings of his small groups. In the bands, they would deal with questions about how they lived their lives, challenging one another to move away from a life shaped by the larger culture and embrace love.[7]

A similar approach is promoted in the work of Greg Ogden. People are empowered to have conversations in groups of three or four, working through a book. Ogden developed the book *Discipleship Essentials* for this purpose. They meet for six to nine months together. Afterwards, they encourage each person to connect with three others and repeat the process.[8] The Spirit of God is in the midst of our dialogue, and this is the way that God shaped us for mission.

Spiritual Formation of Leaders

God refers to the people of God as "saints," that is holy or set apart for him, and this identity is to shape how we think about leadership. Think of it this way: to be holy is a bit like those special dishes that were passed down to your mom that you only used once a year at Christmas. They were distinct from the everyday. They were treated with special care. God's church, God's people, are his group of saints, God's advertisement to the world.

Of course we don't look like saints. And by the way, neither did the people in churches during the first century, but Paul addressed them as "God's holy ones" nonetheless.

However, we live with the myth that the success of the church depends upon heroic leadership. Since we are far from looking like saints, the clarion call to heroic Christianity, to zealous discipleship, and to radical mission looks so appealing to serious Christians. Being that the average church is so average, we feel compelled to make sure that someone does something about that.

Leading flourishing community is about embracing our identity as saints whether we look like it or not. The way we do this is to simply walk the path with Jesus taking the next step along the way by the presence of the Spirit. It's not about great leaps of faith, wild acts of love, or renegade efforts against the status quo. It's not about being a spectacle. It's about making space for the Spirit to help us walk the next step in the presence of Jesus.

Heroic faith calls for success and triumph on the journey. It leaves no room for failure because heroes can't fail; they have to be the ones who make things work. Yet if there is anything I've learned on this journey, it is that the failures along the way teach us more than the successes. Life involves suffering. It means hitting walls and falling down. We so often talk about getting up every time we fall, but what about when we just don't have it in us to get up again?

We like to talk about leadership successes, but we don't talk so much about the difficulties, the failures, or when doubt or fear overwhelm us. We have bought into a triumphal view of God's kingdom that assumes God works through leaders more when they are on the mountain than when they are in the "valley of the shadow of death." However, it's in the valleys where God shapes us in ways that are not possible on the mountain tops. In the valleys, God shapes our "who-ness" so that we live into our sainthood and we are broken from our need to be heroic.

There are some leadership lessons that we can only learn through the school of hard knocks. Honestly, I wish this weren't the case. I had much rather learn the right way to lead—whether it's a small group, a church, at work, or in my family—from a book or a sermon and simply avoid the personal struggle. However, God does not invite us into a rule-following contract. He does not expect us to follow the five steps to being a great Christian leader as some kind of external standard of heroic Christianity. That only puts the work of Christ back upon us, which is not, after all, the work of Christ. He invites us to learn to love him and others, and since there is no formula for love, we are invited on a journey to have love woven into our being. This requires the work of the Spirit.

Learning to love like this will break us. There is just no other way because following Jesus involves serving others. As we serve, we begin to see that the needs are too big and our weaknesses are too great. Heroism turns serving others into a way that "I" get the attention, which is not love. Zealotry stirs up energy that I produce something for another. Again, that's about me not the other. And radical service tries to stand out against the status quo. Yet again, that puts me at the center of attention. Such an attitude might cause us to feel like we are rising above the norm of failure, but the facade can only carry us so far. Our most heroic efforts will eventually cause us to beat against the rocks of the needs in the world, where instead of the rocks breaking, we are broken.

We don't like this. We try to avoid it. We work harder and we search for alternative strategies. But eventually reality sets in. Brokenness comes.

We are not heroes. We are simply saints.

When we come to the end of ourselves, we have a choice between three options. We can be broken apart, which means that our pain controls us and usually spills out on others at their harm. We can be broken but bandaged, which means we cover up the pain while pressing on, trying to rise above. Or we can be broken open. We can embrace our brokenness and allow God to create a new future out of it. This third option is the only way to embrace our identity as saints.

Leaders need basic practices that will help them flourish in their leadership in a way that depends upon their identity as saints. This is why I wrote *Leading Small Groups in the Way of Jesus*. The eight practices I identify there provide a path that any leader can embrace and move forward in Jesus' way.

21

How Will You Support Groups So They Flourish? Part 1

Priority: Establish the Hidden Support Systems

Grouping your church in the way of Jesus is not simply founded upon doing obvious, overt things that promote effective groups. The stories of *Relational Re-vision* and *Missional Re-creation* are, at least in part, manifestations of support systems that operate beneath the surface. The tangible measurables come in the form of the life within groups. However, that which is tangible is a product of all kinds of hidden processes that support the life of those groups.

If we think about it, this is true of any aspect of life. A great basketball player does not simply play well because he chooses to. Behind the scenes, people and processes help that player perform at a high level. Or consider the mundane daily reality of purchasing vegetables from the grocery store. We see the end result of food on the shelf. However, without the various hidden systems that extend back to the farmer's ability to purchase the seeds to plant in the fields to the truck drivers who deliver the vegetables to the store, we could not pick up the produce and purchase it.

In chapter 17, we identified how groups are part of an open system that are integrated with other parts of the church, and we introduced how those other parts influence the development of groups, especially in the early stages. This priority focuses on specific support systems that must be developed to stimulate ongoing life in groups.

Pastoral Support System

Few people have sought to understand the role of a group pastor the way Karen Hurston has. Her father was a missionary in the 1960s and 1970s in South Korea. As such he served as the mentor to David Yonggi Cho who was the pastor of Yoido Full Gospel Church, which at its high point, had over 25,000 small groups.

Karen claims that the small groups were effective, in large part, at YFGC because the small group members and small group leaders received direct, hands-on personal support, prayer, and ministry from staff pastors. This ministry comes in the form of proactive, daily prayer visits in the homes and in the businesses of small group leaders and small group members. The staff pastors are constantly recruiting and mentoring new leaders by modeling ministry to those leaders who go with them on these prayer visits. Their ministry is aggressive, intentional, and planned. Above all, it is rooted in prayer. Pastor Cho required his staff pastors to spend three hours each day praying.

In contrast, the typical church staff pastor spends his or her time in the church offices, administrating programs, teaching in classrooms, and waiting for people to come to them for counseling. While the YFGC pastors focus on ministering to people by making five to seven visits per day, the typical American staff pastor is focused on organizing tasks, sitting in meetings, and enlisting people to do other tasks.

Now, one might argue that this is just not the way pastors pastor in America. However, the challenge Karen Hurston offers is worth consideration before we write it off. Consider the various practices proposed in chapter 13 and begin to weave them into your role.

In order to help pastors build these practices into the regular rhythms of pastoral leadership, there are three simple ministry tactics that can be adopted that will have huge impacts upon leadership development. The first Carl George calls a "structured debriefing interview." Also called "one-on-ones," they are monthly meetings between a small group pastor and each of his coaches or small group leaders. In these meetings, the pastor aims to discover how the coach or leader is doing personally, receive feedback about their ministry, problem solve, and pray together.

Karen Hurston trains pastors in a second ministry tactic that she calls "leader (or coach) of the day." Each day, the small group pastor will identify a specific leader and pray more intently for that leader. Then they will make a caring phone call, with no discussion of a task unless the leader initiates an issue. Even then, the focus on the phone conversation should lie not on the task or ministry issue but on ministry to the leader. The small group pastor should probe to find areas of concern so that he can pray for the leader and then continue to lift up that person throughout the day.

The third ministry tactic is practiced when pastors focus on their small group responsibilities on one or two days each week. On these days, they devote all their attention to the coaches, group leaders, and the groups, while on the other days, they focus on traditional ministry responsibilities.

The question about the pastoral oversight system is not merely about how such pastors spend their energy, but also about the span of care. A pastor whose sole responsibility is group oversight can effectively care for up to twenty-five groups on a forty-hour work week.

However, in most churches, this is not possible. A pastor will most likely be required to spend his or her time on other endeavors. For instance, if a full-time pastor is charged with the task of being the small groups point person (as outlined in chapter 13), he or she may only be able to give fifty percent of their time to pastoring groups. Or, in the case of most churches which are less than three hundred, the groups point person may serve in a part-time role. Therefore, if pastor works twenty hours per week and half of his energy is spent on strategic development, he has ten hours to serve as a pastor for groups. This would mean he could effectively oversee up to ten to twelve groups.

The constraints that churches often face means that pastors often must oversee more than twenty-five groups in forty-hour work week. This is simply one of the realities pastors must face. However, we must also recognize that when pastors are required to work with these constraints, they will be forced to focus on reacting to problems instead of pastoring according to the practices proposed in chapter 13. The results will be more programmatic in nature. Flourishing groups that produce the organic fruit of community and mission will arise from groups led by self-initiating, Spirit-led individuals. However, in most cases, the results will depend upon the program that has been developed. Flourishing groups are the result of life-on-life investment that is far less programmatic. Therefore, if pastors are required to care for more than twenty-five groups for every forty hours of work, then primarily focus on the connecting groups introduced in chapter 18. A pastor that is focused on supporting the life of organic groups that is more experimental (chapter 19) can do so on a smaller scale, but the fruit will be richer. This is directly related to the role of a coach.

A Coaching Strategy System

As more than fifteen groups are developed, a church needs to think about how the groups will be organized and networked. While there is a great deal of creativity as to how churches organize group oversight, there are three basic structures that guide most of the creativity.

Five by Five (5x5)

In the structure, a coach oversees five group leaders and a staff pastor oversees up to five coaches. Therefore, a full-time staff pastor would oversee up to twenty-five groups. In larger churches, another level is added, sometimes called a district pastor. This person would oversee up to five staff pastors or 125 groups.

Groups of 12

Most churches will not adopt this structure as a whole, but I include it here to illustrate a prominent oversight system. The International Charismatic Mission in Bogotá, Colombia developed this structure. It is called "Groups of 12" because the goal of each coach—called a G-12 leader—is to develop twelve small group leaders. When this goal has been reached, this coach then reports to an overseer—usually a staff pastor—who has developed a network of twelve coaches. Therefore, a coach (G-12 leader) would oversee up to twelve groups or 144 people and a pastor up to 144 groups or 1,728 people.

Groups of 12 and 3

This structure is an organic combination of both the 5x5 and the Groups of 12 models. In this structure, the volunteer coach would develop three small group leaders, while reporting to a staff pastor who oversees up to 12 coaches. This structure does not fixate upon numbers the way the G-12 model dictates. If a person has the capacity to coach more than three groups, then they are freed to do so.

Oversight System Questions to Consider:

To think through the kind of oversight system that might fit your church consider the following questions:

- How many group leaders does the volunteer coach oversee? In the G-12 model, the coach will mentor up to 12 small group leaders. In the 5x5, he will mentor up to five. In the G-12.3, three is the goal. The principle: raise up coaches who have experience leading groups and allow them to coach as many groups (up to 12) as they have the time and skills to coach. The more groups the coach oversees, the greater the commitment and time will be required. Therefore, in busier metropolitan cultures, it is wise to limit the number that a volunteer coach would oversee to no more than five.
- How often do they meet in coaching huddles? Frequency of coaching huddles varies from once per week to once per quarter. The pure G-12 model requires the coach to meet with his 12 leaders every week to model what they should do in their small groups that week. In other models, the frequency is not fixed. The most effective models meet at least once per month. The principle: Discover what your people need. Leaders that require lots of hands-on mentoring will appreciate weekly meetings.
- Does the coach continue to lead a small group? This is a distinc-

tive of the G-12 model. The G-12 leader, who plays the coaching role, also continues to lead a group. In the 5x5 model, coaches typically hand their groups over to new leaders. In other models, both options are viable. The principle: Talk with each leader and ask them what they want to do. Many effective small group leaders have been promoted to the role of coach and become frustrated because they enjoyed leading a group. Good leaders are often able to lead a group while coaching two or three others.

- How many coaches does the small group pastor oversee? The number of coaches directly under a small group pastor is a key differential between the various models. The 5x5 model dictates that the small group pastor oversees up to five coaches (up to 25 small groups). In the G-12, the small group pastor will oversee up to twelve coaches (up to 144 small groups). In the G-12.3 model, the pastor for small groups oversees no more than 12 coaches and 50 groups. Other creative models have various numbers between five and twelve coaches under the small group pastors (See Joel Comiskey's book *From 12 to 3*).

- How do the groups multiply? Traditionally, the 5x5 model embraces the split approach where 14 people divide into two groups of seven. The G-12 model practices small group planting, a process where one small group member is launched out to start a new group, leaving the old group intact. The reality is that there are many ways to multiply a group. Three people can launch out to plant a new group. The old leader might start a new group, handing off the old group to an apprentice. Two groups might work together to start a third. All of these are used in the different oversight strategies.

- Are groups homogeneous or heterogeneous? For churches that follow the G-12 model, groups are organized homogeneously (by gender or age). In most 5x5 churches, the groups are heterogeneous family groups. But there are also many churches using the G-12 model to oversee heterogeneous family groups, and the same is also true for the 5x5 model. Some churches have a mixture of both.

- Are groups organized geographically or by affinity? It has been assumed that the 5x5 model is the geographic model and the G-12
  model is the affinity-based model. While this is often the case, it is
  false to assume these connections as a basic principle. Many 5x5
  churches have groups based around affinity, such as youth small
  groups, groups that meet at lunch breaks, or men's and women's
  groups. In the same way, many G-12 churches organize their
  small groups around geography. Once again, in some churches,
  the small groups are organized around either type, depending on
  the passion of the small group leader.

Organic Development of an Oversight Model

Most pastors would love to have a prescribed model that works in
all situations. To have a clearly articulated destination, a final product
directly from the hand of God would be most comforting. However, no
such model is given in the New Testament. Instead, the Bible only lays
out principles that elders (coaches) and pastors are to follow. The Bible
seems to emphasize the journey more than the final destination.

The popular small group oversight models were not predetermined
structures that pastors received from God in a vacuum. They arose
through the journey of trial and error, through following God's leading
in the messiness of ministry. In such organic development found on this
journey, God shapes his people into the Bride he desires. You can and
should learn lessons from these models; you don't have to recreate the
wheel. But you cannot short-circuit the journey and arrive at a perfect
oversight model without going through the process of following God to
see what kind of model he wants to create in your church.

Use these questions as guideposts on your journey. See what kind
of oversight structure is developing in your church, one that works in
your culture at this time. It will share characteristics of other models,
but as it organically develops, it will possess unique traits that uniquely
fit your context.

New Leader Training System

Two parts comprise the equipping of small group leaders. First, potential leaders require basic training in the technical aspects of leading a group. These topics include what a small group is, how to facilitate a meeting, how to care for people, how to reach out to non believers, and how to raise up and mentor future leaders. Small group leaders do not have the time or qualifications to train their interns or apprentices in these techniques; therefore an experienced pastor should facilitate this training through a course or in a retreat setting. When a person completes small group leader training, it is the equivalent of graduating from the eighth grade. Eighth grade graduates are usually not ready to work. They are ready to go to high school.

High school in this case is mentoring from a small group leader, the second piece of small group leader equipping. As future leaders are mentored, they are released to do more and more ministry in the group. This process allows the future small group leaders to practice what they learned in training with someone who can back them up if they do it wrong. It also continues the learning process, as the small group leader serves as a spiritual mentor and guide to help the future leader enter into and discover what God is doing in their life. Small groups depend upon relationships. Equipping small group leaders is no different. *Leading Small Groups in the Way of Jesus* sets an introductory process to set new leaders on the right track.

Group Multiplication System

Group multiplication comes in many forms; there is no one right way to do it. The best approach is to listen to what God is doing in the groups and then develop a multiplication strategy from there. Groups seem to struggle when a predetermined form of multiplication is forced upon them. Here are five multiplication options that have proven effective:

New Leader Launch. In this strategy, the old leader remains with most of the small group members and the new leader launches a new group with a few other small group members. This approach is advantageous because it is vision driven. The small group members that start the new group feel called to do so, not forced to do so. This strategy also keeps the core of the old group in tact, thereby retaining a sense of community.

New Leader Plant. In this strategy, a new leader recruits three or four people who are not part of the original group to start a new group. This is a very exciting approach to launching groups. The greatest strength of this strategy is that it keeps the original small group in tact, while at the same time sending out those who are ready to lead. It seems to work best after the small group system is developed and more people understand the kind of ministry that makes small groups work.

Old Leader Launch. In this approach, the leader of the original small group launches a new group with two or three small group members and gives the original group to an intern, who is now a new leader. This strategy allows exceptional leaders who like to start new things to do what they like to do. It also helps a novice leader get a strong start with an established group.

Organic Multiplication. In this approach, the new leader takes half of the group and the old leader takes half of the group. For many, this experience feels more like group "division" than group "multiplication. This is the downside. The upside for this approach is very high. It makes room in both groups for growth, whereas the other strategies only make room in one group. It provides the opportunity to start two new groups. This can be very exciting for group members because the emphasis is not on the multiplication of one group, but the birth of two new groups.

Group Reorganization. Reorganization comes in many forms. Two groups can work together to start a new group. Three groups might become five groups. A small group leader might step down for a season and a new leader step up.

Group leaders need to know the multiplication strategies that best fit the church and specific resources to facilitate that strategy.

Children's Group System

One time, I led a group with 12 kids. At times it was frustrating, but the adults knew a few secrets about children and ministry. The group had shifted its paradigm so that the adults could love and include the children instead of viewing them as nuisances. Before small groups can develop strategies to incorporate children, they must begin to shift their views regarding ministry and children. If these views do not change, the new strategies will prove frustrating. Let's explore a few of them:

Children are part of small group life, not an impediment to it.

The small group leaders who confess that the children have been an interference to small group meetings are being honest. Children are children and they don't always understand that adults want their meetings to be orderly. A baby cries when someone begins to share a deep need. A toddler spills juice on the carpet, disrupting the post-meeting conversation. Someone has to make plans every week for the time when the kids break off to minister to one another.

Children interfere only if the group expects to have a dignified and uneventful small group meeting experience every week. But such expectations are divorced from the realities of life. The small group meeting is not like a Sunday worship service, nor is it like a board meeting. It deals with real life, and children are a part of that real life. Children should not be entertained so that the adults can have a sterile experience without any interference.

True learning focuses on values, not just knowledge.

Much of children's ministry focuses on teaching cognitive facts about the Bible. Children need more than information; they need a place to copy or imitate others who are living for God. If children are left to learn about Jesus from age-graded curriculum, they will be deprived of the privilege of learning from adult models. When they have adult models, "children have the benefit and privilege of an extended 'family,' of seeing others who have strengths that their parents do not have. They can copy whatever they see going on, because their parents are doing it and because they see others too!"[1] Children learn from models by watching others, questioning the things that trouble them, receiving instruction, and laughing with others.

Children are ministers of the present, not just ministers of the future.

Most adults assume that God is preparing the children for use when they become adults. While this is partially true, it does not relegate children to a secondary role of ministry in the church. The Holy Spirit wants to move through every member of the church today. The prophet Joel said, "Your sons and daughters will prophesy." This does not mean that they have to wait until they are 21 to do so. The best people to reach out to elementary-aged students are elementary-aged Christians. They see each other every day at recess, at lunch, and in the classroom. The church doesn't equip the children to minister because it has limited its children's ministry to ministering to the children, rather than showing them how to minister.

On a practical level, there are specific steps to take to support groups that have children participating. Group members need to understand the three basic principles stated above. In addition, group leaders need a basic structure for how children will be involved. For instance, in many cases, the kids join in the ice breaker and the worship time but then they break off into their own Bible discussion and ministry time. The way this is organized will be a part of the system provided to the group leaders. See the resource provided at the end of this chapter.

Counseling Support System

When people feel safe in groups, they begin to open up about their pain. With that personal issues often come to light which are beyond the ability of the group to address. I've seen groups slowly die because marital problems were confessed and the group tried to rally around the hurting couple because their compassion drove them to try and fix the situation. Sharing a history of abuse, chronic sin, or mental illness can take over the group and stall it out. The reality is that there are many issues that are beyond the ability of the leader or the group to address. The group can be a support to these hurting individuals, but providing other resources is needed.

Administration System

The following introduces a few organizational issues that must be addressed:

A way to track small group members

When a church has fewer than 10 groups, tracking members can be accomplished by memory or on paper, but as the groups continue to grow and multiply, keeping up with which groups contain which people will prove increasingly difficult. Such a tracking system should record small group membership, attendance, and the level of equipping each person receives. It is even possible to merge this information with donation records so that all information is integrated. Web-based and local computerized tools have been specifically designed to help small group-based churches develop such a database.

An annual calendar of events

Such calendars should be created and published well in advance so that people will be able to plan their activities. This calendar usually includes dates for small group leader training, group member retreats, monthly small group leader meetings, and any other activities planned by the church.

Church budget

The budget should address the projected personnel requirements, needed training materials, and a special money pool for supporting small group leaders. This discretionary pool should fund special gifts for small group leaders, an annual appreciation banquet, and all the materials to train new small group leaders. Small group leaders are front-line ministers and the church should support them by blessing them in this way.

Prayer System

More than anything, prayer is central to flourishing community. Prayer is our means for communing with the Father, Son, and Spirit. Prayer is the language of the church. It is the ultimate activity that determines whether our churches will enter into God's relational kingdom. Unless we speak the language of the kingdom, how will kingdom life enter into his people?

The church can only be the church as it prays. It is more than a ministerial program of the church. The prayer life of the church in God's kingdom cannot be promoted by a prayer department or by hiring a prayer pastor, although these activities are not bad in and of themselves. If we see prayer as a ministry alongside all the other ministries of the church, how will those other ministries operate? If prayer is the job of the prayer pastor and her team, then how will the small group leader lead? How will the coach invest life into her small group leaders? How will the small group overseer establish a life-giving small-group system? If we don't pray, then trying to do all the other stuff that produces relational kingdom living will fall short of the goal.

Chapter 23 addresses how prayer can be fostered on five levels within the group system. These include the personal, group, networks of groups, church-wide, and staff.

System for Removing Anchors

Pastoral oversight, coaching, counseling support, new leader training, children, administration, and prayer are a few of the key systems that help support the life in groups. In every local congregation, there will be unique systems that either hinder or promote healthy group life. Things like exorbitant debt, dated buildings, ill-equipped staff, and other issues could impact the hidden systems. Some of these will serve as systemic anchors that keep groups from moving forward.

Systemic anchors can be illustrated with a rubber band being stretched between two fingers. The right finger represents the way of Jesus; the left represents the old systems of doing church. As groups are developed, the right finger has been stretching the rubber band away from the left, but as long as the left finger remains anchored, the two fingers will remain in tension. This is because the old ways of doing church are rooted in an established system, while the new way has not existed long enough to put down roots.

Kurt Lewin developed a planning and implementation tool called force-field analysis that helps a church evaluate the systems that hinder group development and those that promote it. The goal of force-field analysis is to remove or minimize the hindering forces (the old systemic anchors) to change and maximize the propelling forces. Here is the process for performing a force-field analysis. After picking an issue that you want to improve, take a blank piece of paper and place it horizontally.

- Draw a line down the middle of the page to signify the current location of the church.
- Draw a line down the right edge of the page to represent where you want to be.
- Draw arrows to the right of the center line pointing away from it to represent each force helping to move you toward your goal.
- Place arrows to the left of the center line pointing away from it to signify each force hindering your movement toward your goal.
- Identify the various systems pointed out in this chapter to determine what hinders group development and what promotes it.
- Make the length of the lines proportional to the strength of the helping and hindering forces.
- Develop a clear and simple strategy for removing or minimizing the hindering forces.

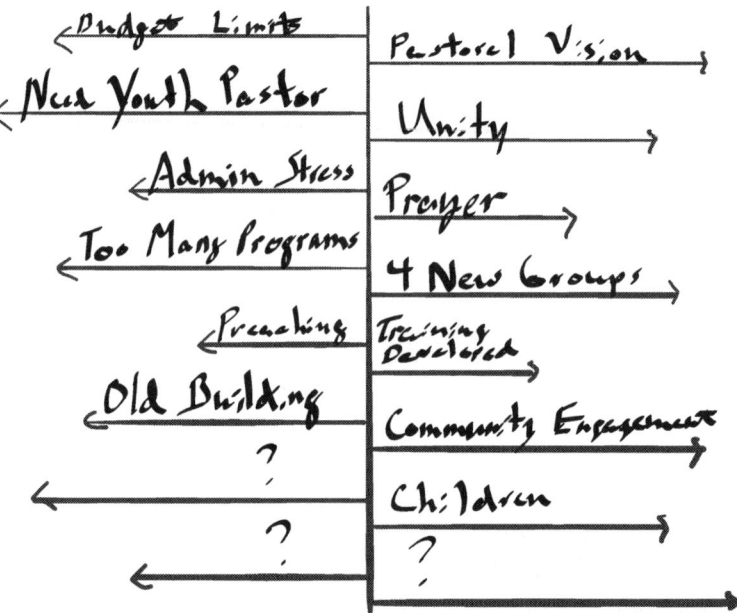

The method for dealing with these anchors will vary from problem to problem. Some of the challenges will call for technical solutions.

Others are adaptive in nature. (See chapter 5 on the difference.) This tool helps you to identify the challenges and how they act as anchors. Then you will be much more likely to deal with them.

System for Re-Anchoring Culture

As these anchors are cut away, there is no time to waste; the new culture must be re-anchored immediately. New behavioral norms and shared values must be reinforced and rewarded. Here are a few practical strategies to re-anchor the culture.

Expand. Expand groups, expand ministers, expand churches. God will reveal many ways he wants to lead the church into expansion.

Concentrate. Contrary to the practices of many churches, this is time to re-emphasize and concentrate on groups more than ever. The pastors and groups team cannot succumb to the temptation to focus on something else because the groups seem to be working so well.

Communicate. Church leaders must communicate the group vision regularly. This communication should come in written and public forms, but the most important form of communication is interpersonal. Group pastors and coaches must re-emphasize the group vision and the important role their group leaders play.

Celebrate. The pastoral team must provide specific ways to celebrate and reward those who have made the shift into group life. Ideas include a group banquet, rewarding group leaders for their service, and public praise that reveals how the groups have advanced.

Refine. At this point, the church leaders should refine materials and methods that they have copied from other churches. Writing training materials is especially important.

Communication System

One of the keys is the system that leaders develop to guide people from Connecting Community that is depending upon programmatic systems and into Missional Community that develops in organic ways. This is the topic of the next chapter.

22

How Will You Support Groups So They Flourish? Part 2

Priority: Establish the Hidden Support Systems

This chapter could have been included as a part of the previous one, however, this one topic is too important to get buried alongside the other points of that chapter. It merits its own chapter because most people who connect with your church will not have the ability to immediately see and understand what it means to live out the dream of Communion, Relating, and Engagement. They need to be brought along a journey so that they can change how they see what God is up to in your church and in small groups.

Leading People through the Stories

Throughout this book, I've been using the image of sailing as a metaphor for the organic, Spirit-led way of *Relational Re-vision* and *Missional Re-creation*. In contrast, a motor boat represents groups that live out *Personal Improvement* and *Lifestyle Adjustment*. One of the questions pastors and leaders must answer pertains to the process that a church adopts to help people re-imagine what it means to participate in the church, and thus make the shifts necessary in their lives to get involved in the next steps of group involvement. How will they board a motor boat and then move from a motor boat experience onto a sailing vessel? In other words, people needs ways to get connected in programmatic groups and then they need a clear pathway to move from that experience into God's missional community that sails with the winds of the Spirit.

For most, jumping straight into a small group that lives out the dream of Communion, Relating, and Engagement in such a way that members participate in the story of *Missional Re-creation* is a bit like attempting to board a large yacht and sail the open seas. *Relational Re-vision* and *Missional Re-creation* are so different from normal church life and our common life experience that the leap may never be attempted.

Experiencing the stories of *Personal Improvement* and *Lifestyle Adjustment* can be used to prepare people to move beyond the typical small group patterns. In other words, programmatic group experiences can prepare people for moving beyond small groups. Something like a 40-day campaign can provide environments to help people learn aspects of God's mission so that some will embrace the call to move beyond them.

Leading people through the stories is not about getting people to commit to a strategy. Leaders cannot announce a new vision of the four stories, expecting people to line up, sign up, and live up to the vision instantly. The four stories provide leaders with an interpretive grid for leading people from where they are today and into the next steps.

When we see the journey of leading people through the four stories, we create room for all four stories to exist within any one church. Actually, they are already happening because the stories are about how people live, not about their being a part of a program. We just have not organized our structures to facilitate movement through the stories.

The following diagram illustrates how strategies for all four stories can exist side-by-side in an established church. The horizontal triangle is wider on the left because there are more people who live out *Personal Improvement*. It gets smaller with movement toward the right because fewer people will count the cost to move into the stories of *Relational Re-vision* and *Missional Re-creation*. Also note that the triangle is open to the left, meaning that all are welcome to take this journey and go as far as they choose.

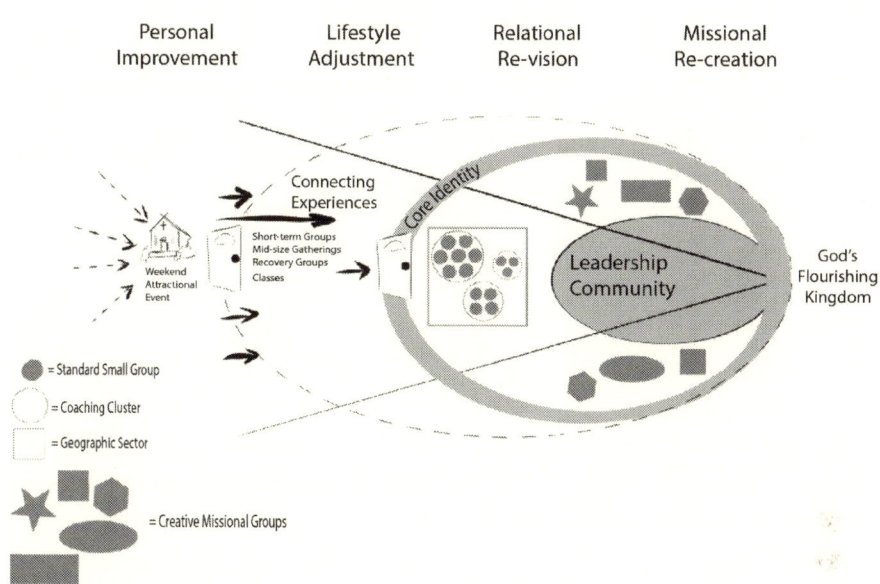

While there is not a one-to-one relationship between the various structures in this diagram and the four stories, there is a loose affiliation. *Personal Improvement* can be affiliated with the weekend services and the small group programs that are directly connected to and driven by those services, like 40-day church-wide campaigns.

The *Lifestyle Adjustment* story can be affiliated with various connecting strategies from semester groups, common small groups, discipleship classes, service opportunities, and even affinity-based recreation groups.

Relational Re-vision is depicted by the small circles where small communities are intentionally working together to learn to be missional while *Missional Re-creation* is depicted by the various other geometric shapes as they are more creative and trying to engage the context.

Examples of Journey Pathways

Example #1: A Church of 3000

A church that has been built upon the speaking gifts of a lead pastor is now trying to lead people into mission. The church has developed an extensive recovery and counseling ministry and has numerous ways for people to get connected. However, they want to make sure that they are challenging people to move beyond their typical programmatic forms of connection. The process that they have developed includes these five phases:

- Hear the call: This occurs through the weekend preaching and forty-day small groups campaigns that occur during the fall and spring to help people get connected.
- Recover: For those who have a specific felt-need to address, i.e. substance-addiction, divorce, etc., there are groups that meet weekly.
- Connect: For the connecting stage, people can either participate in various semester-based small groups or they can attend classes provided during the week at the church.
- Discover: At this stage, someone who wants to explore the difference of living out the Embrace phase, as opposed to traditional forms of Christianity, attends a series of classes that explains what it means to participate in a house church. The goal is to make sure that people who have been formed by established church patterns understand what they are committing to.
- Embrace: Those who enter into the home groups that live out this part of the vision commit to a specific set of practices to support this life together. Of course, those who enter faith in Christ through the home groups do not have to go through all the other phases. They are instead discipled organically by the members of the home groups that are living out the Embrace vision.

This process is simple enough to make the steps clear, while at the same time providing options for various ways to get connected and move forward on their journey.

Example #2: A church of 250
One church developed a simple four-step journey that can easily work in smaller churches:

- Envision: Through weekly worship and monthly church-wide "town meetings" people are given insight into what the church is called to be.
- Envelop: People gather in three-month groups based around various topics of study.
- Equip: "Equipping for Mission" classes prepare people for the ministry calling that God has uniquely created him or her to do.
- Engage: Mission groups are empowered to engage the neighborhood.

Example #3: A small organic church

Over the years, I have found various small organic churches that do a good job of helping people walk through the four stories, even though they themselves might not use this language. A summary of what I've observed looks like this:

- Relate: Most people begin participating in an organic church through a relationship. They are free to ask as many questions about the church with any leader or member of a group.
- Welcome: For those who want to go a little deeper, they are invited to a monthly Welcome Conversation, which meets in the home of one of the church leaders. This is a short ninety-minute meeting that gives a basic introduction to what the church is about.
- Learn: An introductory six-week class provides an opportunity for people to talk about their previous church experiences and how this is different from this new organic version.
- Participate: Most of the learning occurs through simple participation in group life. As this occurs, there are a series of discipleship resources to help people along the journey.

Organic churches do not need to develop all of the programs to walk people through the various stories; they can walk through those stories within the relationships in their small groups, house church meetings, and discipling relationships. However, they do need a clear process to help them get started on the right track.

Common Elements

Entry Points to Church Life

An established church might initially move people through the sto-ries in a linear fashion, assuming that people will almost always begin the journey through the Sunday service. As the number of groups that live out *Relational Re-vision* and *Missional Re-creation* grows, people will enter into the life of the church in all kinds of organic, unpredictable ways. Many churches today are being built from the beginning upon or-ganic life and therefore the points of entry into church life are as varied as the kinds of relationships that people have.

Introduction to Church

Whether in a programmatic or an organic church situation, there must be a doorway for people to be introduced to the life of the church. In a programmatic situation, this doorway might be something like a membership or introduction to church life class. (One of the most effec-tive is the Growth Track developed by Church of the Highlands. This is an introductory process which I help churches adapt and customize for their contexts.)

In an organic situation, it might be something informal between a house church leader and the person joining the group. The goal of this doorway is to introduce the journey and help people take initial steps.

At this point, it is crucial to communicate what your church is about and the long-term vision to equip people to move beyond the typical patterns of cultural Christianity. You don't want to water down the vision. However, at the same time, you want to validate the initial steps required to help people take the next step. The emphasis of the first door is the communication of the core identity of the church and the desire to equip people in the basics of doing relationships in a healthy way.

Connecting Experiences

On the other side of this door are the connecting experiences. Again, these can be either formal and programmed or they can be organic and highly relational. The goal of these connecting experiences is to provide opportunities for people to become awakened to a new reality, to discover a different way of living. They might hear about the vision as they pass through the first door, but they won't actually grasp this new reality without a new experience. (This is the focus of chapter 18.)

Identity Formation

At the second doorway, the goal is to help people discover the core identity of what you are becoming as a church. (Please note that I used the word "discover." I specifically did not say that people are taught the core identity of the church. Most churches don't need more information explaining theological nuances. Instead, what is needed is a shaping of our lives around the biblical story so that we can enter into an imagination of God's mission in the world.) It's vital to your success to help people see themselves in that story so they can envision what it means to participate in moving beyond church programs. This cannot be prescribed to people by communicating loads of information. Instead, it must be caught as people discover together what their core identity is as God's missional people.

At this point people need to enter into a "reshaping process" so that they understand what it means to move beyond typical patterns of cultural Christianity where they are merely consumers of spiritual goods and services. The content of identity formation is based in the practices of Communion, Relating, and Engagement. This is where a line is drawn in the sand and people see that moving ahead involves counting the cost, discipleship, spiritual formation, and self-sacrifice.

Missional Communities

Inside the Core Identity oval are various groups that are living the stories of either *Relational Re-vision* or *Missional Re-creation*. Such groups will come in two forms. First, there are the groups that appear on the surface to look like any other standard small group; however, they have moved beyond basing their group around the weekly programmatic meeting. They are flourishing as practices of Communion, Relating, and Engagement shape their life together.

The second form is found in groups that have morphed into creative patterns that are based in the life of their local contexts. Because their life is based in the practices of Communion, Relating, and Engagement, they can think "outside the box" and develop groups that fit the life of their neighborhoods. For instance, a group of shift workers might meet in the middle of the night at a breakfast diner. Ten ladies might walk together as a form of exercise three times per week. While they walk, they talk and they pray, and this leads to the Spirit empowering them to serve their neighbors together. While the form the group takes will vary, the core of the groups are shaped by the practices of Communion, Relating, and Engagement.

Leadership Community

The oval to the far right of the diagram represents those who are committed to be the spiritual leadership of the church. They include small group leaders, house church leaders, coaches, and pastoral staff. This is not merely a functional community. It is a spiritual community of leaders, both novices and the experienced, who are committed to practice a set of disciplines shaped by the way of Christ. Here, there might be more technical training involved like how to lead a small group, pastoral skills, or basic theology. But the development of leaders through practicing the disciplines of the faith shapes them to be the leaders that reflect the life of God revealed on the cross.

Conclusion

Today the church finds itself in a unique time. On the one hand, people expect the church to provide spiritual goods and services, as it has done in the past. On the other hand, people have lost respect for the church because it has only been a vendor of spiritual goods and services. It's as if the average person knows that the church is called to be more, to go beyond, but old expectations and habits have a way of keeping us tethered to the past.

We live in a time of searching for what it means to be the church in a new era, in a new context that cares little about what the church, as it is commonly practiced, has to say. This process of leading people through the four stories is a way to help people re-imagine how life in God can be, and therefore they can reimagine what the church can be. Even more, it is a way of immersing people in the reality that God is at work in the world and through the church. It's far more than simply placing people into groups and expecting them to flourish. It's about guiding them into a new reality of knowing God, of participating in God's story, and of loving one another. When we see this, our story changes.

23

How Will Groups Impact the World?

> *Priority: Invest in the Hidden, Indirect Work of the Spirit*

Much energy is spent on how to get groups started in a church that has a regular flow of new people attending worship services. Some energy is spent on how to get groups going in established churches that don't have many new people. However, significantly less is invested in empowering groups to organically influence the world around them and thereby foster flourishing life by participating in God's mission in the world. In other words, how do groups get involved in what God is doing in neighborhoods, with friends and family members, and in the workplace? The answers to this question aim to advance both the programmatic groups developed in chapter 18 along with the organic experiments suggested in chapter 19.

The Unexpected Impact

Before we talk about specific ways that groups can impact the world, it is important to articulate an imagination about impact that is rooted in the revelation of God in Christ. This will curtail futile attempts to change the world through worldly means.

The Old Testament stories speak of how the Israelites were trying to copy the cultural patterns of the reputable nations of their period. The most obvious example of this is found in 1 Samuel when the Israelites asked for a king so that they could be like other nations. They wanted the privilege, the possessions, and the power that they observed in Egypt, Assyria, and Babylon. King Solomon embodied the pursuit of these three things as he led Israel to its apex of glory as defined by the standards of the world.

The idols of privilege, possessions, and power continue to shape life in our neighborhoods. When we idolize privilege, we cut off the weak, the widow, the orphans, and the sick. When we idolize possessions, we work too much and live in fear of losing what we have amassed. When we idolize power, we run over others, fight for ourselves, and treat one another with violence and manipulation. It's the story of how one is against the other, one group over another, trying to secure a position above others.

The church can try to impact the world through this same pursuit of privilege, possessions, and power. This is a form of syncretism, where the gospel is mixed with cultural patterns that are inherently antithetical to the nature of who God is. For instance, the church has a long history of adopting worldly patterns with the intention of promoting the gospel. One of the most extreme was the practice of forcing people to convert to Christianity with the threat of violent death. But today, the syncretism is much more subtle. Privilege, possessions, and power are used to make good things happen in the world. They aim to produce overt results that substantiate the truthfulness of the gospel on the terms set up by the world.

As an alternative, the gospel impacts the world in a way that is illustrated by the story of Jesus washing the feet of the disciples (John 12). Instead of coming with domination over others that produces obvious results, he took on the role of a servant who washed the feet of the disciples. On the surface, washing feet seems insignificant on the scale of world history. How does this produce conversions, justice for the poor, racial reconciliation, church planting, and care of creation? These are the kinds of things that get celebrated at annual denominational meetings. One could argue that Jesus' efforts would have been more effective if he had had a consultant to help him develop a strategic plan.

What if the consultant advises to focus on the hidden work of Christ because God changes the world by washing feet? This is why Paul said that the cross appears scandalous and foolish (1 Corinthians 1:23). Every culture in history has expected their god to work through overt, visible acts that directly shift the course of history. The cross reveals how God acts indirectly. God works to bring about conversations, justice for the poor, inclusion of the outcast, healing of the sick, deliverance of the demonized, equipping of new Christians, formation of Christian leaders through the hidden work of the Spirit. This is rooted in the theological claim that the cross is the climax of God's work, and if this is the case, then Jesus did not change the world through direct force, but by the indirect act of allowing his enemies to crucify him. This is the mystery of foolishness and the hiddenness of truth beneath the scandal. It does not look like it will have an impact on the surface, but the reality is that it changes everything.

If we don't identify this distinction, it is too easy to ignore the cross by laying a Gospel-sounding message on top of the ways of our dominant culture. We inform people about the basic tenants of the faith, and we tell people how to live morally-upright lives. We must also manifest a way of life that confronts the ways of our secular, normal, day-to-day activities.

We do this by offering a foot-washing, cross-shaped alternative. Instead of fighting for privilege where we try to climb to the top, we offer hospitality where we use our time to invest in others. Instead of power where we try to wield our influence, we offer forgiveness where we release others from any debt owed because of wrongs done. Instead of the pursuit of possessions, we offer generosity where what we have is used to bless others. Hospitality, forgiveness, and generosity—these don't seem to have much significance, but when we live them, they free us to participate in God's world-changing mission.

Groups do this through unexpected, even hidden patterns of life together that may or may not seem—on the surface—to have that much potential to impact the world. The five patterns of impact introduced here are practical ways to enter into the cross-shaped way of having an impact. Instead of finding a cause to attack or a world to save, we create space in our life as a group so we can see what God is up to and move in that direction. We change the world through beneath the surface actions instead of trying to fix others or the world's patterns directly.

Pattern #1: Love One Another

We embody this foot-washing pattern of impacting the world through our love for one another. After Jesus washed the disciples feet, he told them: "A new command I give you: Love one another. As I have loved you, so you must love one another. By this everyone will know that you are my disciples, if you love one another" (John 13:34-35). The world is changed by the gospel as the church embodies a way of life that sets an example of hospitality, forgiveness, and generosity.

This is the reason that Jesus sent the disciples out two-by-two in Luke chapter ten and why Paul traveled with a team to plant churches. The point was not merely to announce the message of the cross. It was first to manifest Jesus' kingdom so that people might see a different way of living. The way that groups pray and worship together, and the way that groups love and sacrifice are not internal activities that make a church healthy. They are acts of witness to God because it shows the world that there is another way to live that is not filled with the pursuit of privilege, possessions, and power.

The patterns of life exhibited by Jesus's followers would have expressed the truthfulness of the cross. The New Testament scholar Rita Finger writes, "Many neighbors would have overheard activity around a communal meal in a small room or an open courtyard that was characterized by great joy (singing? laughter?). In the midst of the urban chaos and misery that characterized every ancient Mediterranean city, such a gathering must have sounded inviting indeed."[1]

We change the world not because individual Christians decide to make something happen, but because groups of Christians enter into the love of God for one another. As such, the church becomes a sign that there is an alternative in the midst of the chaos, loneliness, and secularity that dominates common life.

Practically, one of the most important elements to living out this pattern is the art of learning to waste time with one another. We have cluttered souls because our lives are so over saturated that we do not have time to love one another. (This was discussed in chapter 20 under the heading of "simplicity.")

Pattern #2: Pay Attention to God's Work

The Scriptures make it clear that God gets involved in the mundane activities of life in creation. In the narratives of the Old Testament, the Incarnation of Jesus, and the churches of Acts, God is known through verbs. The acts of God reveal the adjectives about God. God is faithful because he acts faithfully. Before we know how to talk about God's character, we read of and now see God's assertive action.

Too often, the church has assumed that impacting the world is first the work of the church itself, that it is up to the church to adopt specific activities in order to accomplish God's work. It's as if the church feels the pressure to act as if God is not present, does not speak, and cannot work in our midst. When this occurs, the church becomes the center of the message.

However, if God is at work in our world as revealed in the Scriptures, groups must learn to read what the Spirit is doing by paying attention to the whispers and hidden cues. It can be seen in a conversation with a neighbor or co-worker, by trying to understand the neighborhoods in which we live, and by taking the time to listen deeply to the needs that God wants to address.

Paying attention to what God is doing is similar to reading a good novel. The story unfolds. The reader does not make it happen. Good readers enter into the story and, in some ways, become part of that story. This is what we do when we attend to the world around us. We observe, listen, and ask questions. We give ourselves time to let everything sink in.

In *Cultivating Community in the Way of Jesus*, I introduce how to use a tic-tac-toe diagram to help groups identify and pray for their neighbors and those in their networks. A few group members might even host a party for inviting a few people.

Another action that can train us to pay attention is community exegesis, which was introduced in chapter 15.

On a simplified and less organized level, group members can use the power of a shared meal or meeting for coffee to embrace the stranger. The entire small group need not be involved, possibly only a couple or a single member from the group.

As groups do this, they are simply listening to what God is already doing in their neighbors, friends, co-workers, and family members. We must listen to the needs that are being expressed, which could be as simple as a wife needing help with her chronically-ill husband or to something as complex as racial tension in a specific part of town.

Pattern #3: Pray

There is an invisible war that permeates how God is at work in the world. Paul wrote, "For our struggle is not against flesh and blood, but against the rulers, against the authorities, against the powers of this dark world and against the spiritual forces of evil in the heavenly realms. ... And pray in the Spirit on all occasions with all kinds of prayers and requests. With this in mind, be alert and always keep on praying for all the Lord's people" (Ephesians 6:12;18).

We can implement all of the right elements to move people into groups, but if we miss the reality of the spiritual war, we will fall short of flourishing. Imagine a haze that infiltrates everything you do to lead people into groups, and it grows darker and heavier the more people are released into God's mission. If we don't see this haze, we will remain under its control and fail to do things to combat it.

Jesus fought against evil in a way that demonstrates that our world is caught in the middle between God's love and Satan's lies. The apostle Paul speaks about this in terms of "principalities and powers of the air" who shape the way we do life, the patterns of our thinking, and the systems of relating to others.

Satan and his minions love it when we deny or minimize their existence. When you go to a church in Africa and people make a first-time commitment to Christ, there are often manifestations of demonic possession that make it clear a spiritual war exists. Most of us in the West don't encounter such manifestations. Instead, the lies of Satan are revealed in much more subtle ways—ways that have become so commonplace to the Western way of life that it just seems normal. Think about ways that small groups have been undercut because people started rumors about fellow members or they cast judgment on other group members because of personal struggles. Disunity, lack of trust, and an unwillingness to work through relational difficulties disempower churches.

A part of this warfare includes the spiritual strongholds that keep individuals bound. Paul wrote, "The weapons we fight with are not the weapons of the world. On the contrary, they have divine power to demolish strongholds. We demolish arguments and every pretension that sets itself up against the knowledge of God, and we take captive every thought to make it obedient to Christ" (2 Corinthians 10:4-5). You might not use this kind of language, but you have experienced its reality. You've known people who are entrapped by "strongholds in their minds" (lies) that keep them in bondage. These could be rooted in unforgiveness toward someone from the past or believing a lie that an authority figure told them when they were a child. A middle-aged woman in our church shared how one of her elementary teachers told her that she wouldn't amount to anything because of her learning disability. She carried this lie around for over forty years.

These lies, if not confronted and repented of, will control us and keep us from the flourishing life that God has for us and for the world around us. If we walk around our neighborhoods and do an exegesis, we can see the "strongholds" that keep people in bondage, the lies that shape their daily living. We do not fight these things through direct confrontation. That would be "weapons of the world." Instead, we pray and we "take every thought captive."

Prayer changes things. Prayer releases those in small groups to flourish, and it empowers them to engage their community with the gospel. This is often missed in current conversations about small groups, even though it was central to their development twenty years ago. Churches around the world that were known for their ever-expanding network of groups were just as well-known for their extensive investment in prayer. Some may have ignored this because most of those early proponents of groups were charismatic, but there is something about the fact that prayer was so essential, no matter the tradition. Senior pastors of these churches were known to pray for hours per day. Small group pastors had a one-hour block built into their daily schedule to pray for their groups. One pastor told me how she regularly organized prayer events for all the people in groups under her care. For instance, they would rent a bus and drive through the city praying for specific needs. They also trained groups to prayer walk their neighborhoods.

This is illustrated by the following observations by Ralph W. Neighbour Jr. regarding early model churches that were built upon small group life. He observed how prayer is fostered on five levels:[2]

1. Personal Prayer: In his discipleship resources and teachings, he trains group members to enter daily into what he called a "Listening Room." He encourages people to keep a journal to record impressions and thoughts which flow from God's throne during those times. In the Listening Room, group members learn to hear from God and receive his guidance.

The Listening Room experience differs from the traditional "Quiet Time." Neighbour teaches that members' time with God is not a private experience that only pertains to personal needs. The awareness of other group members while in the Listening Room fosters intercession and hearing God's voice for ways to encourage one another.

2. Group Prayer: In the group meeting, prayer becomes a vital part of the time of Worship. In addition, the Word portion of the meeting is facilitated with space to pray for one another. Often members surround an individual who needs God to work, calling out for physical healing or for God to address a serious problem. During the Witness times of group meetings, members share about those they are ministering to in everyday life so that they can support one another as they listen to God about how to serve co-workers, family members, friends and neighbors.

3. Network Prayer: Neighbour also emphasizes how multiple groups within a network under the care of a coach or a pastor can gather together on a regular basis (perhaps every six weeks) for a half-night of prayer. The sessions begin with worship, testimonies from groups or members about what God has done through prayers for healings, deliverances, etc. Then people can get in groups of two or three and pray over a specific area as they walk through the neighborhood. Usually worship is interspersed throughout the evening.

4. Church-wide Prayer: Gathering all the groups from the church for prayer is also vital. For example, Neighbour writes about some churches that call members together on Friday nights for a half-night of prayer. He recounts how one church holds a full hour of prayer during their worship services about once every three months. The pattern used included ten minutes each for worship, prayer for the nation, prayer for the church, prayer for one's family needs, prayer for the unsaved, and prayer for one's own needs.

5. Staff Prayer: Neighbour explains how one church gives each staff member three days of prayer leave every three months. A small stipend is given toward the rental of a hotel room, and staff members go in pairs for this time of quiet meditation and prayer. While most of the time is spent alone, there are seasons of prayer and sharing between the two during meals.

The staff in one church builds prayer into their regular schedule in this way: On the first Tuesday of each month, the employees of the church pray from 8 a.m. to 1 p.m. Part of this time is spent praying individually, another part as an office staff event, and finally all the staff gather for worship and prayer warfare. On the other Tuesdays, the entire staff prays for two hours. Other work days begin with an hour of prayer within each department. Thus, the staff is saturated with prayer events that were done on "company time."

Developing prayer on these five levels illustrates how these early experiments began and have continued to build groups on union with God and not just doing things for God. After all, our ultimate goal is knowing and loving God, and as we do this in prayer, doors are opened for the church to participate in God's work.

Pattern #4: Practice Hospitality

God is the great neighbor. Being Father, Son, and Spirit, God is what some theologians call "roomy," having enough room in his triune love for every neighbor. God does not need to dominate because God is welcoming. God is not threatened by difference, because God finds difference intriguing. God is not limited by others, because God has unlimited love for others.

While we live as strangers to our neighbors, we are instructed to "offer hospitality to one another without grumbling" (1 Peter 4:9). The Greek word for hospitality is *philoxenia*, which means love of strangers. The word *xenia* has a dual meaning, as it was used to identify both the stranger and the host, signifying that a host is just as much a stranger to the stranger as the stranger is to the host.

The love of the stranger is not a love which seeks to convert or change. Instead, it is one which receives people where they are. Our neighbors are not objects to be won over to a prescribed way of thinking. They are people loved by God. The art of hospitality allows others to enter our hearts without expectation of change. Henri Nouwen states, "Honest receptivity means inviting the stranger into our world on his or her terms, not on ours." When we say, 'You can be my guest if you believe what I believe, think the way I think and behave as I do,' we offer love under a condition or for a price. This leads easily to exploitation, making hospitality into a business."[3]

"By definition, hospitality involves some space into which people are welcomed, a place where unless the invitation is given, the stranger would not feel free to enter."[4] To embrace a stranger, the one who must take the first step is the host. The host is the one who must change, who must go out and draw in the stranger. Therefore, the only way hospitality works is if the group members change, opening their hearts to receive strangers as they are.

Receptivity is only one side of the coin of hospitality. Receiving the stranger does not mean one should abdicate what he believes, becoming neutral because of the fear of offending. In true hospitality, the host enters into dialogue with the stranger. Again, Nouwen steers us correctly: "When we want to be really hospitable we not only have to receive the strangers but also to confront them by an unambiguous presence, not hiding ourselves behind neutrality but showing our ideas, opinions and life style clearly and distinctly."[5]

There are two basic spaces for practicing hospitality. The first occurs when the group plays the host by inviting others to see the presence of God in their midst, offering people the opportunity to taste and see that the Lord is good. This often occurs in informal ways as the group demonstrates love in such a way that outsiders can tangibly see. In most cases, this occurs over meals. Hosting meals—something which taps into a life practice that all people must do, i.e., eating—creates a place for conversations, which leads to the opportunity to see where God might be at work. Of course, this also happens in small group meetings where people gather to talk about the Scriptures and pray.

The second occurs on the neutral ground of third places which have been previously mentioned. This involves God's people going out as guests and entering into the territory of their neighbors. This is illustrated by the sending out of the 72 by Jesus in Luke 10. In that story, Jesus' followers were sent out as guests who embodied the gospel on the turf of their neighbors. We enter into work, neighborhood events, coffee shops, bars, grocery stores, children's activities, schools, and community centers with the assumption that God is already at work there.

Once we enter as a guest, we listen. We don't go with answers, telling others how life and God works. Instead, we ask great life questions, and thus we make space for God to open conversations. There are four basic questions that have been asked throughout history, and they continue to permeate our lives today. Cultures around the world answer these questions in different ways at different times as there are no universal answers to these questions. The following is a simple introduction to how these four questions can create space for hospitality.

"Where do I belong?"

Our world categorizes people into social classes according to their financial worth and their possessions. The kind of car we drive, the size of house, and the plethora of other toys we work hard to purchase put us in a category. As a result, we end up belonging to our things more than we belong to other people. People are looking for places to talk about where they are connected to others not based on what they have produced, but because they are loved.

"Who am I?"

In the culture of individualism, some assume that the way to answer this question is to become somebody significant, to rise a level of admired stature in the eyes of others. Therefore, self-promotion and self-development become central to one's life. This question drives people to take care of "me" and "mine," to look out for "number one," because no one else will. As a result, we are trained to be competitive. People get into college because they have test scores that are better than others. Athletes are venerated because they defeat other athletes. Pretty girls feel pretty until a prettier one moves next door. We live in a world where there are winners and losers built upon comparison. People are asking, Where can we be ourselves without having to prove ourselves, without having to perform for others' approval?

"What do I have to offer?"

People need places where they can talk about what they are called to offer the world. Each person has a vocation, a calling as they do their jobs as accountants, grocery store clerks, or elementary school teachers. To hear this calling, we need to listen to each other so that we invite people into a place of freedom to offer our unique gifts.

"What is next for me?"

Many people have been told that the future is nothing more than an extension of today. Circumstances, mistakes, and cultural limitations keep people fenced in without any hope. Although America is the land of opportunity, opportunities primarily come to those who already have them. People need more than personal salvation and a promise of a mansion in heaven. They need a place to talk about their realities. They need others who can make space for their struggles and offer the possibility that the future need not be simply an extension of the past.

Pattern #5: Innovate

The goal of the experiments introduced in chapter 19 is to move people into the life of being neighbors with God, with one another, and with the world so that they might have an impact. Or to state it another way, groups are learning to participate in God's mission to redeem all things. When groups do this, they discover the Spirit's creative movement that cannot be predetermined or developed as a strategy from the church office. A group might meet at a coffee shop on Saturday mornings. Another might meet over lunch at the office. Still another might gather at a park while their toddlers are playing. This is illustrated below by the re-emergence that arises out of death. Here the dependence upon the Spirit generates space for innovation and creativity.

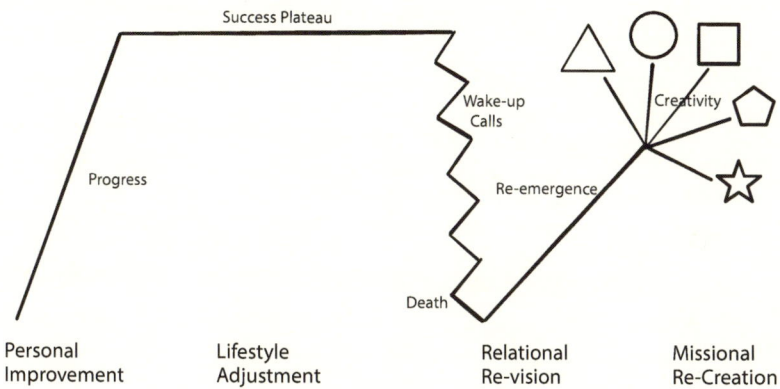

| Personal Improvement | Lifestyle Adjustment | Relational Re-vision | Missional Re-Creation |

Or consider two or three people who catch a vision for seasonal migrant workers or a specific part of town where there is a high rate of homelessness. Two groups might partner with each other to take on a project that will cause them to be present in a neighborhood. For instance, two or three groups could work together on a Habitat for Humanity project. They might partner with established ministries like homeless shelters, ministries to orphans, and battered-women's homes. When we do this, we discover new and creative ways to be God's people in different contexts. As stated previously, when groups move from the story of *Relational Re-vision* into *Missional Re-Creation,* the actual form that groups take will evolve in unpredictable ways. Groups that emerge as a part of the story of *Missional Re-creation* cannot be controlled. They will emerge out of the gifts of those involved and the local context in which they are set.

Flourishing in the Conversations

God created us for conversations, with him and with others. Because God is personal, he speaks with us, and therefore we are invited to respond personally with him. This is most obviously exemplified in the way that Jesus manifested the life of God when he walked the earth. God is a conversational God.

Not only do we find God in our conversations with him—through prayer, spiritual disciplines, worship, etc.—but we also find God in the midst of conversations with others. This is how we typically discover anything new. We learn by interacting with a person, a group, a book, or listening to someone speak. Instead of assuming that we already have all the abstract facts lined up—as if we can plummet the vast truths of God completely—we are walking with Jesus by the Spirit to discover new aspects of God's love. The heart of this is captured by this confession of Henri Nouwen,

> More and more, the desire grows in me simply to walk around, greet people, enter their homes, sit on their doorsteps, play ball, throw water, and be known as someone who wants to live with them. It is a privilege to have the time to practice this simple ministry of presence. Still, it is not as simple as it seems. My own desire to be useful, to do something significant, or to be part of some impressive project is so strong that soon my time is taken up by meetings, conferences, study groups, and workshops that prevent me from walking the streets. It is difficult not to have plans, not to organize people around an urgent cause, and not to feel that you are working directly for social progress. But I wonder more and more if the first thing shouldn't be to know people by name, to eat and drink with them, to listen to their stories and tell your own, and to let them know with words, handshakes, and hugs that you do not simply like them, but truly love them.[6]

Such conversations create space in our lives to flourish, for groups to flourish, and for God to breath forth his love into God's body. May we receive what God is doing through these conversations.

Conclusion

Thirty miles north of Dallas, you will find a few hundred acres once owned by my grandparents who operated a dairy farm. That property is now covered with houses. My grandfather sold the property in the 1960s. When I was a kid, my father rented the land for raising beef cattle. We also raised sheep, chickens, and even rabbits at one point of my childhood. We cultivated wheat, oats, and hay as well. Through my veins runs the dirt, sweat, and tears of generations of farmers.

I learned many lessons about life on the farm, one of which applies to groups. Farming is not spectacular. In fact, to some it is quite boring because it is so repetitive. Every year, a farmer repeats the same patterns: cultivating the ground, planting the seed, fertilizing the plants, and then finally harvesting the crop. With animals it is the same.

Developing groups in the way of Jesus is similar. It's not about a quick fix. When we expect immediate results and spectacular activity, we succumb to the temptation to jump from idea to idea. The fads that come with regular waves of the new and the next entrap us. When the excitement wanes, we move on to the next ministry idea that sparkles.

Many churches have fallen short of flourishing because they wanted results quickly. When I read the promises made by God to Abraham, Isaac, and Jacob, one question returns to me almost every time. Why did it take so long? God created his people by calling one family. When Abraham died, there were not many people worshiping Yahweh with him. In addition, the one person who did leave Ur and travel with him—his nephew Lot—parted ways and found himself surrounded by sin. Even when we jump forward to the end of the Pentateuch, it seems like so little was accomplished.

Of course, all of this is pointing forward to the coming of the Messiah. However, the coming of the Messiah took far longer than any modern leader would ever put in their strategic plan. God is always in

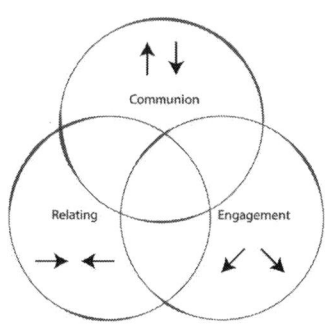

a hurry to love but never in a hurry to produce the spectacular. He is always loving and drawing people into his love so that we might be a people who live out Communion, Relating, and Engagement from the core of our being.

He wants to create a people who actually get God's way that was manifest in the life, death, and resurrection of Jesus, and that takes time. From our perspective, time is limited. We think that faith is displayed as we make things happen quickly, but from God's perspective faith is about trusting that the Spirit is at work, even when we don't see immediate results.

The Flywheel Effect

In the business leadership book, *Good to Great*, Jim Collins writes about companies that stand out and what they do that is different than those that are average. He and his team of researchers discovered that great companies practice patterns that result in the "flywheel effect." Imagine a huge flywheel, one three stories high and weighing over 5000 pounds. The goal is to push the flywheel so that it rotates by simply leveraging your strength against it. By pushing once, it moves slightly. You realize that it will require multiple, consistent pushes to get it moving. After some pushing, it turns once. Then you keep pushing, and it turns again and again and again. Collins writes:

> Then, at some point—breakthrough! The momentum of the thing kicks in your favor, hurling the flywheel forward, turn after turn ... whoosh! ... its own heavy weight working for you. You're pushing no harder than during the first rotation, but the flywheel goes faster and faster. Each turn of the flywheel builds upon the work done earlier, compounding your investment of effort. A thousand times faster, then ten thousand, then a hundred thousand. The huge heavy disk flies forward, with almost unstoppable momentum.
>
> Now suppose someone came along and asked, "What was the one big push that caused this thing to go so fast?"
>
> You wouldn't be able to answer; it's just a nonsensical question. Was it the first push? The second? The fifth? The hundredth? No! It was all of them added together in an overall accumulation of effort applied in a consistent direction. Some pushes may have been bigger than others, but any single heave—no matter how large—reflected a small fraction of the entire cumulative effective upon the flywheel."[1]

Collins then boldly proclaims, "There is no miracle moment. ... Rather it was a quiet, deliberate process of figuring out what needed to be done to create the best future results and then simply taking those steps, one after the other, turn by turn of the flywheel."[2]

After over two decades of helping churches develop groups, I've observed that groups that fall short of *Relational Re-vision* and *Missional Re-creation* are often found in churches that look for the magical group strategy that will make everything fall into place within a budget cycle or school year. Collins observed a contrasting pattern in companies that were not able to move toward effective implementation of their goals. He writes:

> Instead of a quiet deliberate process of figuring out what needed to be done and then simply doing it, the comparison companies

frequently launched new programs—often with great fanfare and hoopla aimed at "motivating the troops"—only to see the programs fail to produce sustained results. They sought the single defining action, the grand program, the one killer innovation, the miracle moment that would allow them to skip the arduous buildup stage and jump right to breakthrough. They would push the flywheel in one direction, then stop, change course, and throw it in a new direction—and then they would stop, change course, and throw it into yet another direction.[3]

Churches that develop flourishing communities don't stand up and announce that they will change the church by mobilizing everyone in

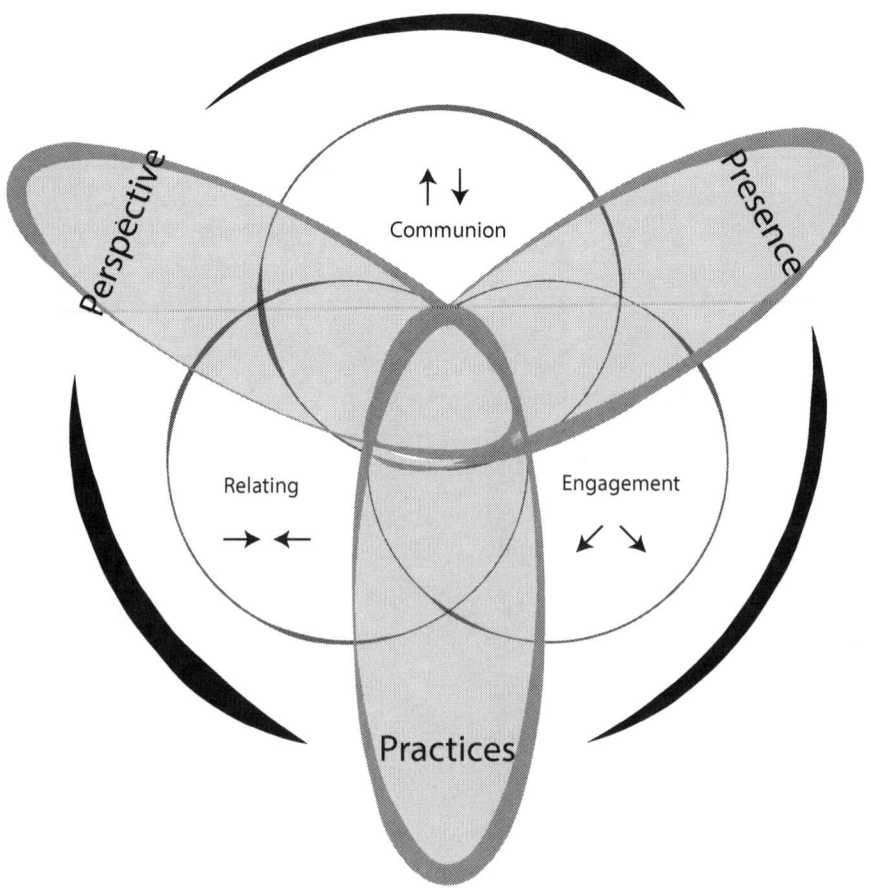

a new small group program. Instead, leaders invest their energy in the right places to produce tangible results that reveal the power of being a part of a community on mission. They recognize that moving the flourishing community flywheel will take time (in most cases a few years). They keep at it, pushing forward in little ways that only produces small results at first, and they celebrate those small results and even the turtle-slow pace of the process. They have learned something very valuable: this is God's way of building community and mission momentum.

This is the way of entering the waters of the Spirit with Jesus as we shape the Perspective of the way of Jesus, as we embrace the Presence of Christ, and as we put a set of Practices in motion. We also have the Spirit to work through us to push the flywheel, and then the life of Communion, Relating, and Engagement generates new life on its own.

To see a movement of group life that goes beyond a program that we have to prop up with effort and administration and into an organic group experience, we must consider how to best apply the right kind of leverage to the flywheel of Perspective, Presence, and Practice and then go about it quietly. We have to stay the course.

This will move people into the stories of *Relational Re-vision* and *Missional Re-creation*, if we keep sailing.

Appendix
Grouping Models
By M. Scott Boren
& Jim Egli

The contemporary church is challenged with a plethora of different small group models. Some of the most popular models contradict each other on fundamental points. Very few pastors and church leaders have the time to understand and compare the divergent models. They typically read one or two small group books and possibly attend a small group conference. Most books and conferences, however, present only one model—yet they do it in a very convincing way. This book has introduced a different way to think about how to develop groups. The key is not to try to figure out which model best fits your own church, leadership style, and community. Instead, look at models others have developed in order to learn from their experiences and be responsive to the Holy Spirit's guidance and your own unique situation.

The purpose of this article is to offer a quick overview of the key models so that you can understand the basic principles, common patterns, and differences.[1]

The Cell Church Model

The roots of the contemporary small group movement extend back to 1964 in Seoul, Korea. After collapsing from exhaustion, Yonggi Cho—then pastoring a church of 2400 people—sought God over a period of months to discover how to lead the church differently.[2] He was struck by how Moses divided the millions that he cared for into groups of 100s, 50s and 10s (Exodus 18:13-26). He also noticed how the young church in the book of Acts was able to enfold thousands of new converts by using home group meetings (Acts 2:46). Cho also sensed God saying, "I am destroying your ministry and giving it to others." To this day, the church remains based on a small group system. Yoido Full Gospel Church has over 20,000 home groups and it is actively planting churches throughout Korea and around the world. There are several important points to understand about Cho's small group model:[3]

- Small Groups exist for the dual purposes of edification and evangelism. Cho emphasizes that groups can fulfill and must fulfill these two objectives simultaneously.
- Group meetings include Bible study, but they are more than just Bible study groups. Initially, group meetings were two-thirds Bible study and one-third prayer and it was determined that they did not work very well. When they reversed the format to be one-third Bible study and two-thirds prayer, growth escalated.
- There is an emphasis on relational evangelism, serving the needs of unbelievers in practical ways. The church tells its members to show Jesus' love to those around them by saying, "find a need and fill it."
- The church established what has come to be known as the 5x5 oversight model. Every five to seven groups are overseen by a "section leader." Over every five or so section leaders are staff pastors. This pattern of oversight is apportioned according to geographic areas.

One innovative leader who was influenced by Yonggi Cho is Ralph W. Neighbour Jr. He was the primary practitioner and scholar who refined and wrote about Cho's models in a way that could be adapted for the Western context. In the 1990s, it became popularly known as the cell church model, which was set up against what Neighbour called the Programmed-Based Design of the church.[4] He emphasized a way of doing church that promoted:

- the centrality of evangelism to cell life and growth;
- the necessity of a clear discipleship path to enable continual leadership and group multiplication;
- the centrality of home groups to New Testament Christianity.

Neighbour's collaborative partner, William Beckham, further explicated this model by calling it the Two-Winged Church, which provides a word picture of a balanced church that equally emphasizes the importance of the small group "wing" alongside the large-group wing.[5]

While the popularity of this model has waned in North America, it remains a very influential strategy in South America, Asia and Africa. Joel Comiskey has been the primary researcher, writer, and promoter of this strategy.[6] One of the most significant churches that has continued to thrive on the basics of these cell church principles is the Elim Church in El Salvador. Led by Mario Vega, this church promotes a system that consistently sees annual conversion growth and the birthing of new churches. They have done this by staying the course and discipling people year after year.[7] A more recent exposition of the foundational dynamics of thriving cell groups can be found in Jim Egli and Dwight Marable's 2011 book *Small Groups, Big Impact*.[8]

Meta-Church Model

Parallel to the development of the cell church model in the 1990s which Neighbour introduced and promoted, the Meta-Church model came upon the scene through the writings of Carl George, specifically his book *Prepare Your Church for the Future*. The Meta-Church Model provides an interpretive lens that allows the leadership to see how the church is already organized into small groups so that they can facilitate the groups that are present and move them toward more intentional experiences of community. The saying, "becoming a church of small groups instead of a church with small groups," popularized this model. Within this church of groups, there are a variety of types of groups: "loving (pastoral care), learning (Bible knowledge), deciding (internal administration), and doing (duties that serve those outside the group)."[9] Willow Creek Community Church was directly influenced by Carl George and began to promote a variation of this model. In their book *Becoming a Church of Small Groups*, Bill Donahue and Russ Robinson write about five major types of groups: disciple-making groups, community groups, service groups, seeker groups, and support groups.[10] In a later resource, they argue that one of the major "deadly sins" of small group ministry is a "narrow definition of a small group." Instead of a one-type-fits-all approach that they identify as a 301-level group, they shaped all of their ministries to have varying levels of "spiritual intensity and meeting frequency." Those that required less were identified as 101 or 201 level groups and those involving more commitment as 301 and 401.[11]

This illustrates how the Meta-Church model embraces a wide variety of small group types. This is the primary attribute that sets it apart from the cell church model. In the cell church, all groups emphasize a balance of edification and evangelism, whereas the Meta Church provides different kinds of groups for different kinds of people. Carl George view of small group variety is clarified in his latter book when he wrote, "Cells include Sunday-school classes, ministry teams, outreach teams, worship-production teams, sports teams, recovery groups, and more."[12]

Common to this model and the cell church model as exemplified by Cho and Neighbor is the emphasis on leadership development and formation. These groups were designed to develop leaders from within and birth new groups as a result.

Recent Models

Even though there are many different models and approaches to small groups, all of them can be traced back to or have striking similarities to the cell church model or the meta-church model. Though not always acknowledge by small group experts, what is now called small group creativity is simply a repackaging of the basic principles outlined in these two approaches. However, while different models offer unique contributions and combine elements in creative ways, it is worthwhile to dig deeper into how they emphasize different things. In this section we will introduce three models that stem from the roots of the cell church approach and three that seem to derive more of their strategy from the meta-church point of view.

The Groups of 12 Model

A direct derivative of the cell church model is that developed in Bogotá, Columbia by International Charismatic Mission (ICM). In 1990, after seven years of founding and pastoring this church, Castellanos was frustrated because it had plateaued at 3000 members. Part of his frustration was how long it took to produce small group leaders. Few people completed the two-year process they were using and those who did had few non-Christian friends left to win once they became leaders. Castellanos sought God for a breakthrough to release unlimited growth. He recounted:

> But the moment came in my life when I said, "Lord, I need something that will help me accelerate the purpose." And in my times of spiritual retreat God ministered greatly to my heart. In one of those moments he said, "I'm going to give you the ability to train people quickly." And then he removed the veil and showed me the model of 12.

The "Groups of 12" or "G12" model is a combination of principles and methods that enabled ICM to become the fastest growing church in the world. What are the characteristics of the G12 model?

- A "consolidation" process to disciple new believers that immediately sends them on a weekend "Encounter" retreat to help them be set free from spiritual bondage and be filled with the Holy Spirit, then into a "School of Leaders." This discipleship system equips every member to start his or her own evangelistic small group within the first year of coming to Christ.

- An emphasis on the external multiplication of homogeneous groups targeting specific populations such as businessmen, women, students, couples, and so forth. External multiplication means that instead of splitting existing small groups, new groups are formed by individuals by gathering new people from their own circle of influence.
- A system of oversight that has group leaders in "Groups of 12" where they are discipled on a weekly basis. Leaders of the Groups of 12 are also members in another Group of 12 led by someone else. The central point in the system is the pastor and his own Group of 12.

The G12—short for "Groups of 12" or "Government of 12"—model is intense. In time, a leader is involved in three weekly meetings—the small group that they lead, the G12 group where they are discipled by their leader, and a G12 group where they are encouraging and equipping the leaders under themselves. Joel Comiskey, in his book *From 12 to 3*, has suggested ways to apply the strengths of the G12 model—specifically that of intentionally investing in leaders—in a way that is more flexible and less intense.[13]

The Geographic Model

This approach is best illustrated by Randy Frazee's book, *The Connecting Church*.[14] According to Frazee, leaders found three things that caused them to move toward a geographic approach to group life:

- Their problem was not the size of the groups. Community can best be experienced in small groups.
- Their problem was not the people in their groups. Those involved in their small group system sincerely wanted to experience community and grow in Christ.
- The problem with their groups was that people were not experiencing genuine community.

Their conclusion that the problem of groups was a lack of genuine community set in motion a study on the ingredients of true community and how churches could cultivate and experience it. Frazee performed extensive research on community as it occurs in a wide diversity of settings, such as kibbutzes, gangs, monasteries, work teams, and fraternities. He argues that close geographic proximity is essential for community because it allows people to be more available to one another and to interact frequently and more spontaneously. Consequently, he concluded that small group community happens more deeply and naturally when people live closer. This motivated his church to shift to a geographically based model where members joined groups according to where they lived. Congregational units are also formed according to geography. They found that using school zones is one of the most effective ways to organize congregations because it provided for natural connections and spontaneous interaction for both building community and reaching out to neighbors.

The nature of the group has much in common with those in the cell church model as they focused on both edification and evangelism and encouraged groups to grow and multiply. They have two foci: "to function in interdependent relationships, assisting each other in growth toward Christlikeness" and "to practice their growing faith by reaching out to others outside the group."[15] As groups multiplied, they did so in a way that grouped people living in closer proximity.

One unique attribute of this model is the weekly gathering of the congregational units. Usually occurring on the church campus during the traditional Sunday school hour, these mid-size groups connect groups with other groups, provide an avenue for gifted teachers to equip the people, and alleviates the stress of home group multiplication.

Missional Communities

With the publication of the book *Missional Church* in the mid-1990s, what began as theological reflection about the church shifted to extensive practice and implementation, as well as extensive writing on the nature of what it looks like to be missional.[16] There are numerous variations and ways of doing missional communities, as is illustrated in the examples recorded in Reggie McNeal's book *Missional Communities*. He writes about one group called Soma Communities who declare that "missional community consists of a committed core of believers (family) who live out the mission together (missionaries) in a specific area or to a particular people group by demonstrating the gospel in tangible forms (servants) and declaring the gospel to others—both those who believe it and those who are being exposed to it (learners)."[17]

While proponents of missional communities often claim that they are distinct from small groups, they do in fact come in the shape of a small group of sorts. They simply subsume the small group form to a missional thrust. Some missional communities organize people in mid-size groups of 20-50 people and sub-divide the group into smaller groups for personal ministry either during the group meeting or in a separate meeting. Those who take this approach often organize the entire church around this missional calling and leaders are usually very clear about this up front. Some churches recognize the need for missional communities but also see the reality that not everyone is ready for such radical forms of church life. Therefore they set up a system where traditional small groups parallel the more radical, experimental missional communities.

The Semester Model

This approach, which is derived from the Meta-Church model, comes in two forms: the multiple focus option and the single focus option. The first provides many options for study or group focus, while the second provides one option for small group studies.

The multiple focus option. The multiple focus option is called the semester system and is promoted by Nelson Searcy of The Journey Church in New York. Searcy, along with Kerrick Thomas write about how they have been able to make small groups a central priority to the life of their church. Small groups do not simply receive verbal promotion. They are a priority. Searcy and Thomas indicate that, "We require all of our staff members to be in a small group. Most of them lead groups on their own initiative. In addition, most of our staff have small group administrative responsibilities that require them to help form small groups each semester and give staff oversight and support to those groups."[18]

The unique contribution of this model is highlighted in the above quote. All groups are semester based and are programmed from the central office as they are organized into three semesters per year. All groups have a distinct launch point and the launch dates are scheduled and promoted on the Sundays leading up to the launch. When there are many groups in larger churches, a group catalogue is published each semester, which provides the details about the dates, curriculum, and location.

New Life Christian Church in Colorado Springs, Colorado has practiced an older version of this model.[19] Three procedures characterize their approach:

- Groups are organized around common interests rather than geographical proximity, so as to draw both church members and the unchurched into relationships.
- Groups have a clear start and stop with three small group semesters or cycles a year, so that people can easily join and leave groups.
- Discipleship is "by choice"—meaning that people will join groups or take classes that they need when they need them.

The key assumption behind New Life's small group and discipleship philosophy is that people in the twenty-first century do not want to be told what to do—they want choices. Another assumption is that like businesses in a free market economy, healthy groups will flourish while unhealthy groups will die. So we should encourage a diversity of different types of groups and allow things to naturally thrive or whither.

The single focus option. North Coast Church, led by pastor Larry Osborne, has developed this variation of the semester model. Like those found in the above model, these groups have definitive beginnings and endings—they are 10 weeks long. The uniqueness of these groups is that they all study the same sermon-based content.

The focus of the meetings lies in the spiritual formation practices such as Bible discussion and application, the sharing of needs, and prayer.[20] The primary goal of these groups is to assimilate the members into the full life of the church. Consequently there is less emphasis on serving and evangelism. As the book that explicates this model illustrates by its title, *Sticky Church*, the strategy is to close the back door of the church.

The strategic discipleship option. National Community church in Washington, D.C. has developed a variation of the semester model, as outlined by the strategic leader of the groups, Heather Zempel, in her book *Community is Messy.* Their approach is to lead people on a discipleship journey by creating various kinds of small groups. They want people to move from seeking groups to learning groups, then to influencing groups, and then on to investor groups. They use a discipleship map that encourages people to start with the Alpha experience and then move to different metaphorical "islands" that house the different kinds of groups. This allows people to identify the kind of discipleship that they need and then join a group that meets that need.[21]

The North Point Model

One of the most passionate champions of small groups is Andy Stanley, senior pastor of North Point Community Church in Atlanta, Georgia. His strategy is helpfully outlined in the book he co-authored with Bill Willits, *Creating Community: 5 Keys to Building a Small Group Culture.* North Point has a clear strategy for guiding visitors who come to their worship services into their small groups. They liken it to moving a guest from the foyer to the living room to the kitchen table.[22]

In the foyer—their worship services—their goal is to change peoples' minds about church. In the living room—affinity groups for marrieds and for singles—they aim to change peoples' minds about community. And at the kitchen table—their small groups—they aim to change people's minds about priorities.

One unique aspect of North Point's strategy is how they methodically guide people into groups. Four times a year the church hosts "GroupLink" meetings where people are invited to meet with other people in their geographic area who are also in the same phase of life.

The two-hour meeting is carefully orchestrated to introduce people to the church's small group ministry and what it offers them. People are then introduced to other individuals who are launching new small groups near them. Two weeks later "Starter Groups" are launched which last eight weeks and allow people to try out group life. If these groups go well, they are continued and people are invited to join them by signing a group covenant.

The church uses a strategy that has "closed groups that multiply." When people join a group, they are committing to be together for one and half to two years. People can't invite their friends to their small group but they are encouraged to invite their friends to the worship services of the church. The groups are expected to multiply into several groups at the end of their life cycle.

The Church-Wide Campaign Strategy

Steve Gladden, the Small Groups Pastor at Saddleback Church, notes this about one of the most influential small group models: "Our small group ministry is not just another program. It is an embedded and integrated piece of everything we do as a church. It's our infrastructure. It's where care happens. It's our delivery system for all spiritual formation. It's our method of balancing the biblical purposes and fostering healthy lives."[23]

In many ways this model falls between the cell church model and the Meta-Church paradigm; therefore we have placed it last. The goal of all groups is for them to practice the five purposes (Worship, Fellowship, Discipleship, Ministry, and Evangelism) as set out by Rick Warren in his landmark book *The Purpose-Driven Church*. Therefore the stated intent of the groups line up with those of the cell church. However, they also embrace the flexibility of the Meta-Church approach, especially with their emphasis on church-wide campaigns. And with these, we find their most unique contribution. The goal in church-wide campaigns is to start as many short-term groups (six weeks) that are based on a sermon series and all of the resources for hosting the groups are provided to what they call a H.O.S.T., meaning "Have a heart for people, Open their home to a group, Serve a snack, and Turn on a video."[24]

The campaign strategy focuses on launching groups by lowering the bar as far as possible for the H.O.S.T. This is done by:

- a sermon series that sets the stage for the entire church;
- aligning the children's and youth ministries along with the adult focus;
- small group video curriculum so that leaders do not have to facilitate traditional discussions;
- a programmed, centralized promotion and member recruitment process that provides members for the H.O.S.T;
- a devotional guide for group members (the most popular illustration of this is found in the best-selling title *The Purpose-Driven Life*);
- providing an out for the H.O.S.T and the group if they want to only meet for six weeks;
- providing a plan for supporting the H.O.S.T and the group if they want to continue as a group.[25]

The goal is for these groups to get started and continue on after the campaign as groups that experience all five of the purposes. And then a leader will arise and receive training. Instead of training leaders upfront, they provide experimental H.O.S.T experiences and then later provide the training.

Observations and Cautions

Small group models are a lot like diets. Everybody is looking for the magic diet that will help him or her lose weight, feel great, and stay healthy. Almost any diet will work in the short term, but seldom does a diet alone bring the long-term results that you seek. To be healthy and trim takes discipline and discovery. Mostly likely you cannot find an easy diet solution. You are going to have to exercise, eat healthy foods, avoid lots of calories in a consistent way over a long period of time. There are no quick solutions that bring lasting results. Like the person who jumps from one diet plan to another looking for the one that really works, many churches that jump from one group model to another find themselves in a constant state of disappointment. If only it were as simple as reading the right book or going to the right conference.

Here are our observations and cautions about small group models:

- All models look like the ultimate model when you are reading a book or attending a conference.
- Any model can work for 10-18 months.
- Some things that work great in the short run actually work against long-term effectiveness. For example, lowering the qualifications for group leaders might increase the number of groups in the short term, but long-term growth and health of groups depends upon mature leaders, a thoughtful leadership development strategy, and an integrated support system.
- Too often, the information about models found in books and at conferences focuses on external characteristics and tangible results that stir up excitement and promote the strategy. They often fail to delve into the factors that are crucial to long-term success, i.e., proactive coaching, spiritual formation of group members, leadership development, pastoral investment in group life, and how to lead people through change. These factors do not sparkle and sizzle as much, but they are crucial to effective groups.

Because of these observations, it is important that you ask probing questions about the differences between the models which lie beneath the surface. Getting to this level of understanding about a model will help you to see how the models actually work and to determine what aspects of a model might best fit your context.

Interpreting the Differences

Since small groups are part and parcel to so many different church strategies, and because so many seem to claim to elevate the importance of groups to their strategies, often using the same language to declare how central groups are to their approach, how then do you understand the differences between various approaches? To state the obvious, not all small group strategies emphasize groups in the same way. To understand the differences, one need not digest every detail about grouping strategies. Instead, you only need a list of key questions that will go straight to the heart of the differences. There are four broad questions that pastors and the Groups Team should ask of the various models. The following introduces these four categories of questions.

Question 1: What is the purpose of the small group?

The label "small group" is used for many different kinds of groups in the church, including home groups, evangelism target groups, task groups, and even Sunday school classes. Because different churches define their "small groups" differently, comparing groups from different churches is like comparing apples to oranges. If a leader claims to have 80% of the church in groups, the question is not whether we compare that percentage to that of another church and the grouping strategy they adopt. Instead, we should first ask "What's going on in these groups?" A group that meets once per month to play volleyball and pray together is different from a group that lives in community and is working together to bring redemption in their neighborhood.

This question relates to the difference between groups that are designed for Connecting Community and groups that are designed for Missional Community. This question has two layers. First we must ask what the intended purpose of the group is according to what is promoted by the stated vision for groups. Then we must ask what is really going on. Here are some specific questions to use:

- What's the stated purpose of the groups?
- What are the various types of groups that are provided?
- What is the feeder for the groups? What percentage of group members come from the Sunday service? What percentage come from relationships outside the church?
- What "story" is actually being told by the groups? (See chapter 2)

Question 2: How are small group leaders supported?

All of the successful small group models have developed extensive strategies for supporting their small group leaders. They dedicate resources, time, personal relationships, and money to the support and care of group leaders. But the methods for providing this support vary between the models. Here are a few questions to probe this issue:

- How is the senior pastor involved in the oversight of the small groups?
- What kind of personal support do small group leaders receive from the pastoral staff?
- Does every small group leader have a coach who invests personal time in mentoring him or her?
- How are networks of small groups organized?
- How often do the small group leaders meet for continuing training?
- How often do small group leaders meet with their small group coaches?

Question 3: What priority is given to small group life as compared to other activities in the church?

This third question is one of emphasis and integration. Few churches will state that small groups are unimportant, but many will argue about the priority they should have in the ministry of the church. Some place a very high priority on small groups, even stating that you cannot be a member of the church without participating in a group. Others hold groups up as the priority but set group participation alongside many other options. Here are a few additional questions:

- What degree of priority is given to the small groups?
- Do other ministries compete with small group participation?
- Are non-small group members allowed to take on ministry roles in the church?

Question 4: How does the church equip small group members and raise up new small group leaders?

Almost every church that starts small groups complains about a shortage of leadership. Model churches have developed patterns for equipping every member for ministry. This means providing more than leadership training for new small group leaders; it means creating a spiritual formation track that will take small group members from "new Christian " to "minister" to "leader." In other words, model small group-based churches do not expect disciples and future leaders to develop out of thin air. Instead, they have an intentional development process that disciples each person according to his or her level of maturity: new believer training for new believers, ministry training for growing Christians, and leadership training for future leaders. Additional questions include:

- How does the church equip new believers who join the small groups?
- How does the church prepare small group members to minister to other people in the small group and to non believing friends?
- How does the church train new small group leaders?

There is much you can learn from other churches, but long-term group development is going to take diligence, humility, and seeking God. Learn from others as well as from your own mistakes. If God has put a passion within you for thriving groups, you can see it come to fruition as you persist and continue to invite the Spirit to enliven your church and penetrate your community.

Notes

Chapter 2: What Do We Desire from Groups?

[1] David Reisman, *The Lonely Crowd*, Revised Edition (New Haven, CT: Yale University Press, 2001), Robert Putnam, *Bowling Alone* (New York: Simon $ Schuster, 2001), Kenneth Gergen, *The Saturated Self* (New York: Basic Books, 2000).

[2] Robert Bellah, et. al., *Habits of the Heart* (Berkley, CA: The University of California Press, 1996), 146.

[3] Bill Donahue, *The Willow Creek Guide to Life-Changing Small Groups* (Grand Rapids, MI: Zondervan, 1996), 82.

[4] Steve Gladden, *Leading Small Groups with Purpose* (Grand Rapids, MI: BakerBooks, 2011), 41-42.

[5] Joel Comiskey, *Myths and Truths of the Cell Church* (Moreno Valley, CA: CCS Publishing, 2012), 98.

[6] Reggie McNeal, *Missional Communities* (San Francisco: Jossey-Bass, 2001), 45.

[7] Dietrich Bonhoeffer, *Life Together* (Minneapolis: Fortress Press, 2004), 38.

Chapter 3: What Do We Get?

[1] Bonhoeffer, 36.

Chapter 5: How Do You Get Something Different?

[1] J. R. R. Tolkien, *The Hobbit* (London: HarperCollins Publishers, 1991), 13-14.

[2] N. T. Wright, *Scripture and the Authority of God* (San Francisco: HarperOne, 2011), 122.

[3] This table is adapted from Ronald Heifetz, Alexander Grashow and Marty Linsky, *The Practices of Adaptive Leadership* (Boston: Harvard Business Press, 2009), 20.

[4] Ronald Heifetz, *Leadership without Easy Answers* (Cambridge: MA: Belknap, 1994), 73.

[5] Dean Anderson and Linda Ackerman Anderson, *Beyond Change Management: Advanced Strategies for Today's Transformational Leaders* (San Francisco: Jossey-Bass, 2001), 37.

[6] Robert Quinn, *Building the Bridge as You Walk on It: A Guide for Leading Change* (San Francisco: Jossey-Bass, 2004), 10.

[7] Ronald Heifetz and Marty Linsky, *Leadership on the Line* (Boston: Harvard Business School Press, 2002), 14.

Chapter 6: How Do You Get Something Different?

[1] M. Scott Boren, *Missional Small Groups* (Grand Rapids: Baker Books, 2010), 39.

[2] Ibid., 40.

[3] Ibid., 41.

[4] Ibid., 43.

Chapter 8: Why Do We Need Christ's Presence?
[1] This diagram is a development and an explication of various teachings given by Greg Boyd.
[2] Samuel Wells, *A Nazareth Manifesto: Being with God* (Malden, MA: John Wiley & Sons Inc., 2015), 24-25.

Chapter 9: Where Is Christ's Presence?
[1] Edward T. Hall, *The Hidden Dimension* (New York: Achor Books, 1969,1990), 155.
[2] Wayne Meeks, *The First Urban Christians* (New Haven, CT: Yale University Press, 2003), 75.
[3] Joseph Myers, *The Search to Belong* (Grand Rapids, MI: Zondervan, 2004), 143.
[4] Ibid.
[5] Will Miller, *Refrigerator Rights* (New York: Perigee Trade, 2002), xii.
[6] Bonhoeffer, 44.
[7] Ibid., 44.
[8] Myers, 68.

Chapter 10: What Do Flourishing Groups Practice?
[1] N. T. Wright, *After You Believe* (San Francisco, HarperOne, 2010), 19-20.
[2] Tim Morey, *Embodying Our Faith* (Downers Grove: Intervarsity Press, 2009), 111.
[3] Craig Dykstra, *Growing in the Life of Faith* (Louisville, KY: Westminster John Knox, 2005), 66.
[4] Joel Comiskey with Jim Egli, *Groups that Thrive: 8 Surprising Discoveries about Life-Giving Small Groups* (Moreno Valley, CA: CCS Publishing, 2018).

Chapter 11: What Do Flourishing Leaders Practice?
[1] Dave Early, *8 Habits of Effective Small Group Leaders* (Houston: TOUCH Publications, 2001).

Chapter 12: What Do Flourishing Coaches Practice?
[1] Jim Egli, "Successful Small Groups: Critical Factors in Small Group Growth" (Ph.D. diss., Regent University, 2002), 92.

Chapter 13: What Do Flourishing Pastors Practice?
[1] Lynn Anderson, *They Smell Like Sheep* (West Monroe, LA: Howard Publishing, 1997), 29-30.

Chapter 14: What Does the Pilgrimage Look Like?
[1] Leonard Sweet, *AquaChurch* (Loveland, CO: Group Publishing, 1999), 73.

Chapter 15: What Is the First Step?
[1] Adapted from Simon Carey Hold, *God Next Door* (Victoria, Australia: Acorn Press, 2007), 104.

Chapter 16: Who Guides the Pilgrimage?
[1] Adapted from *Leading Change* (Boston: Harvard Business Press, 1996), 57.
[2] Peter M. Senge, *The Fifth Discipline* (New York: Currency Doubleday, 1990), 247.
[3] Ibid., 241.
[4] Peter Block, *Community* (San Francisco: Berrett-Koehler, 2009), 29.
[5] Ibid., 11.

Chapter 17: How Do You Prepare the Church for Groups?
[1] Joel Comiskey, *Reap the Harvest* (Houston, TX: TOUCH Outreach, 1999), 62.

Chapter 18: How Do You Get People Connected?

[1] R. T. France, *The New International Greek Testament Commentary, The Gospel of Mark* (Grand Rapids: Eerdmans, 2002), 196.

[2] Eugene Peterson, *The Contemplative Pastor* (Grand Rapids, Eerdmans, 1989), 32-33.

[3] Ibid., 27-28.

Chapter 19: How Will You Initiate Organic Missional Experiments?

[1] Everett Rogers, *The Diffusion of Innovations*, 4th ed. (New York: Free Press, 1995), 398.

[2] The basic framework introduced here was developed independently, however, after developing it, I found that Bill Beckham had written extensively about a triad strategy that is quite similar to that which is introduced here. See William A. Beckham, *70: Jesus' Expansion Strategy* (Moreno Valley, CA: CCS Publishing, 2015), 367ff.

[3] Alan J. Roxburgh, *Joining God, Remaking Church, Changing the World: The New Shape of the Church in Our Time* (New York: Morehouse Publishing, 2015), 86.

[4] James Dunn, *The Theology of Paul the Apostle* (Grand Rapids, Eerdmans, 1998), 559.

Chapter 20: How Will You Form People for Flourishing Community?

[1] Elizabeth O'Connor, *Call to Commitment* (San Francisco, CA: Harper & Row, 1985), 34.

[2] Ibid., 128.

[3] Ibid., 128.

[4] Dennis McCallum and Jessica Lowery, *Organic Disciplemaking* (Houston, TX: Touch Publications, 2006), 19-20.

[5] Jimmy Seibert, *The Church Can Change the World* (Waco, TX: Antioch Community Church, 2008), 164.

[6] Neil Cole, *Search and Rescue* (Grand Rapids, MI: Baker Books, 2008).

[7] John Westley, *John Wesley's Class Meeting* (Napanee, IN: Francis Asbury Press, 1997).

[8] Greg Ogden, *Discipleship Essentials* (Downers Grove, IL: IVP Books, 2007).

Chapter 21: How Will You Support Groups So They Flourish?

[1] Daphne Kirk, *Heirs Together* (Suffolk, England: Kevin Mayhew, 1998), 43.

Chapter 23: How Will Groups Impact the World?

[1] Reta Halternman Finger, *Of Widows and Meals: Communal Meals in the Book of Acts* (Grand Rapids, Eerdmans, 2007), 242.

[2] Adapted from Ralph W. Neighbour Jr., "The Cell Church Is a Praying Church" in *"Cellebrating" CellChurch Magazine* compiled by M. Scott Boren (Houston, TX: TOUCH Publications, 2000), 79-85.

[3] Henri Nouwen, *Reaching Out* (New York, Image Press, 1986), 98.

[4] Christine Pohl, *Making Room* (Grand Rapids: Eerdmans, 1999), 39.

[5] Nouwen, 99.

[6] Nouwen, *The Inner Voice of Love* (New York: Image Books: 1999), 68.

Conclusion

[1] Jim Collins, *Good to Great* (New York: Harper Business, 2001), 164-165.
[2] Ibid., 169.
[3] Ibid., 178.

Appendix

[1] M. Scott Boren, *How Do We Get There From Here?* (Houston, TX: TOUCH Publications, 2007), 53-66.
[2] Jim Egli, "A Second Reformation?: A History of the Cell Church Movement in the Twentieth Century," *Journal of the American Society for Church Growth*, 11, 3-16.
[3] David Y. Cho, *Home Cell Groups* (Alachua, FL: Bridge-Logos, 1984).
[4] Ralph W. Neighbour Jr., *Where Do We Go From Here?: A Guidebook for the Cell Group Church*, 10th Anniversary Edition (Houston, TX: TOUCH Publications, 2000).
[5] William A. Beckham, *The Second Reformation* (Houston, TX: TOUCH Publications, 1995).
[6] Joel Comiskey, *The Church that Multiplies: Growing a Healthy Cell Church in North America* (Moreno Valley, CA: CCS Publishing, 2007).
[7] Joel Comiskey, *Passion and Persistence: How Elim Church's Cell Groups Penetrated an Entire City* (Houston, TX: TOUCH Publications, 2004).
[8] Jim Egli and Dwight Marable, *Small Groups Big Impact: Connecting People to God and One Another in Thriving Groups* (St. Charles, IL: ChurchSmart, 2011).
[9] Carl George, *Prepare Your Church for the Future* (Grand Rapids, MI: Revel, 1992), 90.
[10] Bill Donahue and Russ Robinson, *Becoming a Church of Small Groups* (Grand Rapids, MI: Zondervan, 2001), 183.
[11] Ibid., 153.
[12] Carl George, *The Coming Church Revolution* (Grand Rapids, MI: Revel, 1994), 69-70.
[13] Joel Comiskey, *From 12 to 3: How to Apply G-12 Principles in Your Church* (Houston, TX: TOUCH Publications, 2002).
[14] Randy Frazee, *The Connecting Church* (Grand Rapids, MI: Zondervan, 2001).
[15] Ibid., 99-100.
[16] Darrell Guder, et. al., *Missional Church* (Grand Rapids, MI: Eerdmans, 1998).
[17] Reggie McNeal, *Missional Communities* (San Francisco: Jossey-Bass, 2011), 67.
[18] Nelson Searcy and Kerrick Thomas, *Activate* (Ventura, CA: Regal Books, 2008), 60.
[19] Ted Haggard, *Dog Training, Fly Fishing, and Sharing Christ in the Twenty-first Century* (Nashville: ThomasNelson, 2002).
[20] Larry Osborne, *Sticky Church* (Grand Rapids, MI: Zondervan, 2008), 82-83.
[21] Hearth Zempel, *Community is Messy* (Downers Grove, IL: Intervarsity Press, 2012).
[22] Andy Stanley and Bill Willits, *Creating Community* (Sisters, OR: Multnoma Press, 2004).
[23] Steve Gladden, *Small Groups on Purpose* (Grand Rapids, MI: Baker Books, 2011), 47.
[24] Ibid., 214.
[25] Ibid., 218-220.

About the Author

M. Scott Boren began helping churches develop groups in the early 1990s. Since that time, he has written ten books and numerous articles on group life and church leadership. He holds a masters in New Testament Studies from Regent College and doctorate from Luther Seminary. He has served as a pastor at three churches, and now he is the president of The Center for Community & Mission, a non-profit consulting and training organization which provides leadership coaching for the practices introduced in this book. A native Texan who grew up working a farm, he now lives with his wife, Shawna, and their four children in St. Paul, MN.

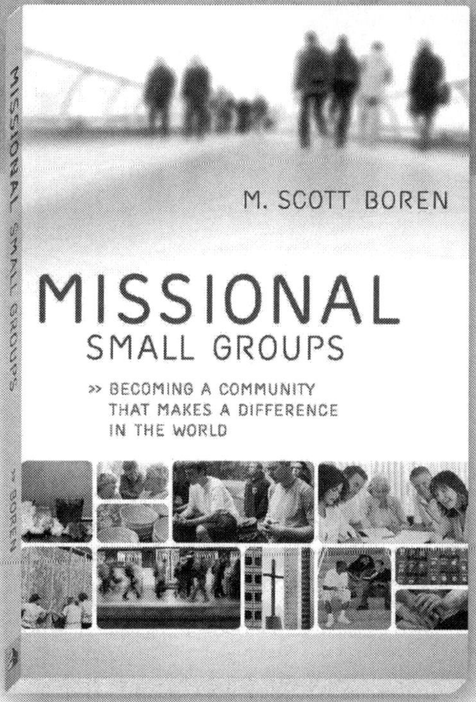

Become a leader that
FLOURISHES

LEADING SMALL GROUPS IN THE WAY OF JESUS

M. SCOTT BOREN

This book introduces eight practices of leaders that will form them to love their group the way that Jesus did and lead others in that way. These eight practices include:

1. See the Way of Jesus
2. Gather in the Presence
3. Lead Collaboratively
4. Be Yourself
5. Hang Out
6. Make a Difference
7. Fight Well
8. Point the Way to the Cross

Discover the Future of a
FLOURISHING CHURCH

This process works with the visionaries of the church to shape a future, along with the practical steps for moving toward that future. The eight priorities to discovering the future of your church include:

1. Discern Reality
2. Discover the Sense-Making Team
3. Dream a Future
4. Develop the Systems
5. Enable Action
6. Experiment on the Fringes
7. Embrace Conflict
8. Establish a New Imagination

As you walk through this process, your church will discover how God is at work already and the various new ways that God wants to work. This will form your church to participate in God's life and mission in the world.

Comprehensive Equipping for Your Church?

Church Leader Events

These one-day events introduce the eight priorities and provide tools so that you can put them into motion in your local congregation.

Group Leader Training

This customized leader training provides an introduction to *Leading Small Groups in the Way of Jesus,* or it can go deep into any of the leadership practices you choose.

Group Member Equipping

This interactive workshop for both group leaders and members provides hands-on equipping that will take your groups to the next level.

Pastoral Coaching

Monthly coaching supports pastors through problem solving, directional equipping, and work on the church's practices of group development.

Church Consultations

These are designed to identify specific issues and give recommendations to a congregation regarding the process of putting the eight priorities introduced in this book into motion.

Free Resources

Curriculum, videos, blogs, and more that will support you on the journey.

www.mscottboren.org

The Center for Community and Mission

Rethinking How Churches Flourish

Equipping and Empowering Churches to Flourish through:
- *Consulting*
  - *Coaching*
    - *Training*
      - *Resources*

Rethinking Future Church

Rethinking Pastoral Leadership

Rethinking Small Groups

Rethinking Spiritual Formation

www.mscottboren.org

Made in the USA
Middletown, DE
20 December 2021

56752266R00203